94602

W9-CBB-292

A FURNACE AFLOAT

THE WRECK OF THE HORNET
AND THE HARROWING 4,300-MILE
VOYAGE OF ITS SURVIVORS

JOE JACKSON

FREE PRESS

New York   London   Toronto   Sydney   Singapore

*f*P

FREE PRESS
A Division of Simon & Schuster Inc.
1230 Avenue of the Americas
New York, NY 10020

For information about special discounts for bulk purchases,
please contact Simon & Schuster Special Sales:
1-800-456-6798 or business@simonandschuster.com

Book design by Ellen R. Sasahara

Manufactured in the United States of America

1   3   5   7   9   10   8   6   4   2

Library of Congress Cataloging-in-Publication Data

Jackson, Joe
A furnace afloat : the wreck of the Hornet and harrowing
4,300-mile voyage of its survivors / Joe Jackson
p. cm.
Includes bibliographical references (p.).
1. Hornet (Clipper-ship) 2. Shipwrecks—Pacific Ocean. 3.
Survival after airplane accidents, shipwrecks, etc. I. Title.
G530.H82J33 2003
910'.9164'9—dc21   2003052756

ISBN 0-7432-3037-X

TO KATHY AND NICK

Man springs from nowhere, crosses time and disappears forever in the bosom of God; he is seen but for a moment, wandering on the verge of the two abysses, and there he is lost.

—Alexis de Tocqueville, *Democracy in America*

CONTENTS

PREFACE

W HO CARES ABOUT a handful of castaways adrift on the ocean more than a hundred years ago? What does it matter that, in another century, 31 men in tiny lifeboats struggled desperately against their own private apocalypse with little hope of survival?

On May 3, 1866, the American clipper ship *Hornet* caught fire and burned approximately 1,000 miles due west of the Galapagos Islands in the Pacific Ocean, literally out in the middle of nowhere. She was a smartly manned ship, an "extreme" clipper, which, in the few years left before the 1869 completion of the transcontinental railroad, was still viewed as the greatest symbol of American commercial might and drive. The *Hornet's* complement consisted of 29 officers and crew, commanded by veteran ship-master Josiah Angier Mitchell, and two extra passengers, the brothers Samuel and Henry Ferguson, scions of a family soon to become among the most influential private bankers in the nation. Samuel was dying of tuber-culosis at age 28; his 18-year-old brother, a college student, was impatient for his life to begin. The three formed the ship's upper crust, and with them sailed a crew that mirrored all the prejudices and nuances of America's In-dustrial Age. There was Henry Chisling, the ship's black steward, who'd survived more sea disasters than anyone else aboard. Antonio Possene, an immigrant "Portyghee," despised by the others for his foreign ways. The three mates—the ship's rising middle class—jealously guarding their rights from the common sailors who berthed "before the mast" in the fore-castle. And Frederick Clough, part of that labor force, a 20-year-old sailor who planned to seek his fortune in the goldfields once the *Hornet* reached San Francisco.

Together, they headed west. Those who survived the trip ended much farther west than they'd ever imagined, sailing straight into the cross-hairs of a young and unknown journalist, Samuel Langhorne Clemens. His nationally published account of their ordeal made them famous, and served as a springboard for his transformation into Mark Twain.

As in other famous disaster epics, the story of the *Hornet* became in its time the symbol of something greater, a floating opera of sudden disaster, wasted life, and endured privations. It is fashionable today for scholars to call ships a "total environment," a human ecology so isolated that it forms a world of its own. This is an elegant concept, one that casts God as both the grand inquisitor and chief experimenter, but perhaps a more practical way to view ships and shipwrecks is what historian Greg Dening styled in his study of the *Bounty* as a kind of tragic theater, for it is in theater that we see the hopes, fears, and working myths of an age.

In the latter decades of the Age of Sail, three castaway tales were recounted again and again. In 1789, Lieutenant William Bligh and 18 loyal crewmen were set adrift on a 3,600-mile voyage by the mutineers aboard the *Bounty*, achieving in their successful navigation a triumph of discipline over nature. In 1820, the whaleship *Essex*, the source for Herman Melville's *Moby Dick*, was rammed by a whale: the tale of its less fortunate survivors, forced to eat one another, became a nineteenth-century metaphor for the breakdown of civilization. And there was the *Hornet*, whose castaways struggled to live for 43 days on 10 days' rations while sailing on a meandering, 4,300-mile course to Hawaii. What Melville called "the full awfulness of the sea" seemed focused on these men: they were stalked by sharks, swordfish and waterspouts, desiccated by heat and thirst, and maddened and weakened by starvation. In the end, they pre-pared for that lottery preceding cannibalism, the ritual mariners called the "custom of the sea." The *Bounty* and *Essex* are still remembered, and until the 1930s the story of the *Hornet* maintained a special place among the sea's devotees. In 1934, Charles Nordhoff and James Norman Hall dedi-cated the second volume of their *Bounty* Trilogy—*Men Against the Sea*, about Bligh's ordeal aboard his lifeboat—to Captain Mitchell and his achievement. But like so many tales of endurance and privation, Mitchell's achievement was forgotten after the murder and torment of World War II.

One facet of the *Hornet* saga that seemed evident in the old accounts but which was rarely explored was the social gaps and tensions separating the castaways. As the ordeal continued, these divisions erupted into class war. The first important commentator to ignore this was Twain, who avoided moral complexity to create a fable of moral leadership. Yet the fact remains that the survivors participated in what was apparently the only recorded account of mutiny aboard a castaway boat in the literature of the sea. Even Bligh's men stayed loyal to their volatile captain once they were banished from the *Bounty:* to do otherwise would have been suicide. Twain and other writers cast the *Hornet* revolt as a kind of temporary madness, yet the war of nerves that developed between the haves and have-nots on the clipper's lifeboats played out a drama that unfolded repeatedly across America in decades to come.

This, in addition to the sheer power of the journey, was what drew me to their tale. I had written two books on American justice and mercy, and in both cases, class was the hidden theme. The war between haves and have-nots raged so murderously in America and Europe during the late nineteenth and early twentieth centuries that one historian called it the "era of dynamite," and Americans have conveniently forgotten that the United States had the bloodiest and most violent labor history of any industrial nation in the world. Affluence wipes away many bad memories. But no longer. Today, the war between the haves and have-nots is intensely global, played as a kind of doomsday theater on television.

The hatreds on the *Hornet* reached such a point, transformed beneath the sun's tropical furnace into a pure kind of rage that sees no future and dreams only of ruin. Yet perched on the edge of self-immolation, something in the castaways made them turn aside. This was what ultimately drew me to the forgotten story of some lonely men in a lifeboat more than a century past. "The long habit of living indisposeth us to dying," said Sir Thomas Browne in his posthumous *Letter to a Friend*. Life was ultimately what mattered, even in the face of doom.

So this is a meditation on the forces conspiring to keep men alive. Although this is a reconstruction of the past, every event actually occurred. The main sources were the journals of the haves—Henry and Samuel Ferguson, Captain Josiah Mitchell and his family—but the have-nots spoke, too. Fred Clough, especially, left a narrative in a 1900 article, while Mark Twain left unpublished notes on the accounts of several sailors. In addition, countless others have been castaways, and I've dipped into the literature of disaster to help understand what occurred. The men of the *Hornet* are long gone and cannot be interviewed, but they left behind a theater that is still relevant. Trapped together in an unforgiving environment, they chose to live.

Finally, a strange mysticism is common in the accounts of sailors and shipwreck survivors, one hard to comprehend for landlubbers like me. Yet there is no denying that deep-water sailors have always shared a bond with the world's oceans that they themselves call spiritual. They insist they see God on the face of the deep, but He is often neither gentle nor benign. Those sailors who feel closest to such truth are those who come closest to death, and castaways are ranking members of that fraternity.

One of the best expressions of this was written by Stephen Crane, a castaway himself, in the last line of his classic story "The Open Boat": "When it came night, the white waves paced to and fro in the moonlight, and the wind brought the sound of the great sea's voice to the men on the shore, and they felt that they could then be interpreters."

All castaways interpret that voice. They learn that life, too short, is a gift. They learn, as has every generation, that when it comes to survival, we are all at sea.

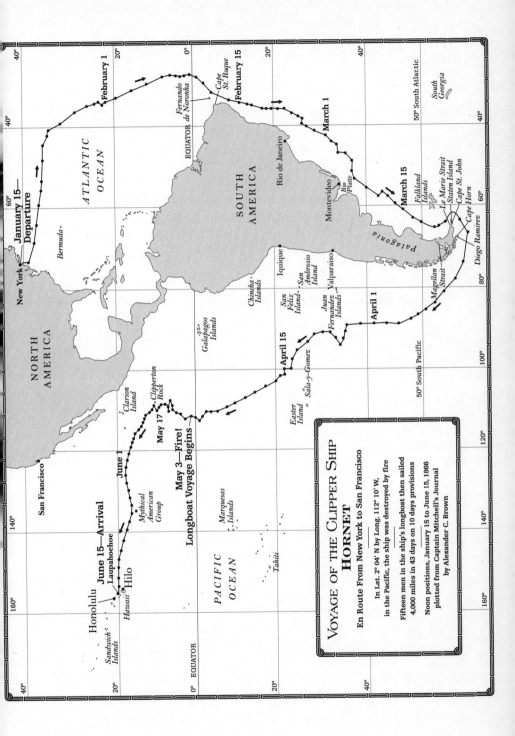

VOYAGE OF THE CLIPPER SHIP
HORNET

En Route From New York to San Francisco

In Lat. 2° 04' N by Long. 112° 10' W,
in the Pacific, the ship was destroyed by fire

Fifteen men in the ship's longboat then sailed
4,000 miles in 43 days on 10 days provisions

Noon positions, January 15 to June 15, 1866
plotted from Captain Mitchell's Journal
by Alexander C. Brown

NORTH
AMERICA

ATLANTIC
OCEAN

SOUTH
AMERICA

PACIFIC
OCEAN

New York

San Francisco

January 15 —
Departure

February 1

February 15

March 1

March 15

April 1

April 15

May 3 — Fire!
Longboat Voyage Begins

May 17

June 1

June 15 — Arrival

Honolulu

Laupahoehoe

Hilo

Hawaii

Sandwich
Islands

Bermuda

Cape
St. Roque

Fernando
de Noronha

EQUATOR

Rio de Janeiro

Montevideo

Rio
Plata

Patagonia

Falkland
Islands

Le Marie Strait
Staten Island
Cape St. John
Cape Horn

Magellan
Strait

Diego Ramirez

South
Georgia

Iquique

San
Ambrosio
Island

Valparaiso

Juan
Fernandez
Islands

Chincha
Islands

San
Felix
Island

Sala-y-Gomez

Easter
Island

Galapagos
Islands

Clipperton
Rock

Clarion
Island

Mythical
American
Group

Marquesas
Islands

Tahiti

EQUATOR

50° South Atlantic

50° South Pacific

The dangers of accusation and trial are human,
but the dangers encountered at sea are divine.

—HORACE, "Third Ode"

A FIRE AT SEA

T HE GREAT SHIP BURNED for 22 hours, illuminating the eternal sea and sky. She blazed like a giant lamp, fueled by the 20,000 gallons of kerosene and 6,000 boxes of candles stored in her hold. As this was consumed, she rose higher in the water, as a ship does at dockside when discharging cargo, in this case lightened by the blaze. The flames popped and crackled, and the 31 men of the *Hornet* watched helplessly as the ship became her own funeral pyre. Surely, another ship would spot the smoke rolling up in black masses. Surely their clipper ship's death would signal salvation from this empty, watery desert, where nothing else seemed to exist but the burning hulk of what had been one of the world's fastest ships, the white clouds skating above them, and their three tiny lifeboats adrift on the sea.

But no help came.

The *Hornet* burned from 7:00 A.M. on Thursday, May 3, 1866, until 5:00 A.M. the next morning. After so many hours, the men grew resigned to their position: a thousand miles from any landfall, with barely 12 gallons of potable water in the scuttlebutt and ten days' short rations for 31 men. How quickly life changed from routine calm to desperate uncertainty. They'd crossed the equator, heading north, on the previous evening, scudding along under a six-knot southeast breeze. They were 111 days from their home port, following the usual track of the California clipper trade. No speed record, true, but the passage around Cape Horn had been a picnic, the entire journey easy and uneventful.

Too easy, some feared, the captain included. In Victorian-era America, superstition was thought the province of the lower classes, but aboard ship such distinctions washed away. "Of all classes of men, the mariner is most inclined to superstition," a ship's steward once observed. The constant threat of an unpredictable environment and sudden death made even the most rational 19th-century man prone to "magical" thinking. The *Hornet's* captain told his crew that he'd never made such a pleasant run through the South Atlantic and 'round the Horn, but he mentioned to the first mate that the voyage was made under such strange circumstances that he feared something would mar it. Good luck had consequences.

Yet even the most superstitious could not predict that it would end this way. Clipper ships were the embodiment of speed in the mid-19th century, and in 1866 still the most reliable route to California. The overland route took months; trips across the isthmuses of Panama and Nicaragua knocked 7,900 miles off the Cape Horn route but were notorious for malaria, cholera, and yellow fever; the golden spike at Promontory Point, Utah, was still three years away. Rounding the Horn was perilous, but there was something romantic about a clipper passage, its masts and yards a tower of white canvas, the sails set high and wide to catch every breath of wind. This was still the heyday of sail in the United States Merchant Marine, and as an "extreme" clipper, with an emphasis on streamlined hull, large sail area, and fast passages, the *Hornet* exemplified America's growing presence on the world stage. American clipper ships were even faster than the China tea and opium clippers of the British, who owned the seas. She was part of a technological elite combining speed with grace, designed by premier shipbuilder Jacob Westervelt in New York City and launched on June 20, 1851.

To Captain Josiah Angier Mitchell, the *Hornet* was a world within herself where he reigned supreme. For all his vague misgivings about this passage, she was still the finest ship he'd mastered during his 40 years at sea. He'd walk the deck, tortured by the thought of placing too much strain on her spars, sick with worry that they'd snap in the wind. He'd place his hand on the rigging and feel the ship vibrate with life, then look overhead at the sails billowing like a fleet of white clouds. She was a marvelous ship, and now as he watched her burn it was as if he knelt by the deathbed of his own wife. She was too fine a ship to deserve this. Let it end quickly, he prayed.

The *Hornet* was many things to many men. To passenger Samuel Ferguson, she was a final chance at life itself. "Only an ocean voyage can save you," advised his doctor, who'd diagnosed tuberculosis and prescribed a tropical climate as the best known means to clear his lungs. To his younger brother Henry, the *Hornet* was an open door to adventure. To Fred Clough, a farm boy turned sailor, she was an escape from the grinding poverty of a seaman's lot. To Henry Chisling, the *Hornet*'s black steward, shipboard life was the closest thing to job equality he and other African-Americans, including cook Joseph Washington, could hope to find in 19th-century America. For over half the ship's crew, the *Hornet* mirrored the hopes and ironies of the dream that brought them from Europe to America—the vague promise of a better life, the reality of hard, unending labor, and the inseparable gulf between the rich and poor.

The disaster struck so fast it hardly seemed fair, and still felt unreal. James Cox, one of the apprentice crewmembers, or "boys," had told Henry Ferguson early in the voyage that disaster could strike at sea without warning. Coal ignited spontaneously; overloaded holds of grain took on moisture and expanded until the timbers burst. A greater danger was that of inadequate stowage: too many ships left port too soon after loading, since cargo needed time to settle in the hold. In the 1870s, when marine insurers first categorized the cause of high ship losses, they found that 93 British and American grain ships had foundered or gone missing in a single three-year period, with a loss of 833 lives; coal shifted with equal rapidity, and from 1874 to 1877, 314 coal vessels were lost, with 1,849 dead.

At the time, Henry suspected that Cox was trying to scare him, a common sailor prank, but Cox proved right, for disaster struck when the sea was smooth as glass and danger was the farthest thing from their minds. May 3 was one such lazy day. At daybreak, they'd lain becalmed in the doldrums; as was customary, Mitchell ordered every stitch of canvas set from the bulwarks high up to the royal yards, hoping to catch enough wind to keep steerage way. The larboard watch, commanded by first mate Sam Hardy, had tarred down the rigging and mainmast with buckets of "slush," the gray, smelly grease made by boiling and skimming off fat from salt meat, while men in the off-duty watch trailed hooks overside to lure bonito. Windsails were set over the open hatches, and every skylight, porthole, and window was fastened out for ventilation. As the sun poured down on the deck, a ripple crossed the water. The breeze caught in the sails and the ship began to move.

Samuel Ferguson listened to the bulkhead creak in his cabin as the *Hornet* rolled gently. He'd rarely known such peace, a restful lethargy said to be found only in the tropics. Three double strokes of the ship's bell announced seven in the morning, this answered by a second bell on the main deck. He nudged Henry and told him to rise.

Samuel's younger brother groaned. Yesterday had been momentous for Henry, if slightly disturbing, a change from the long and boring passage of hours. As always, it was a grand sight to see the ship under a full spread of canvas, the royals, staysails, topgallants, topsails, and courses soaring overhead. Deep-water sailors were prone to hyperbole when describing ships—clipper captains and crewmen the worst of all. They described the ascending sails as everything from moonrakers, cloud cleaners, skyscrapers, and stargazers to puffballs and "angel's footstools." As one watched a clipper ship grow from the horizon, he observed the sails rising row by row: first the skysails, high atop the masts, then the royals, topgallants, wide topsails, and closest to deck, the mainsails, or courses. Outrigged at the tips of the yards came tiers of studding sails; staysails were set between the masts, and triangular jibs at the bow. Sailors in the shrouds sounded like birds to Henry; they filled their territory with chatter and strange nautical song. Admirers of clippers said they "walked the waters like a thing of life," and they were certainly faster than anything else on the water, reaching speeds of 21 knots and making 400 miles a day to set sailing records still unbroken. The *Hornet* swooped through the air like a giant raptor to Henry—a magnificent, man-made bird of prey.

Henry caught a glimpse of the sea's brutality during the voyage. Yesterday morning he'd watched as crewmen caught nine bonito; that evening, they tried unsuccessfully to hook an enormous shark skimming beneath the surface directly astern. Mariners believed sharks could sense sick men and followed in hopes of feasting off the corpse if a sailor were buried at sea. They disemboweled each shark they caught, cut off his tail, and threw him back as a way to "give him a passage" to the other world. One monster they'd landed measured 12 feet from tip to tip, and Henry counted eight rows of teeth in its mouth. The shark's fellows feasted on his mangled remains when the crewmen dumped him over the side.

Such raw brutality was alien to Henry's world of merchant banking and academe. As he rose from the bunk, his first hope was that they'd catch another monster today, maybe the one that had stalked them astern. What if they cut it open and found inside its stomach a half-digested castaway? What a thing to tell his friends back home! He was imagining their reactions when he heard bare feet patter overhead and a voice cry, "Fire!"

The accident was a stupid one, more so for being so avoidable. Minutes earlier, Mr. Hardy had descended through the booby hatch with two other hands to search for a barrel of varnish stored in the hold. Below decks grew darker the deeper one descended, so they'd taken an "open" lantern to light their way. Captain Mitchell had ordered that the heavy barrel be lugged on deck to the sunlight before drawing the varnish, but what a chore that was when all they needed was a canful. Hardy was an experienced seaman, trusted by his captain, yet even good men grew lazy in the tropics. It was so much easier to open the bung and draw the varnish there.

He'd cut corners like this before and nothing happened—but not now. In the dim light the lantern tipped and lit the varnish; one accident instantly compounded the other. They dropped the can and left the spigot open; the flash of flaming varnish ignited a nearby wooden sail locker; suddenly the entire area between decks was burning. Hardy beat at the fire with blankets as flames raced toward casks of kerosene and boxes of paraffin candles. The seamen with him rushed up the ladder to spread the alarm.

When Samuel Ferguson smelled a whiff of smoke, he yelled for Henry to pull on his clothes. They grabbed the first things handy: leather pocket journals, stubby pencils, three bottles of brandy and their overcoats. Samuel added to this his pocket-sized The Book of Common Prayer and his pistol and cartridges for more worldly protection. They bounded on deck and found the forward area alive. Smoke rose black and thick from the booby hatch; three sick bay invalids had crawled through the smoke and lay gasping by the rail. Hardy emerged from the hatch, covered in soot, clothes singed. He yelled for the ship's carpenter and another man to grab axes, then all three chopped at the deck above the fire. "We need water!" cried Hardy. "Pour it down the hole!"

Yet even as he spoke, Mitchell ran up and countermanded the order, screaming instead for the men to close the hatches and smother the flames. By then, however, it was too late for either remedy. The blaze raced through the hold faster than the men could jump to orders; when it hit the kerosene and candles, flames shot through the hatch to the crossjack sail, ten to twenty feet overhead. Mitchell cried for his men to douse the burning canvas and clew up the other sails before they ignited, too, but as the sailors clawed up the ratlines the flames outpaced them again. A crimson column of fire erupted from the main hatch and ignited the great mainsail. Its tarred canvas exploded; the sailors screamed and slid back down the lines. They watched, transfixed, as wildfire leaped from spar to spar as if endowed with mind and purpose, enveloping the rigging until the entire ship aloft was one huge sheet of flame. The holocaust created fiery vortexes that wailed eerily as they sucked up surrounding oxygen; Henry remembered biblical passages in which the voice of God issued from a pillar of flame and the ancients prostrated themselves with fear. Now he understood. A vision of God was also a vision of Hell.

Even the undemonstrative Samuel was stunned. Ten years ago, he'd been a student at Trinity College in Hartford, Connecticut, like his brother; he'd danced around the bonfires with his classmates at the revels for All Hallow's Eve. In the bonfire's glow, the faces of his friends were lit in red and black, as if a more primitive version of themselves emerged from deep inside. Like Henry, he'd thought that nothing could harm him, long before he felt the first touch of TB. His friends had been the same way. That was in 1856, five years before the conflagration that scourged the Union, decimating the ranks of classmates and friends. How many had witnessed a similar emergence before they died on the battlefield, or killed another man?

Samuel and others considered fire the symbol of their age. There were the fires of the Civil War, fires of the great blast furnaces driving Industrial Age America, the consuming fire of disease that burned within his lungs. He could have taken a packet to Panama, crossed the Isthmus by rail and boarded a disaster-prone Vanderbilt steamship to California, but the clipper route was more appealing, no fire in the boilers, just the clean breath of God in the sails. Even so, there were times on this trip when the sun beat down on their ship with a malevolence that forced Samuel inside his cabin. The whole world was like a vast furnace afloat, bobbing in a sea of stars, fired by the sun.

As his condition worsened, Samuel would occasionally drift into strange reveries. His mental state outpaced his "white fever"; he changed from the practical son of a banking clan into a visionary. This was such a time. The entire ship was cloaked in a nimbus and an unearthly roaring filled his ears. He fought off the vision and cried to his brother, "Henry, we must get to the boats, now!" Mitchell yelled to abandon ship: he ordered the ship's carpenter to grab tools from his shop, directed two crewmen to haul sails from the sail locker, told Henry Chisling and Joe Washington to save all the water and grub they could from the galley and load it in the lifeboats. Each man returned to report that all was burning—the shop, sail locker, galley. "Go back!" Mitchell screamed. "Save what you can! Our lives depend on it," even as he realized they'd be doomed without the ship's navigating instruments, books, and charts stored in his cabin. He dove through the aftercabin to his chartroom, grabbed what he could, then stumbled blindly back on deck where the crew hauled provisions to the rail. Pitch boiling between the seams of the deck timbers stuck to the bare soles of their feet. Burning rope and canvas rained from above.

The *Hornet* had three lifeboats—a longboat and two small quarter-boats—and into these they must fit 29 crew and officers, two passengers, a water barrel, stores, oars, what sails and spars they could rescue, and other supplies. The two quarter-boats were already launched and tied along the ship, and crewmen lowered stores into them. But the longboat caused problems. It had been partially loaded on deck and was heavier than usual. The men heaved and strained at the painters but could not lift her up; they grabbed the lines and heaved with a unified curse, raising the boat about a foot before it dropped back to deck and an eyebolt stove in her bottom, tearing a hole the width of a man's head. John Sidney Thomas, the third mate, ordered the longboat lightened as he plugged up the hole with sheets and a blanket, then he jumped out and ordered the men again to the lines. "All together!" he cried. "Heave!" This time the longboat swung from the rail and lowered smoothly from the davits; it settled beside the burning ship on the ocean swells. Thomas and another man leaped into the boat as it rose up; they threw the line back on the deck and unhooked the deadfalls. The boat dropped astern and the crew threw down supplies.

A desperate calm guided their efforts now that all three boats were free. Their survival depended on the provisions and stores they managed to save from the fire. Although no larger sails had been pulled from the sail locker, they did salvage a studding sail, a main royal and some canvas that could be turned into sails. All were tossed into the longboat, while the water barrel was lowered more gingerly by four men holding a rope sling. The three men from sick bay were lowered in the same fashion. One of them, Antonio Possene, the Portuguese sailor from the Cape Verde

Islands, was caught stuffing bread in his mouth; Mr. Thomas roared in outrage when he spotted the theft and ripped the loaf from Possene's hands. The feverish sailor grasped for the bread, his arms flailing above him as he was lowered into the longboat beside another sick man.

Suddenly, they all heard a cheer. Harry Morris, a French sailor from Havre, appeared on deck holding the ship's mascot, a rooster, which flapped in his hands. It seemed a strange vision of madness—the singed and blackened sailor, the singed and crowing rooster, and other sailors laughing as the deck crackled with fire and burning spars crashed down. "*Le Chanticleer!*" cried the Frenchman, holding overhead the symbol of his native country. He laughed as he tossed the rooster into the longboat, then dove from the rail to the sea.

THE FLIGHT OF the bird and the Frenchman signaled the final exodus for everyone left aboard. Stragglers leaped from the rail and scrambled down lines hanging over the side. Samuel and his brother climbed, wet and dripping, into the stern of the longboat; they watched as Captain Mitchell looked back one last time at his burning ship, then glided down a painter and took his place at the tiller by the Fergusons. Mr. Hardy took charge of one quarter-boat, while John Parr, the second mate, sat at the tiller of the other. Mr. Thomas, as third mate, positioned himself amidships in the longboat, a buffer between his captain and the crew. Flaming shreds of sail fell hissing to the sea around them; if any entered the boats and ignited the salvaged canvas, they were doomed. "Cut the painter and shove off!" Mitchell cried. "Pull away to windward." A shadow crossed above them and the *Hornet*'s massive stern reared up like a cliff, threatening to crash down on them with the next swell. "Back!" Mitchell yelled and the crew strained at their oars. The ship's stern slapped the water where a moment earlier they had been.

The three boats pulled out of harm's reach, then came together quietly as mourners do. A weariness fell over them as they watched the ship burn. It was 8:00 A.M. and a quick check confirmed that all hands had survived. Henry Ferguson watched billows of smoke rise from the deck, punctured by sharp bursts of flame from deep in the hold. At 9:00 A.M., the weakened mainmast cracked, groaned, and fell back against the mizzen topmast, the mast closest to the stern. The two clung together for an instant, then the burning yardarms, spars, masts, and spiderweb of rigging twisted sideways and crashed into the sea. Sparks flew up from hissing clouds of steam. Only the foremast rose in the bow from the plumes of smoke, alone on the deck, wreathed in flames.

"That cloud of smoke can be seen for a hundred miles," Mitchell assured his men. "We'll stay here. With luck, another ship will come."

Henry glanced at his fellow castaways and wondered what would happen should Mitchell prove wrong. The men in the boats lay slumped across the gunnels, blank expressions on their faces. They'd been goaded into nearly superhuman effort in the rush to save themselves, but now they had collapsed, bitterly tired. Some were scorched and blistered where the fire had eaten through their clothes; one man's hand was severely burned. They were all experienced seamen, accustomed to pain and discomfort, but that also meant they were a hard lot, living in poverty along the waterfront, and were picked by the captain more for their brawn than brains.

Henry had learned some of their histories during his three months and three weeks aboard the *Hornet*. In some ways, the ship was both a snapshot of America and a preview of what it would become. From 1865 to 1900, the nation's population would more than double, growing from 34 million to 76 million, and most of that increase was due to European immigration. The *Hornet*'s crew presaged that change. Fifteen sailors, more than half, were recent immigrants or wandering sailors from England, Denmark, Sweden, Germany, France, Portugal, and Spain. Only one foreigner was an officer—John Parr, the second mate, from North Shields, England. The rest were regular seamen who could expect little advancement during their years at sea.

Of the rest, three were from New England and four from New York. One New Yorker, William Laing, was a wealthy stockbroker's son, while the *Hornet*'s two black crewmen, Henry Chisling and Joe Washington, came from far different social circumstances. Although their histories are unclear, Chisling was apparently a former free black living along the New York waterfront, while Washington was married to a woman who worked as a servant in a mansion on New York's Catherine Lane. Beneath the black crewmen in this rigid hierarchy were the apprentices—Jimmy Cox, who never stopped talking, and Thomas Tate, considered a whiner, from Portsmouth, New Hampshire. Both were younger than Henry, little more than boys.

The ship's managers and patricians all hailed from New England, a geographical dividing line in lives and careers. Samuel and Henry hailed from Stamford, Connecticut, sons of a wealthy businessman; in normal circumstances, their background held no meaning on ship, since a natural barrier existed between crew and passengers. But in the face of starvation, dehydration, and death, such social barriers would break down. Mr. Thomas, the third mate, hailed from Richmond, Maine, and was the youngest of the officers, barely in his 20s. He was single, hotheaded, and jealous of his precarious position between the older, more experienced officers and the seamen. Sam Hardy, the first mate, was in his 30s, a husband and father from Chatham on Cape Cod, Massachusetts. Before the accident, his future looked good: the *Hornet*'s owners looked ready to appoint him master of his own brig. Faithful service to such merchant firms meant steady progression up the ladder of success, often as quickly as after two profitable runs. Sam Hardy dreamed of his own ship and of the share of profits that came with command, but in one careless moment, all that had changed. Now he had two worries: surviving the shipwreck, and losing his prospects if he did. Either way meant certain poverty for his wife and child.

That left the captain. Josiah Mitchell was unassuming and laconic, and if anything looked a dour, puritanical fellow in the black overcoat and starched white shirt worn by so many clipper ship captains. His gray-streaked beard and deep-set eyes added to the image, but Mitchell's looks belied his character. He was not a "driver," as captains who beat their crewmen were called; he was neither cruel nor harsh, as was common in the world of merchant ships, where absolute obedience was expected and corporal punishment a given for anything less. In port, sailors "yarned" among themselves about captains, mates, and ships before signing a ship's articles, a form of comparative shopping before tying their fates for weeks and months to any one particular man. Mitchell was known among sailors at New York's South Street as a non-drinking family man and a captain who "came up through the hawse-hole," or started in the forecastle like them. Most important, they judged him "a man of rare caution, with a well-balanced Scotch head." He was mindful of the rights of mates and comfortable with delegating authority, issuing orders quietly and intervening only if they were not carried out, which was rare. Mitchell was fair

in his reports to owners, disinclined to exaggerate daily speeds and quick
to praise good work, the latter especially beloved by young mates with
ambitions of their own.

Mitchell was so considered a man of level head and steady tempera-
ment that Mark Twain would later call him a "New Englander of the best
seagoing stock of the old capable times," but in this he was wrong.
Mitchell *was* a New Englander, but did not come from a race of seafarers.
If anything, he was a romantic, like William Laing and young Henry Ferguson. He was born in 1812, the son of Josiah Whitman Mitchell, better
known as "Squire" Mitchell, a prominent lawyer of Freeport, Maine, a
shipbuilding village on the state's southern Casco Bay. Squire Mitchell
envisioned a legal career for his son and with that in mind sent him to the
pricey Hebron Academy, a preparatory school 25 miles upstate in Hebron.
But Josiah's health failed him after graduation, and he was sent to live in
nearby Bath with "Captain Maxwell," a family friend, who invited him to
sail aboard his ship for a year. Mitchell returned from the voyage restored
to health, and to his father's horror, in love with the sea. The younger
Mitchell never looked back: by age 21 he was made captain of a brig, and
two years later was awarded command of ships bound for China, Australia,
California, and other destinations in the Pacific merchant trade.

The captain and crew were capable seamen, but the challenges con-
fronting them now would dampen the spirits of anyone. The longboat, the
hole in its bottom plugged with more blankets and secured with canvas,
was starting to leak and might have to be replugged. Mr. Parr's quarter-
boat had acquired a hole above the waterline when an oar jammed between
the ship and the boat as she lay alongside. Since there were no sails or
spars, they'd have to jury-rig their own if they hoped to reach land. The
greatest problem, however, was the scarcity of their stores. Their 40-gal-
lon water barrel was less than one-third full, while the four one-gallon
demijohns divided between the smaller boats were empty. They had 100
pounds of bread; seven small pieces of salt pork, each weighing about four
pounds; one half-box of raisins; 12 two-pound cans of oysters, clams, beef
bully and soup; six buckets of raw potatoes, already rotting; four hams; and
a keg with four pounds of butter. They'd saved pipes, matches, and 100
pounds of twist tobacco, while the Fergusons added the three bottles of
brandy they'd snatched from their cabin. All had to be divided among 14

men in the longboat, nine in Mr. Hardy's boat, and eight in the quarter-boat under Mr. Parr.

The *Hornet* burned until twilight, and still no help arrived. A black pall of smoke rose up until flattening like an anvil top in high-level winds. The setting sun burned blood-red through the smoke; flames rose from the deck and hatches, replacing the light of the sun. The men's faces split into planes of red and black, reminding Henry of a host of mottled demons. Luckily, the sea was gentle. As the boats rocked, their shadows flickered across the red and gold water.

One advantage of the fire was that they had plenty of light to work by. Mitchell told each boat to fashion makeshift spars and sails for the very real possibility that they'd have to save themselves. Each crew had a hatchet, and they used these to trim salvaged spars into masts, each about 10 to 15 feet long; they lashed the remaining wood to the uprights as yardarms. John Campbell, the sailmaker, and others had saved their leather ditty bags, which contained everything needed for stitching and repairing sails. Henry watched as they rubbed thread across small amber cakes of beeswax to make it more pliable, then passed the thread through the thick sailmaker's needles and cut and sewed the canvas into three large square sails.

Meanwhile, Mitchell wrestled with the problem of food. He concluded that if they cut back to one-third normal daily rations, they might stretch the provisions ten days. They might catch some fish, and though Mitchell prayed for rain to fill the water cask, he wondered whether his boats could survive a storm. He called the quarter-boats over and divided the water and food; he checked that each boat had a sextant, a copy of Bowditch's *Practical Navigator,* and a *Nautical Almanac.* The captain and Mr. Parr had large mariner's compasses, but Mr. Hardy only had a small pocket type, little more than a toy, given to him by Samuel Ferguson. More worrisome was the fact that they'd saved only two chronometers: Mitchell kept one for the longboat and gave the second to Mr. Hardy.

When the stores were distributed, Mr. Parr stared in disbelief at his boat's tiny portion and cried, "This is all?" That's all anyone got, Mitchell countered. He told his mates to give each man half a hardtack biscuit for breakfast, a biscuit and canned meat for the midday meal, and one-half biscuit for tea. They'd get a few swallows of water with each meal.

From this point forward, their survival turned upon the smallest details. Samuel Ferguson watched the third mate and sailmaker push their needles through the seams of canvas, their hands disembodied in the firelight. The leak had grown worse, and he listened to the steady scrape of wooden buckets across the floor as men took their "watch" at bailing, a sound that became as much a part of the background as the wavelets lapping against the sides. He studied Henry's face, wondering if his brother truly grasped their danger: Henry seemed heartened by Mitchell's claim that they lay in the shipping lanes and so would likely be picked up, but Samuel knew that the situation was much worse than the captain let on. They were 1,250 miles due south of California, 2,500 miles southeast of Hawaii, and about 1,000 miles west of the Galapagos Islands. Their boats were woefully overloaded: the longboat itself was 21 feet in length, six feet wide and three feet deep; with 14 men, the water cask and other supplies, they rode dangerously low. The longboat was what sailors called "quick," meaning it rocked easily unless kept in perfect balance, and the quarter-boats, though not as overloaded, were still crowded. If anything, their little boats were built for visiting between ships and taking empty water casks ashore for filling, not extended use at sea. He felt more vulnerable now than he had in that terrible moment when the doctor diagnosed tuberculosis—the wavelets lapping against the sides of their ark, the cold touch of water on his fingers, all transmitted the truth of their position with a clarity he'd rarely known. In one moment, the disaster on the *Hornet* peeled away every protection of society. Instead, there was the sea: immense, powerful, and indifferent. And there were their tiny boats, bobbing like toys in a floating circle of light. Beyond that lay darkness.

Near dawn, a crash rang from the *Hornet* and all glanced over. The red-hot anchor had broken through the burning cathead to which it was secured and dragged tons of chain with it to the bottom of the sea. The glowing metal raced through the hawse-hole; clouds of steam hissed up where it entered the water. Henry watched in fascination and wondered how many people could say they'd seen such a sight. The chain raced on, two hundred fathoms deep, then fetched up, sending a spray of sparks in the air. There was a pause, then timbers splintered as the windlass pulled up from the deck by its roots and leaped across the deck after the chain. It crashed through the rail and followed the anchor into the sea.

Soon afterward, their vigil ended. At 5:00 A.M., a crewman cried, "There she goes!" The fire had finally eaten through the hull. They watched as the once-proud *Hornet* raised her stern from the water and plunged bow first, leaving behind charred spars and cinders, clouds of smoke and steam. A few bubbles lingered on the surface. Then even they were gone.

THE PICNIC CRUISE

LATER, WHEN THE HEAT and thirst grew so torturous that his tongue swelled in his mouth; when his skin shriveled black and salt-water boils dotted it like smallpox; when Captain Mitchell complained of hearing strange music and the men in the bow stared at him in hunger; then and only then did Henry Ferguson recall his first glimpse of the *Hornet* and the drift ice crunching against her sides. The memory of the cool, white ice tormented him now. It floated in sheets, grinding against the pilings of the South Street Harbor, first appearing on the ebb tide of Saturday, January 13, 1866, then filling the East River from shore to shore. The drifts were large and heavy, making navigation perilous: they'd already hauled down the dock when the pilot refused to tow them past Sandy Hook until Monday. Henry stared at the hundreds of ships and steamers lining the river, their thicket of yardarms and masts like a forest stripped of foliage. He gazed at the low clouds, lit sulphurous by the city lights; at the large, heavy snowflakes that muffled his city in silence. Soon he'd leave this cosmopolis of mansions and opera houses, tuberculosis and cholera. He was already homesick, but longed to be away.

In the days following the disaster, they remembered the delays that held them back, as if in warning not to sail. The unseasonal ice and violent gale. The pilot's refusal to tow them out. The change of masters eleven days before embarking. Captain Prince Harding was slated for the *Hornet*'s thirteenth voyage from an eastern port, its eleventh to San Francisco round the Horn, but clipper captains drove themselves as hard as their ships and such pressure took its toll. On January 2, a telegram arrived for

Mitchell in his Freeport home. Harding begged Mitchell to take command, citing bad health, a request echoed by the shipowners, the New York merchant firm of Lawrence, Giles & Company. Mitchell had commanded the *Hornet* in four straight cruises during 1859–1861—three times on the Frisco route, once from New York to Bristol, England. He knew her better than almost any man alive. Harding was more of a "driver" than the younger Mitchell, his best time on this route an enviable 111 days compared to Mitchell's best of 128, but Mitchell was solid and level-headed. The ship's cargo, insured at $400,000, or nearly $4.4 million in today's dollars, included 45 barrels and 2,000 cases of "kerosene oil," 6,195 boxes of candles, 400 tons of Pacific Railroad iron and three small steam engines, one bound for California gold country. The owners believed their capital couldn't be in better hands.

Reliability defined Josiah Mitchell. He'd received an A1 manager's rating from Lloyd's of London and fit the picture of the "prudent mariner" prized by merchants and insurers: the captain who worked his way across the oceans, avoiding risk as much as possible, but bravely facing whatever came. At 53, Mitchell was quiet and undemonstrative, yet despite the calm surface, he drove his ship like other clipper captains, very much Alexis de Tocqueville's American mariner: "The European sailor navigates with prudence," wrote de Tocqueville. "The Americans are often shipwrecked, but no trader crosses the seas more rapidly."

The weather was an omen, too. Seamen read the atmosphere like Talmudic scholars, and the signs made them uneasy. The conditions on January 13 continued the bad weather that had plagued the eastern seaboard since New Year. A prolonged gale howled from the northeast, blowing from Nova Scotia to North Carolina and filling the shipping columns of the *New York Herald* with notices of wreck and ruin. On Tuesday, January 9, the steamer *Mary A. Boardman* wrecked on the Romer Shoal and broke in two; the brig *Itasca* ran aground off Sandy Hook and five crewmen died while rowing for aid. The brig *Emma C.* struck the beach at East Sandwich, went to pieces, and five of her crew froze to death. On January 11, the schooner *Christiana* sank with all hands missing; the schooner *Warren*, bound for Rhode Island, wrecked off Hatteras. Four of her crew froze to death in the rigging, and two pilots washed overboard and drowned.

The *Hornet*'s course was an old one, charted by explorers, whalers, and sailors in the hide-and-tallow trade. The shortest course from New York to Frisco lay through the Straits of Magellan, a 13,328-mile route that most ships followed religiously. The U.S. Naval Observation and Hydrographic Office estimated 130 days as the average passage for a ship on the east-west route: 120 days was good, while 110 was a miracle. But this was not good enough for a nation obsessed with speed. America at midcentury was in a kind of exuberant adolescence, demanding change in every field. Americans had invented the sewing machine and trip hammer and strung telegraph wire from New York to Chicago, and women demanded suffrage. Speed was the index of change. No more dramatic change occurred than in sailing ships, which doubled their rates of speed in less than a decade—all because of clippers.

For Henry, booking passage on a clipper was like riding the Concorde: the clipper was a sublime technological feat, a gasp-inducing marvel that alters the sense of what humanity can achieve. With long, lean frames and knifelike bows that sliced through waves instead of riding over them, clippers carried loftier masts and wider sails than ever before seen in the history of sail. Their existence depended on speed. Before their development in the 1840s and 1850s, few sailing vessels had gone faster than an average sustained speed of six knots, and seamen considered a 150-mile day an excellent run. Yet by the 1850s, American clippers routinely clocked 250-mile days, and merchants were intoxicated. Conservative firms that once modestly christened vessels for wives and children were suddenly filled with poets who named their ships the *Lightning*, the *Flying Cloud*, and *Sovereign of the Sea*.

All this masked the less-than-glamorous reality that clippers were glorified express freighters, nothing more. All the romance was accident; the beauty, serendipity. It was a matter of trial and error that the shape that moved fastest through the water was streamlined and attractive, and that the cloud of sail needed to move such a ship took one's breath away. Clippers specialized in high-duty freight composed of smaller, more valuable items, many of these charged at an individual rather than bulk freight rate, and the California gold rush fueled the demand for such luxury goods. In 1849, for example, a barrel of flour selling for $6 in New York commanded $200 in San Francisco; a bushel of potatoes sold for $16; a pair of boots, $100; an egg, $1, equal to $23 today. Clippers were the moment's cash cow.

"Extreme" clippers like the *Hornet* were the solution to a nagging commercial problem: how to maximize hull speed while maintaining profitable cargo space in the hold. The answer was to build ships longer, not wider, yet even designers were amazed by the speed of their creations. Passages to California suddenly dropped from 130 to 116 days. Then, in 1851, the *Flying Cloud* cut that to 89 days, 21 hours—a sailing record that still stands.

New York was the center of the clipper world. By the 1850s and 1860s, the city handled five times more freight than all the New England cities, a focus that turned it into the nation's banking and financial center. Henry's family grew rich off this world. In 1790, his grandfather had immigrated to America from County Yorkshire in England, settled in Philadelphia to enter merchant shipping, then moved to New York to found a shipping house with his brother-in-law. In 1802, they formed J&S Ferguson, merchant bankers specializing in import and export shipping, and by the time of his death in 1816, the business was turned over to Henry's father, John, who located the firm at 35 Pine Street in the financial district.

Henry was the youngest of five brothers, all destined for money and power. John Day Ferguson, the oldest, practiced law for twelve years in New York under former senator William M. Everts, then returned to the family's "country" home in Stamford, Connecticut, to serve as state legislator. Samuel, the second boy, was born in New York on February 11, 1837, and graduated twenty years later from Trinity College with a bachelor's degree. By 1866, he listed his address as 35 Pine Street and his occupation as private banker. By then, Edmund, the third brother, and Walton, the fourth, worked for the firm. There were three sisters—Helen, Elizabeth, and Sarah—and Henry, who in truth had no idea what he wanted to do.

Merchant bankers like J&S Ferguson invested heavily in clipper ships, and though there has been considerable debate about their profitability, economic historian Robert Evans, Jr., argued that even after costs, owners earned at least 10 percent on their capital in lean years, and over 50 percent in better times. From 1853 to 1876, for example, the clipper *David Crockett* brought its owners a 37 percent net annual profit, or $500,000 yearly, equal to nearly $8.2 million today. The *Midnight* netted a 12.4 percent average annual return from 1855 to 1860, while the *Mandarin* took in a healthy 38 percent from 1851 to 1859.

All changed with the Civil War. In 1857, the United States slid into an economic slump, and by 1860, shipbuilding had ground to a halt. Then Confederate cruisers dealt Yankee shipping a mortal wound. Raiders like the *Alabama* and *Shenandoah* chased every merchantman they spotted, then put to the torch those registered American. Premiums for war-risk insurance rose out of proportion to real losses, and ships with neutral flags took business from the U.S. fleet. By 1865, nearly 1,600 American vessels had been transferred to foreign owners, a blow from which the merchant marine would not recover until after World War II.

Considering the upward course of their fortunes, it is likely that J&S Ferguson divested itself of most merchant fleet holdings by 1866 and diversified instead in the era's growth industries, including steel. The brothers did well. On his early death in 1877, John Day Ferguson bequeathed $10,000 to the town of Stamford for a public library. Edmund, the third brother, left an estate of $110 million in 1911, equal to nearly $2 billion today. Walton, the fourth, joined the family firm in 1863 and went to Pittsburgh, where he befriended coke and steel magnates Henry Clay Frick and Andrew Carnegie. Through his influence, J&S Ferguson became an early backer of Carnegie's steel empire, while Walton himself was appointed director of Union Carbide. When he returned to Stamford years later, he built a huge mansion the color of gold.

By 1866, Henry had shown no interest in the business world. Not that it mattered, since his future was charted for him. Like his brothers before him, Henry enrolled in Trinity College, attended St. Andrews Episcopal Church in Stamford, and was expected to vote Republican someday. It was assumed he would join the family firm after graduating in 1868. He was a prize scholar, but at 18 he was mostly interested in girls. On New Year's Day, 1866, he made 29 social calls, many including Stamford's eligible young females. On January 4, he visited the young ladies of a sewing society; on January 7, he "went to church with Josie Taylor and succeeded in freezing an ear" in 15-degree temperatures. He seemed particularly interested in Miss Taylor: she was included in his New Year's visitations, and on January 11, she and he ice-skated.

When the subject of accompanying Samuel to Frisco was first broached on Monday, January 8, Henry itched to go. It was raised at supper, a fire crackling in the hearth, the family seated at the silver-laid table, servants in the wings. The choice of a traveling companion was Samuel's. His father cautioned him about falling behind in his studies. *Who cared about that?* Henry thought. *He was going Out West.* "Felt much in favor of it," he wrote, but his excitement was best telegraphed by the speed with which he left for Trinity to arrange his sabbatical.

Of all the brothers, Henry was closest to the introspective Samuel, while Samuel seemed amused by his younger brother's high spirits. An 1866 photo shows the two of them together, the beardless youth and hirsute young man, both in conservative black suits with white handkerchiefs poking from the left lapel pocket, both lean and lanky with high foreheads. The photo does not show the affection shared between them: the way Samuel nursed Henry through his seasickness, or Henry's careful watch over Samuel. They were two oddballs in a clan of high achievers, but both were given leeway: Henry, because of his youth. Samuel, because he was dying.

Riches and power shielded the Fergusons from the Civil War, economic downturn, and the poverty rampant in New York's streets, but it did not save them from disease. John Day, the oldest, died young at 45. Edmund and Walton were forced to leave Trinity early from sickness; the fate of the sisters is not known. Samuel was their harbinger, his curse pulmonary tuberculosis. The rod-shaped *mycobacterium tuberculis* bacillus was mankind's first reported plague, and evidence of its affliction goes back to 5000 B.C. In 1866, Samuel's disease had many names—white plague, phthisis, and most commonly consumption—but Samuel called it "my lung fever" and Henry knew it as "my brother's wasting disease."

Samuel was nearing the final stages of his disease. He'd probably contracted it two and a half to five years earlier in New York, where entire sections of immigrant neighborhoods were known as "lunger blocks" and the bacillus-filled droplets sneezed, coughed, or exhaled by TB victims hung suspended in buildings for days. His slow-growing curse progressed through chest pain, shortness of breath, sleeplessness, loss of appetite, and fatigue; the ruddiness of his face gave way to deathlike pallor; he feared the day his cough transformed into the recurring hemorrhage that started "sweet, insipid, or saltish" and ended with a foul-tasting, rusty-green mucus streaked with blood. His body assumed the classic proportions of the dying: the frame that was "slim, erect, delicate looking, having scarcely any fat"; a gaunt face with bright eyes and large pupils; skin that was soft and transparent, through which the bluish veins pulsed and glowed.

His family watched the change, spellbound and horrified. There was an obsession with death in mid-century America: Lincoln had been assassinated nine months earlier; the 1.09 million war casualties were a constant presence; typhus, malaria, pneumonia, smallpox and tuberculosis killed more soldiers than battlefield wounds. But tuberculosis was the greatest killer of all. Death had a wasting face, seen up close in loved ones. Vital records suggest that by 1800, one of every 250 people on the eastern seaboard suffered some "consumption," accounting for one in four deaths. The Industrial Revolution, crowded slums, bad water, open sewers, moral decay—all were blamed for TB.

A strange inversion of life and death occurred in popular culture, where images of pale, wasting men and women quickened Victorian pulses. "Decay and disease are often beautiful, like the pearly tear of the shellfish and the hectic glow of consumption," wrote Henry David Thoreau, a consumptive himself, in 1852. A wasting beauty in women was called ethereal, while robust health was considered vulgar; in men, tuberculosis was thought to denote creative genius, prompted by the suffering of such artists as Poe, Goethe, Balzac, Stevenson, and Keats. As nothing stopped the epidemic, cures turned desperate and strange. In southern New England, rural families believed that TB victims returned from the grave to feed on their siblings: they were exhumed and cremated, their ashes mixed in a brew for the living. In health resorts like Denver, a blood mania developed called "the slaughterhouse cure." As one observer wrote: "When the doors of the slaughter-houses opened, a throng rushed in ready to catch the ebbing life of the doomed animals. As the warm red current gushed forth, glasses were held to be filled from the stream." Death was a solemn toast when cures were "scarcely ever heard of, and never expected."

One slim hope remained—escape to another place, the most ancient cure of all. The treatment was called Climatology, hearkening back to Hippocrates' *Airs-Waters-Places* and seen as early as 86 B.C. when Roman orator Cicero spat blood, "became thin like a pole," sailed south on a sea voyage, and recovered. The weak and ill based their last, best hope on what TB sufferer Robert Louis Stevenson called "the seeking of life under more gentle skies." As early as 1820, health seekers came to the West in great enough numbers to be dubbed the "one lung army." Miracle cures were promoted in Southern California, Colorado Springs, and New Mexico. "Go West and Breathe Again!" promised one ad campaign.

As a private banker, Samuel had incentive to spread the family fortune to new regions, as Walton did in Pittsburgh. The Southwest in 1866 looked promising—the mineral wealth of the Rockies and Sierras was just being realized, while the California haciendas were open for land speculation. And there was the railroad, the next big thing. J&S Ferguson needed a good man in California, and Samuel was willing to go. He sewed $200 in gold and silver into his coat lining, then packed his stores: two dozen pints of hard cider; four dozen quarts of ale; an equal amount of claret; ten bottles of whisky, eight of wine, four of brandy, and two of sherry; a half-barrel of fresh apples; two dozen cans of peaches in syrup; two boxes of pickled oysters; one keg of tamarinds; one basket of lemons; two boxes of gingersnaps; and two valentine boxes, not to be opened until February 14. One was from his family, the other from his sweetheart, Miss Snow.

He also took his pistol. Its presence would prove critical. It was of polished black metal, had a brown wooden stock, and was small enough to fit in a coat pocket. Early service revolvers were first mass-produced during the Civil War. The 1851 Colt Navy .36, 1858 Remington New Model Army .44, and 1860 Colt .44 were all civilian favorites, but the barrel-length of each was such that they could only be carried comfortably tucked under the belt or in a side holster. Only the Starr Army .44 was small enough to be carried in a pocket; it was also one of the first double-action models, an added advantage since Samuel could fire with a simple squeeze of the trigger as compared to cocking the hammer before every shot. A deluxe kit included mahogany case, ornate silver powder flask, bullet mold, small metal pillbox filled with pellet-sized percussion caps, and five boxes of prefabricated paper cartridges, the latter unfortunately prone to misfire.

Samuel chose Henry to "watch" with him in his final days. Watchers provided comfort and a link to family, but most important, he would not die alone. Henry knew his selection was an honor; he did not know that it could also be a death sentence. By staying in a cramped cabin with his brother for nearly four months, he too stood a good chance of breathing in the free-floating bacillus. If so, he'd continue the deadly tradition, bringing Samuel's disease home to the family.

The last detail was conveyance, and the *Hornet* was a fine ship for the voyage. Built for the California trade, she measured 207 feet in length, 40 feet in width, and 22 feet in depth and weighed 1,326 tons. Only one other clipper built before her was larger—the 1,534-ton *Stag Hound*—and the shipping press described her as a "flush decked ship" of white oak with iron and copper fastenings, a vessel that would be "extremely fast" and was "one of the best modeled and constructed clippers" of her day. Everything about "extreme" clippers like the *Hornet* was gargantuan. Mainmasts towered 190 feet above the deck, main yardarms stretched nearly the length of a football field, lower studding sails stretched 160 feet from end to end, and a suit of sails contained about 1.75 acres of canvas. *American Lloyd's Registry* of 1862 gave her an A1– rating, a high grade reflecting her 15 years of service.

More than that, clippers were judged by the elusive factor of character. Legally, ships have a personality: the idea, agreed upon by custom in 1866, was made official 36 years later by the U.S. Supreme Court. "A ship is born when she is launched," decreed the justices in the 1902 *Tucker* v. *Alexandroff.* "From the moment her keel touches the water she is transformed, and . . . acquires a personality of her own." If so, the *Hornet* was more sturdy and reliable than glamorous and flashy. She'd set a record in 1853 by sailing from San Francisco to Callao in 34 days, and was best known for beating the famous *Flying Cloud* that same year during a 106-day race from New York to Frisco. But she'd suffered bad luck, too. On her maiden voyage, two steamship boilers weighing 49 tons apiece were stowed on deck; they had to be chopped loose and thrown overboard during a gale or the *Hornet* would have foundered. Ten years later, during a trip to Bristol, she was caught in a hurricane for 20 hours. Her lifetime average of 125 days for the Cape Horn run meant she was not among the fastest ships, but in fair and foul conditions, she sailed steadily without the mutinies, death, and disaster that plagued the record-setters.

THEY LEFT ON Monday, January 15, two days behind schedule, when the ice thinned enough that the pilot no longer had conniptions. At 7:30 A.M., they were towed from the pier by the *William Fletcher*, a steam-powered sidewheel tug, and lay in the Upper Bay until 9:00 A.M., when a pilot boat brought the rest of the crew. One unidentified sailor never made it: he'd stowed his gear aboard the previous night, but never returned. The *Fletcher* towed them past the swift pilot boats clustered at the harbor mouth, then three miles out cast off its lines and headed home.

That afternoon, they encountered gentle seas. "No inconvenience so far," Samuel jotted as they unpacked their clothes in a cabin the size of a modern prison cell. Their cabin was on the port side of the "saloon," or messroom, behind Mr. Hardy's; Henry took the upper berth and Samuel the lower. Aftercabins were walled in half: the mess, taken up by a large table, steward's pantry, and small cabins, lay forward, while aft lay the captain's quarters. Clipper cabins could be luxurious: one had six portholes, a full-sized bed with a bookcase, and a full-length suite, while the saloon had polished teak bulkheads, a grand piano, and a caged canary. Though Mitchell was not given to such sumptuousness, Henry called their quarters "very cozy indeed."

That changed at 10:00 P.M. when they ran into a southeast gale. Snow and freezing rain came with it; the ship pitched and rolled drunkenly in the heavy seas. The brothers hid in their bunks as their unsecured trunks crashed from wall to wall; Henry was so "capsized" with seasickness that he didn't care if he lived or died. Samuel could jump around and tie off the trunks if he wished: all Henry wanted was to lie still.

Matters were infinitely worse overhead. Mitchell stayed on deck all night, worried that their journey might end before it even started. The *Hornet* sailed in 30 fathoms of water and the wind shoved them toward the lee shore. Hundreds of ships had wrecked off the Jersey coast: if this gale continued, they'd be dashed to bits on its sandbars like so many other ships in last week's news. All he could do was shorten sails, brace the yards, and sail close-hauled into the storm, which meant every man must go aloft, from the most veteran sailor to the greenest "boy."

There were three "boys" aboard the *Hornet*, a ranking applied to any man who had never before been to sea. In this case, all were young, and two suffered badly. James Cox was the youngest, a wiry fellow of 14 or 15 who gave his father's address as the New York firm of Wellington & Cox at 74 Broad Street. Events suggest he was apprenticed to Mitchell, just as Mitchell had been apprenticed to Captain Maxwell in 1829. Like Mitchell, Jimmy Cox hoped to rise from apprentice to seaman, seaman to mate, then be made master of his own ship by age 21.

William Laing was also green, but older, age 19 or 20, "a gentleman's son who came to sea for pleasure," Henry said. His father, New York stockbroker A.E. Laing of 18 Broad Street, was quite successful. Laing was drawn by a romanticism common among young men of his class, inspired in part by Richard Henry Dana's firsthand account of sailor life 26 years earlier.

The 1840 publication of Dana's *Two Years Before the Mast* was a phenomenon in ways rarely seen today. Before this, nautical literature celebrated the sublimity of the ocean and the freedom of the sailor: Dana's narrative of life aboard a brig in the New York–to–California hide trade included death, near-mutiny, and flogging. Sales were impressive, and imitators abounded. Journey narratives like Dana's were uncommon before 1840; now they sprang up everywhere, including Francis Allyn Olmstead's *Incidents of a Whaling Cruise* in 1841, Herman Melville's *Typee* in 1846, and Francis Parkman's *The Oregon Trail* in 1847. *Two Years Before the Mast* was an American hero quest, the brutal journey from which a young hero emerged purified and reborn. Just as important, it was suffused with the power and mystery of the sea.

Victorians were enthralled by the sea. It transcended all understanding. A ship on a dangerous sea was society in microcosm: it was the ordered world protecting man from chaos. The captain, the embodiment of law, must be obeyed. Man, like the ship, was alone against the elements. Only faith, luck, and obedience helped him survive.

Such metaphors had tremendous influence on 19-century lads, and just as quickly fell apart in the face of reality. "A sailor's life is like a dog's life," old sailors said, and Laing could see why. He felt like a terrified spider as he climbed the tossing ratlines over a white-capped sea. A light-framed youth unused to hard physical labor, his misery was compounded by doubts that he would survive. He too was seasick, at 150 feet, and the rocking increased the higher he climbed. A head sea beat on the bow with a force like a sledgehammer; boarding seas flew in a green sheet over the deck; the wind whistled through the rigging. The hard sails had to be punched into submission as he reefed them up. Soon his hands and fingers bled.

Later that night the wind shifted to the west and the *Hornet* headed for open water; Mitchell ordered the cook to rustle up hot food, and told Mr. Hardy to call the green hands down. It was only then that Hardy saw the red and blistered fingers of Laing and Cox and sent them to their berths. William Laing had gotten frostbite on his first day under sail.

Fred Clough knew what the green hands were suffering. A man learned to climb the rigging's weather side to take advantage of the ship's angle; he learned to keep his eyes glued to his work, since glancing down invited vertigo. There was a choreography to sailing a ship, and sailors learned to dance in the shrouds. Yet learning the dance did not insure survival. In another storm like this, he'd felt the sudden slacking in the footrope and saw the vacant spot beside him on the yardarm. Man overboard! He glimpsed, through lightning flashes, a figure hurtling through space. In the next flash, he saw the crest of an oncoming wave break over an upturned face. A third flash and there was nothing except a watch cap carried off by the wind.

Fred Clough was a typical merchant sailor for his day. A magazine photo shows him posed in a studio, left hand on his hip, derby in his right hand. Such sittings could be stiff but Clough seems at ease, even cocky, a proud Jack Tar at age 20. He has broad cheeks, thick brows, and short dark hair; his jaws clamp down on a cheroot, probably hand-rolled. He wears what could be his only suit, and stands five feet six or five feet seven inches, not tall, but solid. Tattoos were common, but none can be seen. His hands are thick and rough, always "half open, as though just ready to grasp a rope," said Dana, and probably scarred, the result of hazardous work conditions. He'd been a sailor for a year or two before shipping aboard the *Hornet*, long enough to be rated as an "ordinary" seaman, a rating between green hand and "able-bodied" veteran. He was sufficiently accustomed to the ways of the waterfront to hear of Mitchell, and savvy enough to know that a monthly wage of $12 to $15 held no future for him.

This was Clough's last voyage, but for different reasons than Laing. Fred's brother Amos awaited him in San Francisco: they'd pan gold together, then build a farm like home. Clough was raised on a farm outside Thomaston, Maine, where at one time more wooden ocean-going ships were built than anywhere else in the nation. Located 12 miles up the St. Georges River, the town was also a harbor for wealth: three of the nation's seven millionaires in 1840 lived in Thomaston, and all three were sea captains *and* shipbuilders. First landfall there occurred in 1605, and the British captain, George Weymouth, was amazed to find an area overgrown with huge trees with long, straight trunks, the very thing needed for mastheads. From then until the outbreak of the Revolutionary War, all masts and much of the wood for British ships came from Thomaston.

It was nearly impossible for an adventurous young Thomaston lad not to be inspired by the sea. No records remain of Fred Clough's first passage, but by January 1866 he came well-prepared. He wore a checked shirt, baggy trousers, and straw hat when he signed up, and was expected to provide his own mug, plate, spoon, and fork, all of tin. His gear included a "donkey's breakfast," or straw mattress, and quilt; a "cheap jack" razor and strap; one sheath knife and belt; one pound of tobacco and one dozen matches; and, if he could afford it, an oil-sealed jacket and pants for wet weather. This cost about $8, or nearly $82 today, more than half his monthly wage.

If anything illustrated class differences aboard ship, it was the living quarters. The captain, officers, steward and passengers lived aft in the well-appointed afterhouse; the men lived forward, before the mainmast, in the forecastle (pronounced "foc's'le") named for the fore castle in the high-riding bows of early galleons. No man went aft unless ordered, while no officer, including the captain, entered the forecastle except in dire emergency. On the *Hornet*, the forecastle was moved from an area below decks to a deckhouse placed forward, and though well-ventilated deckhouses were superior to the damp forward dungeons of early sailing ships, forecastles were still dank, crowded, smoky, and smelly, home to the crew, cook, ship's galley, carpenter and his workshop, several apprentices, and various vermin. The latter included roaches, biting flies, lice, fleas, bedbugs, mosquitoes, and, in South American traders, tarantulas. Of them all, rats prevailed: they chewed holes in walls, stole socks from sailors' shoes, ate balls of twine and cakes of beeswax, scampered over sleeping sailors, and drowned in water pitchers. One exterminator hired to clean out a nest of rats reported catching 624.

Food was the second great divider between classes. The officers and guests dined off china and ate the best cuts of meat, pies and cakes, preserves, and fresh fruits and vegetables. In the forecastle, meals consisted of four staples: salt meat (beef or pork), hard bread, rice, and beans, and everything ran with bugs. The basis of this daily fare was the salt meat, soaked in a brine laced with saltpeter and kept in 300-pound kegs. Sailors called it "old horse" for good reason. Eating salt beef took the skin off the roof of one's mouth, yet sailors took pride in eating the stuff, using it as proof that they could digest anything small enough to swallow.

Fred could anticipate the food and quarters, but he never knew about his shipmates until under way. There was a certain "Yankeeness" on clippers, but this accounted for only half the crew. The rest were Spaniards, Portuguese, French, English, Germans, and Scandinavians. Prejudice among groups was rampant, but most reviled were Portuguese sailors, despite their nation's history of exploration. "Portyghee" crewmen were thought to lack skills, be physically inadequate, and be prone to moral degeneracy—another term for buggery. There were a number of reasons for such diversity. In times of revolution, nations cleared their jails and workhouses to fill ships, and Europe had been in a state of revolt since 1848. The world was in turmoil, nowhere more than at sea. But opportunities out West and in the growing number of factory jobs also siphoned away sailors. Although industrial conditions were abysmal and workers labored six days a week for 12 to 16 hours, they still provided more freedom and better pay than a life at sea. Captains pointed out to shipowners that if they wanted American crewmen, they must pay higher wages, but owners stonewalled, filling openings with foreign sailors and refusing to upgrade working conditions.

There is real irony in this. The nation's economy was stimulated by wartime production to such an extent that in 1866 the United States was on the cusp of a commercial greatness that had only been a distant dream. The businessman brother of war hero William Tecumsch Sherman marveled: "The close of the war with our resources unimpaired gives . . . a scope to the ideas of leading capitalists, far higher than anything ever undertaken before. They talk of millions as confidently as formerly of thousands." Yet during this gilded era, the shipping industry began to fail. The forest of masts along the East River belied the industry's decline. In 1857, freight rates to California hit rock bottom; in 1863, war-risk insurance rocketed to a high of 8 percent; by 1865, 1,000 ships had transferred to foreign flags, including 74 clippers. By 1866, New England's golden age of sail was over. To pay their debts, shipowners turned to the detestable guano trade.

Clough was lucky for a sailor—he'd not yet signed for a guano cruise, but knew it was only a matter of time. Over the centuries, millions of sea birds lived and died at the Chinchas, three rocky islets a dozen miles off the coast of Peru, forming with their excrement round hills of guano, some 150 feet deep. Bird droppings were pure gold. By 1850, Peruvian guano accounted for 22 percent of all commercial fertilizer used in the United States, and by 1860, guano represented 43 percent of the total despite the then-exorbitant price of $73 per ton. The business was so lucrative that in 1852 a brief "Guano War" flared up between the United States and Peru when a Brooklyn businessman looted a Peruvian island of its guano. The U.S. backed down, but four years later, under pressure from farmers, the U.S. Congress passed the Guano Islands Act, a piece of legislation that, according to economic historian Jimmy M. Skaggs, "deputized each and every American citizen to claim territory for the commonwealth, an act that has no parallel in history." Ships came from all over the world to carry home the stinking stuff, waiting 2 to 3 months to be loaded, then drawing close to a cliff where Chinese coolies, noses and mouths covered with rags, shoveled the guano through chutes that dropped to the hold. Vessels were enveloped in a thick, yellow cloud that penetrated everywhere. Unhealthy as this was for sailors, the trade was deadliest for coolies, who died of starvation, exhaustion, sickness, and jumping to their deaths to the rocks below.

If guano sickened sailors' bodies, the trade in coolies sickened their souls. By the 1850s, shipowners were paid $50 to $80 for each coolie they carried from China to the Chinchas; a shipload of 800 coolies was worth at least $40,000. Yet death rates were staggering. In 1856, the *Sea Witch* piled up on a reef with 500 coolies, most of whom drowned. In 1857, a ship of 1,000 coolies endured flogging, suicide, and mutiny before trying to set the ship afire. One-hundred thirty coolies died on that trip, 70 during the mutiny, the rest from dysentery.

Clough didn't have to be a genius to know that pay and working conditions were improving everywhere in America, except on her ships. At least one-quarter of the crew didn't even want to be here. Faced with a shortage of seamen, shipowners turned to "crimps," agents who kidnaped sailors or derelicts from the waterfront and delivered them to ships in exchange for an advance on their wages. A sailor fresh off a voyage would stroll into a bar or brothel and the next day find himself waking on another ship, his stupor induced by a drink laced with drugs. The most infamous crimp's bars were found in San Francisco, where laudanum-laced "specials" could drop a man in his tracks, but New York's crimps were more sophisticated for having a veneer of legality. Business there was controlled by the Boarding House Keepers' Association, chartered under the laws of New York, which monopolized the supply of seamen for 30 years. A sailor "advanced" a significant part of his wages to a crimp for room, board, and the tribute required to secure a berth. When he arrived at the new berth, he also came with a requisition for "services": the captain deducted this fee from his wages, and it might take months before he ever earned a penny. If nothing remained of his wages when the voyage ended, his only recourse was to leave sailoring altogether or start the debt cycle anew.

Thus, a year after the war that ended slavery, American clippers depended in many ways on forced servitude. Yankee clippers were called "blood packets," "slaughterhouses," and "hellships" with good reason: the Jekyll-and-Hyde contrast between the glamour of the ship and life of the sailor turned their voyages into bitter contests between seamen forced into hard and dangerous work and captains determined to get their ships to port as quickly as possible. As with most forms of slavery, the blame was laid on the slave. Merchant captain Samuel Samuels said the era's seamen were "the toughest class of men in all respects . . . [but] had not the slightest idea of morality or honesty. . . . I tried to humanize these brutal natures as much as possible, but the better they were treated the more trouble my officers had." According to another clipper captain: "They were a class of humans incapable of self-regulation."

It was a rare cruise that sailed without a cargo of discontent and barely suppressed rancor. Although Congress passed laws in 1850 forbidding flogging, the practice continued well into the 1860s. Savage "bucko" mates enforced discipline with belaying pins, brass knuckles, revolvers, handcuffs, leg irons, and whips. Mutiny was a palpable threat: aboard the *Adelaide*, a first mate knocked a seaman overboard to his death, another sailor killed this mate, and the captain hanged the vigilante from the yardarm. Clough knew as well as any sailor that a journey could turn in an instant from a "picnic cruise" into a nightmare. The fact that the *Hornet* had an easy captain dampened the anger. But the sea was a lottery, a ship's fate resting on the whims of the officers, the tempers of crewmen, the randomness of Nature.

AFTER THAT FIRST awful night, the weather abated and all felt more at ease. The crew formed a pool for their arrival time in port: the second and third mate predicted 120 days, and each noon's fix of longitude and latitude made the bets interesting. They went in climate from winter to spring to summer, then back to cold weather near Cape Horn. By January 17, the second day out, they entered the Gulf Stream; on January 23, they "spoke," or hailed, an English brig bound from New York to Constantinople carrying survivors from the shipwrecked *Edwin Reed*.

For Fred, it was a rare and pleasant passage. He'd climb the rigging and see the deep blue ocean in the distance, some mornings dotted with other ships, their white sails glowing in the sun. On the blackest nights, he could follow the ship's path by its phosphorescent wake, or stare overhead and spot the Southern Cross, the brightest constellation in the sky. All made a man forget the petty differences on ship, or the doubts he had ashore.

Samuel felt peaceful, too. "Get more and more in love with the sea and the color of the water which is different from what I ever saw," he wrote on January 19, four days after embarking. He studied shades and hues like a painter. "The waves danced about as if they were having a real good time, not sullen as sometimes," he wrote on Monday, January 22. There was even beauty in storms. "The tremendous seas looked as if they would wholly engulf the ship, but coming up would break, mingling the whites of white foam into almost perfect blue." At midnight on Sunday, February 11, they crossed the Equator and celebrated his 28th birthday, toasting both with a raised glass of Madeira. Yet the greatest gift—restoration of his health—had still not materialized, and perhaps in response his old mysticism reared its head. On January 22, he dreamed of four vessels, a dream that troubled him for days. The only four ships he knew were those of the Pilgrims: the original *Mayflower*, *Fortune*, *Anne*, and *Little James*. Captain Mitchell had mentioned that an ancestor, Experience Mitchell, sailed aboard the *Anne*. Nineteenth-century Americans venerated the Pilgrims, cast as seekers of a purer purpose, outside the daily striving of men.

Henry felt neither peaceful nor sublime. He was bored. Except for the sea and weather, every day was "a repetition of all that have preceded it." At 7:30, they ate breakfast, followed by reading and strolling the deck. At noon they ate, followed by lounging, reading, and walking on deck, or watching the sailors make and mend sails. At 5:30, they had tea, played whist with the captain, and turned in. Everywhere he looked was sky and water, water and sky. He did what he could to escape: he thought of girls, especially the pretty Miss Taylor; he climbed to the mizzentop to study Greek, slid on the jibboom to catch bonito, swung in a hammock beneath the spanker boom. He took potshots at albatross until crewmen warned they were the ghosts of dead sailors.

On February 23, a sailor caught him aloft and made him pay a "footing," an old shipboard code. Passengers were not supposed to climb the rigging, the domain of sailors, a place best not invaded by those aspiring "to raise themselves above their betters by climbing the ratlines," his captor jokingly said. The penalty to return to deck was usually a bottle of rum. "As I had been aloft so much and nothing said, I almost thought it had gone out of fashion," Henry wrote: he did not name the sailor, but later familiarity suggests Fred Clough. Henry took it in good humor: "I gave the fellow half a dollar to drink my health," in the process scoring points in the fore-castle. On April 19, he turned 19 and celebrated with gingersnaps and a glass of sherry; a few days later, he caught head lice, was plagued by toothache, and fell seasick again.

More than anything else, he watched sailors, a species of human he'd never observed. They had a casual acquaintance with violence he found hard to understand. Once the hands sang a sea chanty as they hoisted the topsails. It all seemed romantic until he listened to the words:

> *They say I hung my mother,*
> *And then I hung my brother.*
> *I hung my sister Nancy,*
> *Because I took a fancy.*
> *A rope, a beam, a ladder,*
> *I hung them all together.*
> *They call me "Hanging Johnny," away aye oh!*

In between pulls on the rope, old shellbacks sang out, "Hang, you sons of bitches, hang!!"

It seemed an existence lived without context. Not a man on the ship had, to Henry's knowledge, fought in the Civil War. Many seemed igno-rant of the Thirteenth Amendment abolishing slavery, which became effective in the month before they sailed. Sailors were sealed within their ship, adrift, without ties to women, family, formal religion, or country; they were, in fact, considered apart from society in almost every literate age. They were "to be numbered neither with the living nor the dead," wrote one 18th century cleric. They were a "distant and peculiar species" of human, wrote American consul J. Grey Jewell in 1874. As late as 1900, an observer swore that a sailor "lives in the utmost ignorance of what is going on in the world . . . like the inhabitant of some undiscovered country."

Samuel was dismissive of sailors and easily angered by them. He called the crew "the most complaining set of men I ever saw," adding that they were "pretty scaley." Henry Chisling, the steward, was "an honest sort of fellow though not a very good man for the place"; the Swedish carpenter, B. Laarson, "is rather a butt and not much of a fellow"; cook Joseph Washington's pork was not to his liking, and his hog butchery was "sloppily done." The second mate, John Parr, was "generally down on everything." He even criticized Mitchell, although on the whole he approved of the older man. Mitchell didn't keep Sunday services, didn't hold an Easter service, and did not require the classic visitation by Neptune when crossing the equator. Such laxity toward custom and religion offended the Episcopal deacon in Samuel. Mitchell was "a sort of Swedenborgian," a follower of Swedish philosopher-scientist Emanuel Swedenborg whose ideas of an "inner church" influenced the American transcendentalists; Samuel was offended and angered by the captain's loose pantheism. When he talked to Mitchell about his beliefs, he concluded the captain was "pretty well mixed up and not very well-read."

Henry wished his brother were not so critical; such arrogance did not help his standing with the crew. They already thought of him as a bad-luck "Jonah": all passengers were Jonahs, since their clumsiness and whining affected a ship's efficiency. Samuel doubly qualified by bringing his sickness aboard. Such beliefs seemed ludicrous to Henry, but he was just as subject to prejudices of his class and time. The comical steward was "the greatest specimen of nigger yet met"; the cook was "decidedly the 'greasy old Dark'" mentioned in song. Yet he dropped such remarks after they nursed him through his seasickness, and found himself intrigued by their knowledge of the sea. Joe Washington saved his cook's wages to open a restaurant, and could cook anything from flying fish to soups as varied as oyster, clam, oxtail, bean, pea, and vermicelli. Henry Chisling, the steward, was one of the most widely traveled men he'd ever met. Chisling could whip up a curry he'd learned in China, compare tea prices in different Asian kingdoms, and had survived three shipwrecks, including one on Lake Erie and another off the coast of Iceland, as well as a stint aboard the *Dreadnought*, the famously violent clipper mastered by Captain Samuel Samuels. Of the latter he said, "I saw things that'd open your eyes."

The mates formed a curious triumvirate. Sam Hardy, the first mate, was the first to rise each morning and last to retire each night. First mates were usually young men earning the 60 months' navigational experience necessary for a master's ticket; this accumulated slowly over years of service, and shipowners generally thought that two successful voyages as a first mate were sufficient to qualify a good man for command. First mates were close enough to success that many married, and Sam Hardy was no exception, with a young wife and child on Cape Cod. He was also liked by the men. He rigged hammocks for the Fergusons, invented rattraps during a war against rodentia, and handled the education of the "boys." He organized the port watch, kept 12-hour duty, had final responsibility for the ship's upkeep, and kept the logbook. All had to be perfect: if not, the captain's bad report could end his hopes of command.

John Parr, the second mate, was an English seaman, and English sailors on American ships had a special burden. Since it was assumed they had special skills with ships, they had to be more perfect than other sailors, yet because of this, many considered them conceited and uppity. Parr seemed caught in this contradiction and responded in kind. Samuel observed that the men did not like or trust John Parr, nor he them. Crewmen called him the "sailor's waiter," since he furnished them with spun-yarn, balls of marline, and other seizing stuff when they worked in the rigging. On some ships even the steward, accountable to no one but the captain, was known to treat the second mate in a cavalier way. John Parr had pride, and such treatment rankled him.

The position of John Thomas as third mate was even more confusing than Parr's. He was entitled to the dignities of rank and the indignities of a lackey, yet Thomas withstood such contradictions with better humor than John Parr. Though only 24, he'd been at sea for 15 years, running away from home in Richmond, Maine, when he was nine. He belonged to the port watch and acted as its straw boss when Mr. Hardy was busy elsewhere. Henry liked him best of all the mates: it was Thomas who taught him sailors' superstitions, tried to make him a fisherman, and slid out on the jibboom with him to spear bonito. Of all mates, he seemed most loyal to Mitchell.

Among the crew, Henry was greatest friends with Jimmy Cox and William Laing. The latter would be laid up for nearly two months with frostbite and Mitchell said he would lose a finger, news that greatly depressed the stockbroker's son. He told Henry that he was sickened by the romantic notions that had brought him here: curse Richard Henry Dana and that damned book of his! Henry felt sorry for him and loaned him some books; Laing was genuinely touched and acted as if it were the nicest thing anyone had done for him since he'd come aboard. On February 4, Henry was visiting Laing in his forecastle berth when a boarding sea suddenly filled the cabin with water and nearly washed both young men out the door. It was not the best location to cheer up someone, Henry mused.

Cox, on the other hand, seemed incapable of depression. When the brothers gave him gingersnaps, Cox was so excited that he tried giving Sam all of his cheap twist tobacco in exchange. On February 13, less than a month after his bout with frostbite, Cox was scampering up the ratlines again. It was funny to watch him copy the older hands, a 14-year-old imp who cursed a blue haze to imitate his elders and chewed a quid of tobacco nearly as big as a fist. One day Samuel paid a visit and the boy offered him a cigar, "the first I have had in my mouth since leaving New York," he said. It was also a foul-tasting thing. Samuel thanked the boy, then had a coughing fit. "I find smoking doesn't pay," he said.

As both foremast hand and cabin boy, Cox had a privileged glimpse into the lives of all crew members, traversing the gap between forecastle and aftercabin with ease. He knew of Mr. Hardy's affection for his wife and baby son, of the sailors' boasts of girls in every port, of Harry Morris' contention that French whores were the best in the world. Most poignantly, perhaps, he knew of the captain's longing for his family, and had seen their somber tintypes when he ran chores to Mitchell's cabin. Mitchell had four children: Harry, age 26, who lived in San Francisco, and three daughters— 23-year-old Mary, 19-year-old Sarah Abbie, and 10-year-old Susie, named for her mother. Mitchell had mentioned he'd planned on taking Sarah and Susie on a cruise with him, but the suddenness of his appointment to the *Hornet* meant he hadn't time to prepare. This would have been a pleasant voyage for two young girls, Mitchell said, so unlike a trip in 1861 when his oldest daughter boarded the *Hornet* to Bristol and they sailed into a hurricane.

More than any other, Mitchell wished his wife Susan was here. But Susan Mitchell had never shown an interest in the sea. "Home [is] in all my thoughts," he wrote in his journal, but there were problems at home. The marriages of many "Cape Horn widows" were plagued with worry, ill health, depression, and discord; the long absence did not always make the heart grow fonder, but bred resentment by forcing women to manage households alone. Susan was a handsome woman with dark somber eyes and dark hair pulled tight in a bun. Josiah had married her when he was 25, already a young captain; now he was 55, and on March 12, Susan celebrated her 50th birthday alone. Mitchell did not mention the date in his journal or make any reference of it to the Fergusons. That day, instead, he said they were four weeks out of New York and mentioned he'd take the *Hornet* to China after Frisco. Samuel was invited to come along.

On March 17, they reached Lat. 50° S, beginning the passage around Cape Horn. Though only a gnarled promontory and rocky island at the tip of South America, the Cape was a psychological turning point, such an ancient symbol of hardship and death that its very approach had an effect on the crew. Suddenly Henry Chisling told stories of his many shipwrecks, an unexpected disclosure he could only attribute to nerves. Mitchell said he'd been around the Horn seventeen times but the place still made him nervous. "At first, I thought you and your brother were a pair of Jonahs," he admitted, "but if you bring me the same mild weather we've had so far, I'll give you your passages." Veteran hands called the place "Cape Stiff," a land of blasting gales and murderous snowstorms: they worried most about winds from the southwest that could drive them against the rocks. The Cape was the home of Adamaster, the resident specter, tall, bearded, hollow-eyed, and pale. "Look close," said Jimmy, "and you'll see him on the Devil's Tablecloth," that cloudy promontory of tempest and ruin.

It was as if God Himself had fashioned a special place to kill sailors, and now it was the *Hornet*'s turn. They rounded Cape St. John expecting a deadly southwester, but found instead as fine a day as anyone could wish, clear and crisp like October in New England. A pod of black and white orcas, or "grampuses," came up close like sightseers. They breezed by the Cape "without any weather that could not have been handled by a sailboat," Henry wrote. "I never saw such weather in this latitude," exclaimed Mitchell. The U.S. Naval Observation Office gave the average time for the Cape Horn crossing as 18 days. The *Hornet* did it in nine.

As they headed north, Henry wondered if they'd beat the 120-day forecast made by Thomas and Parr. The seas were empty of other ships, the skies clear. Except for one wild southwester that broke the pin in the mizzen topsail yard and sent it into the rigging, all signs seemed in their favor. Henry watched a total eclipse of the moon on the night of March 31, the first he'd ever seen. Despite the seasickness, he was glad Samuel had asked him to come.

At 11:00 A.M. on April 3, Mitchell called the brothers from their cabin. It was a warm day, with light winds but high, rolling seas. He pointed past the railing at a bottle floating past, "corked and sealed with something white like a paper inside." It was said that a bottle could travel around the world if dropped in the sea off Cape Horn. What ship had it come from? What castaway lost in a lifeboat, or going mad on some desert isle? Henry and Samuel watched it float off with the oddest feeling, but the boats were all up and Mitchell didn't want to lower them. "I am sorry such was the case and think the Captain regretted it afterwards," Samuel said.

Then their luck changed, as if they'd been judged and found wanting for not heeding that message. A rat infestation broke out and no traps worked. A Prussian ship passed to south but would not stop for messages. The studding sail boom of the fore topmast was carried away in a squall. Their headway fell off and Mr. Parr adjusted their arrival time to a dismal 130 days. Four men fell sick: one with a pain in his lungs, one with a pain in his leg, one with fever, the fourth possibly from syphilis. Mitchell worried there might be something infectious at work on his ship, possibly dysentery, or even worse scurvy, the oldest and most pernicious shipboard disease. He purged his men with Opodeldoc, a liniment of camphor and oils that was a Victorian standby, and moved the four into a sick bay between decks near the booby hatch for air. He feared that Antonio Possene, the sickest, would not live much longer, though another part wondered whether this was classic "sogering," or goldbricking, in order to escape Mr. Thomas's hatred of all things Portuguese.

On May 1, they passed the equator going north and entered the green waters of the doldrums, that inferno where a ship could lay idle for days. As they "ghosted along," the sailors were always aloft, trimming sails in hopes of catching the smallest cats-paw of breeze. The doldrums were mind-numbing place and the *Hornet* lay becalmed. The sickness of the four men grew worse, their cries rising from the booby hatch; others showed a listlessness that Mitchell feared would spread. "O, for a lodge in some vast wilderness," Mitchell quoted, only half in jest, "some boundless continuity of shade." A second man among the four, Peter Paulson, grew worse than Possene, and Mitchell did not expect him to live another day. "O Patience, don't desert these men," he wrote. "This hot weather without a breeze will kill them."

On May 2, one day after crossing the line, a gentle breeze started and they began to move. They headed northwest by west, and that night a shooting star traced through the sky. It's funny how quickly luck changes,

Henry thought, watching the meteorite fall.

The next day was the morning of May 3. The ship's position was Long. 112° 10' W, and Lat. 2°, above the equator. The air was humid and hot; no sea, no wind, just a blistering calm. No one wanted to work, much less move. Mr. Hardy went below with an open flame in his hand, a little more careless than usual, and Henry found the excitement he'd craved.

DEAD RECKONING

S O THE *HORNET* BURNED. They stared aghast, watching man's work crash in flames. Fire and fear leveled all distinctions, vulnerability making equals out of men. When the *Hornet* finally sank at 5:00 A.M. on May 4, it felt "as if we hadn't any home anymore," one crewman said later. Each castaway was as alone with his thoughts as their tiny boats were alone on the sea.

Henry was silenced by the sea's immensity. He told Samuel what a grand adventure this was to tell his schoolmates, but when the *Hornet* slid beneath the surface, he wrote, "We are now alone." The boats rowed back and forth at Mitchell's order, salvaging bits of wood for cooking fires. Henry stared at the ocean and wondered whether it was cruel or just indifferent. Its silence frightened him in ways he'd never known.

They were stranded in a desert: one of water, whose scale was too awesome to contemplate. This ocean was different from all others, blanketing a third of the earth's surface, an area of over 68 million miles. A line drawn from Panama to the Malay peninsula stretched 11,000 miles, four times the distance of Columbus's journey to the New World; it measured 9,600 miles from the Bering Strait to Antarctica. In many places the bottom lay 3½ miles beneath them, while four trenches plunged into darkness for six miles. Immense mountain ranges lay under the surface; most of the world's active volcanoes ringed this ocean or capped its islands; some islands rose and sank as if to madden mapmakers. Its waters were bluer, waves higher, weather patterns more massive, and storms more monstrous than anywhere else on earth. It was the most unstable place on the planet, and Henry had to face it in a 21-foot boat.

Samuel was calmer, less afraid of death than Henry because he'd already faced the possibility. "I put full confidence in the Almighty, who will do for us as he thinks best," he said. As an Episcopal deacon, he recognized the religious component of castaway tales. There was Jonah, but more important, St. Paul, whose shipwreck occurred while sailing from Myra, in modern Turkey, to Rome, in A.D. 60. Paul sailed to appeal a judgment before Caesar, but the ship was tossed in a week-long tempest and wrecked off the coast of Malta. "The soldiers' counsel was to kill the prisoners, lest any of them should swim out, and escape," Luke reported, but the commanding centurion ordered all to swim or cling to wreckage and float to shore. All 276 aboard the ship survived, and Paul successfully argued his case before Caesar. Surviving the sea changed one forever, a deliverance both dramatic and demonstrable.

The sea and ships were loaded with religious content for those inclined to look. The albatross in the sky resembled a white cross; the Southern Cross each evening was the brightest constellation. Ancient Greeks believed the porpoises leaping by a ship would escort souls to happiness, a myth transformed by the Church into a metaphor for Christ's saving of souls. The mast and its yardarms formed a giant crucifix, and during the Reformation, men confessed to the mast when death seemed imminent and no priest was near. The sea was the "waste howling wilderness" surrounding civilization, a haunt of demons but the place where God revealed himself to Moses, Elijah, John the Baptist, and Christ. It was the home of lunatics and holy men.

It would seem that social divisions disappear in calamity, but survivors' accounts show otherwise. Shipwreck victims behave rigidly, sometimes suicidally so, and social patterns could already be seen by the men's seating. In Hardy's boat, the two black crewmen sat together in the stern beside the mate, as if to seek protection; amidships and in the bows, two Spaniards, three New Yorkers, and a Londoner grouped themselves by national origin. Except for John Parr and Jimmy Cox, the second mate's boat was filled entirely with Germans and Scandinavians.

Divisions were most apparent in the longboat. Immigrants sat toward the front: Peter Smith and Charles Kaartman of Denmark; Joe Williams, John Ferris, and Antonio Possene of Portugal and the Cape Verde Islands;

Henry Morris of France. John Campbell of Massachusetts sat beside his French friend Morris, but all other Yankees—Mr. Thomas and Fred Clough of Maine; Thomas Tate, the unloved carpenter's apprentice, and Neil Turner of New York—were clumped amidships where they controlled the water barrel. Clough seems to have been especially trusted, since he was assigned to guard the precious cask. The aristocrats placed themselves in the stern by the tiller, the symbolic position of leadership. Mitchell took the rudder seat, while Samuel and Henry sat beside him, thus completing the division of upper from lower classes and placing barriers between themselves and the foreign "rabble" in the bow.

The upper classes feared this rabble, and changes were occurring that were nowhere more apparent than in New York City. Samuel still remembered the Draft Riots of July 1863, when for six days black smoke rose above the city from buildings torched by rampaging Irish mobs. The riot began as a protest against the Conscription Act, passed by Congress that March calling for an additional 300,000 soldiers to fight the Confederacy: the opposition sprang from a clause exempting any man who paid a $300 fee, thus freeing the rich and insuring that the poor would fight the war. Soon the riots became a general revolt against all authority: "The nation is . . . in a state of Revolution," wrote the *Washington Times*, a popular uprising resembling in temper and scope the spontaneous rebellions of 1848 in Paris, Berlin, Vienna, Budapest, Prague, and Rome. "There is a general fight," wrote Lord Palmerston, the British foreign secretary, "between governors and governed, between law and disorder, between those who have and those who want to have." What Samuel witnessed on July 11–16 as 50,000 to 70,000 New Yorkers rioted in Manhattan's streets was similar to the barricades in the capitals of Europe and the mayhem directed against authority.

He remembered the dreadful night the rebellion threatened J&S Ferguson. Undercover detectives discovered that rioters planned to invade the financial district and loot the U.S. Subtreasury, close to the firm's Pine Street address. That night the Ferguson women and children were sent across the East River into Brooklyn while armed family members, employees, and servants manned the windows and doors. Luckily they were spared, but others were not: when the riot ended, at least 2,000 people were dead, another 8,000 injured, and property loss was estimated at $1.5 million, equal to about $20.8 million today.

Merchant captains viewed their crews as rabble, and many believed that the only way to run a ship was through a kind of tyranny. Evidence suggests that captains, as a group, saw their seamen as large, destructive children, and some ships' officers wondered in their journals whether they were not a lower species of *homo sapiens.* When a ship's boy died in 1842 and the captain watched as sailors built his coffin, he wrote, "They have manifested a degree of tenderness and feeling that shows they are not destitute of humanity and sympathy." Such admissions were rare. A framework of statutes controlled the sailor by classifying him a ward of the state, a legal status designed for those unable to govern themselves that included children, the mentally incompetent, and slaves. Laws provided for flogging and death for inciting mutiny; prohibited sailors from leaving their vessel after sundown and from cursing and playing at dice or cards; and empowered every "free white person" to catch runaway sailors. Laws prohibited all acts by seamen that could do "prejudice to masters and owners" or that constituted a "manifest detriment of . . . trade," creating a harsh and circumscribed system that assured a ready supply of cheap labor while making sailors dependent on merchants and masters.

Mitchell was not as disdainful of crewmen as many brother captains: he called them "poor devils" and realized that the discord stowed on every clipper sprang from the inequality of their lives. Morale seemed good at the moment, but more misfortune could bring these old resentments home. "Where are we to go, in God's name, with this small lot of stores?" he wrote in his journal, although writing was difficult since he'd lost his reading glasses. "No chance but to be picked up by some vessel or gain the Windward Islands in the doldrums. At all events we must live as long as we can and trust in God's wisdom to guide and direct us. For this I pray."

He would not give in to despair. That first day, he distributed supplies, saw that the hole in the longboat was repatched, and saw that the gallant studding sail they'd saved from the sail locker was cut properly into a square sail and rigged to the longboat. He divided the boats into watches, four hours on and four hours off, and the officers took the tillers, with each man choosing a relief. Mitchell knew he was fortunate to have Mr. Thomas with him. When he saw that the Fergusons also wrote journals, he ordered that they be kept up as long as life continued. The last survivor was to place the journals in a bottle and lash that bottle to the inside of the boat;

he gave bottles to the other two boats with orders for journals to be kept in them, too.

These needs met, he turned to his charts. Nearly 80 percent of the world's oceanic islands are contained in a wedge-shaped segment of the Pacific whose points lie at Santiago, Shanghai, and Jakarta, a vast triangle loaded with thousands of islands and atolls. But the men of the *Hornet* lay too far north of that triangle, adrift in a gap on the map devoid of any reef or rock on which to land. In all probability they were on the same path as Ferdinand Magellan, who in 1519–1521 sailed 8,000 miles from Santiago to Guam and sighted only two uninhabited atolls. Magellan may have been the unluckiest navigator ever, losing half of his ships and 209 of his 240 crewmen to thirst and starvation, including his own life soon after landing on the Philippines. Mitchell didn't want to repeat such a record. Their food would last ten days, but their 16 gallons of water would last only four at one pint per man per day. So he studied his *Bowditch* charts carefully: the Galapagos Islands lay 1,000 miles to the east, the Mexican coast near Acapulco just short of 1,000 miles to the northeast, the Marquesas Islands and Tahiti more than 3,000 miles southwest. Even farther northwest lay Hawaii. Landfall did not seem an option out here.

Their lives depended on his intuition and seamanship; any mistake, even the smallest, could be fatal. These doldrums were more dreaded by mariners than Cape Horn. This was the region of calms, squalls, and baffling winds that prompted Coleridge's "Water, water, everywhere, nor any drop to drink," a world-encircling ditch into which the trade winds emptied and that expanded with the seasons. In February and March, the doldrums were centered north of the equator and might be only a few miles in width, but by late spring and summer the center moved to Lat. 7 to 9° N and was several hundred miles wide. The French called the doldrums the *pot au noir*, the "pitch pot," a black hole that sucked up mariners and never let go. Strange things happened here. Daybreak came slowly, seawater was lukewarm, and a half-knot counter current ran through the region, so that one actually went backward in the deadest calm. A century after the *Hornet*'s passage, another castaway observed an unclassified water spider skate across the mirrored surface. The air grew so close and oppressive that a sailor could *feel* the region in his body. Wrote Lieutenant Matthew Fontaine Maury, superintendent of the U.S. Naval Observation Office:

"The elasticity of feeling which he breathed from the trade-wind area has forsaken him."

The region was also one of the most essential places on earth, the great humid engine driving the world's weather. The Pacific and Atlantic doldrums were the earth's true equator, Mark Twain later remarked, and not the arbitrary line of mapmakers. It was here that the trade winds came together, canceling each other out in a limbo where neither system prevailed.

One constant in an engine is heat. "The rays of the torrid sun pour down . . . and raise its temperature to a scorching heat," warned Maury. "The atmosphere dances, and the air is seen trembling in ascending and descending columns." The sun hit the waters of the equator, unlike any other large region on earth, from directly overhead; thus, a square foot of sunlight heated a square foot of water. To the north or south, light hit more obliquely and the water was not as warm. Dougal Robertson, who survived the same stretch of doldrums in 1972, measured a sea-temperature rise of at least ten degrees in one 24-hour period, a phenomenal increase across so large a body of water. This assures constant evaporation into the atmosphere, a highly unstable state in which any drop in air temperature causes water vapor to precipitate and creates a sudden change from potential to kinetic energy that is experienced as torrential thunderstorms. Henry could see on the horizon huge cumulus clouds rearing over zones of rising air, thunderheads that were sustained by the constant upflow of warm water and air. It was one of the ironies of their situation that they depended on these storms for water, yet what hope would they have in such violent seas? If they'd sunk farther north in the belt of dry trade winds, the sea would have been more predictable—but they'd die of thirst from lack of rain.

Which heading must they take to escape this purgatory? The Galapagos were closest, yet heading east would throw them even deeper into the heart of the doldrums. A northeast heading toward Mexico would extract them from the region sooner, but they'd run head-on into the Northeast Trades, which would push them back *into* the doldrums or farther out to sea. If they'd had triangular sails like a lateen or today's racers, they could have cut through such wind like a knife, directing air smoothly onto both sides: the resultant forces pulled a boat through the water and allowed it to tack. Unfortunately, square rigs like theirs could not make better than six to eight points into the wind, which meant they were limited to running before it, having no control over their heading but where the wind pushed them.

Mitchell decided that their best bet lay in striking north and slightly west, toward the Revilla Gigedo Islands, discovered in the 16th century. Though these islands were 1,200 miles distant—farther off than the Galapagos or Mexico—the course did have advantages. They'd stay in the shipping lanes and would not hit the Northeast Trades head-on. Clarion Island was the westernmost of four isles in the group, 714 miles west of the Mexican coast and the most directly on their course at Lat. 18° 20' 36" N. and Long. 114° 43' 19" W. It had three prominent peaks that could be seen from a distance, and birds, turtles, and cacti were plentiful, though there was no fresh water. According to James Imray's *North Pacific Pilot*, the standard 19th-century text for merchant captains, the most extreme distress might be relieved, but there was no other reason to land.

A little after 6:00 A.M., one hour after the *Hornet* sank, they shook out their sails and headed for Clarion. Mitchell passed a line to Hardy's boat, and a second was passed to Mr. Parr. The longboat, with the largest sail, would tow the others. They "kept off N. by E.," according to Mitchell's notes, moving so slowly that they seemed to leave no bubbles on the smooth surface. Some occupants looked forward, some back, some stared at nothing. Yet all had the same question: Where would this journey end?

THE NEXT TWO DAYS passed easily. By day there was a broiling sun, beating down from overhead with little chance of relief save the shade of the sail. The breeze held steady at five knots, keeping them on their northeast heading through the first afternoon. Samuel began to see that one curse would be their immobility. Man was made to fidget, performing a meaningless pantomime that kept the joints oiled and blood warmed. But with everyone jammed tightly in the little boat, there was no freeboard and it was possibly the most crowded place he'd ever endured. He could touch the surface of the water by bending slightly, but saw an ominous gray torpedo pass beneath the surface and kept his hands inside. The longer he sat, the more his knees and back began to ache, a pain that grew from general stiffness to focused torment as if an unseen devil dug at one spot with a rusty awl. If he stood to stretch, he overbalanced the boat, threatening to tip them all.

Mitchell's four-hour system of "watch and watch" allowed half to sit up while the other half stretched along the bottom, but even this proved mesmerizing. Every innocent action became an annoyance, the little boat moving in her course, the bailer scraping water off the bottom with a tin cup and flinging it into the ocean, the sail's intermittent pop and rustle, Possene's fevered muttering. The rooster dozed at his perch on the water cask, ruffling his red feathers in the breeze. They all took pleasure in the bird, commenting on his slightest cluck or cackle as if they read their fates in cockerels. Mitchell had the men up front make a drag, or sea anchor, in anticipation of the nightly storms; Samuel watched as they lashed together some bottom boards, then attached canvas shaped like an open-ended cone. They tied it to a coiled rope and stowed it in the bow, ready to run out as needed.

To keep his mind occupied, Samuel calculated where they might possibly go. He borrowed Mitchell's *Bowditch*—more specifically, Nathaniel Bowditch's *New American Practical Navigator*, probably the 1860 edition—and compared it to a map he'd purchased in New York. This map would cause considerable debate between Samuel, Mitchell, Mr. Thomas, and the others, for on its tiny details hung their lives—*Bowditch* and Samuel's map did not always agree. Although the title of the map was never mentioned, it was probably Captain James F. Imray's "Chart of the North Pacific Exhibiting the Western Shores of Asia and the Western Coast of North America" or one drawn from it, since Imray's was the most widely circulated and accurate sea map of the mid-19th century. But such accuracy was relative, for both *Bowditch* and Imray's chart were plagued with "isles of vain hope," islands that did not exist. Nineteenth-century charts and atlases showed nearly 200 of these, most in the Pacific. Some were real, though their positions were poorly determined; others were the result of errors in charting, reporting, or typography. A few rose and sank, others were optical illusions, and a smaller number were the result of fraud or deception.

Samuel felt the pull of these specks, becoming what Lawrence Durrell would call an obsessive "islomane." Most castaways mentally transformed islands into an earthly paradise, places of bounty and peace, uncorrupted by civilization. It rarely worked that way. The history of island refuge ranged from the forced loneliness of Alexander Selkirk, Robinson Crusoe's real-life model, who spent 4 years on Juan Fernandez Island, to the self-destruction and murder of the *Bounty* mutineers on Pitcairn Island. But a man could dream. Samuel copied a list of islands directly from *Bowditch's* Table LIV, recording the names and positions of seven possible landfalls in the back of his journal on a blank page titled "Bills Payable, May":

Clipperton Island	Lat. 10°28' N	Long. 109°19' W
New Blada	Lat. 18°12' N	Long. 114°5' W
Clarion	Lat. 18°21' N	Long. 114°23' W
Cloud	Lat. 19°43' N	Long. 114°57' W
Freshwater	Lat. 19°22' N	Long. 115°08' W
Cooper	Lat. 20°06' N	Long. 131°43' W
Roca Partida	Lat. 19°06' N	Long. 111°52' W

Of these seven, only three existed: Clipperton Rock, a solitary prominence between them and Clarion but too far east to seem reachable; Roca Partida, also in the Revilla Gigedo group; and Clarion, their present goal. The four phantom isles were apparently separate sightings of Clarion by navigators whose reckoning was faulty. The list of so many possible landfalls was heartening, although in truth they reflected a fatal lack of accuracy. If the castaways followed their charts to the letter, they'd miss salvation by miles.

The breeze held up till 6:00 P.M. then slacked off, shortly replaced by rain. It was as if someone flipped a switch: light gave way to dark, breezes ended in weird silence. The quiet was replaced by an approaching hiss that brought the smell of rain. "Clew up the courses," Mitchell called as the first drops fell. The squall came at them as a solid line of darkness, its slow approach bespeaking less than violent winds. Yet the deluge that broke was like nothing Samuel or Henry had ever experienced, so like a cataract pouring down upon them that they gasped for breath, half drowned. On the *Hornet* they'd ghosted through such squalls like magic, the drum of the rain on the cabin roof quite soothing, the ship pushed along by breezes way up in the topsails. But here on the surface there was only water pouring into their boats, while through the darkness they heard Mitchell and Thomas screaming, "For the love of God, bail!"

Suddenly the water was over their ankles, an unbelievable weight of water falling each minute, greater than anything in New England. Sud-

denly Henry lost sight of the men in the bow. The longboat seemed to vanish except for the shadows of Mitchell and Samuel, glimpsed through the
curtain of rain. Henry grabbed a carboy bumping along the bottom and
bailed with desperation, rising and falling like a piston in some desperate
piece of machinery. But still the water gained: the pure, sweet rainwater
they needed for the casks, now threatening to sink them. The rain
streamed down his hair and into his mouth, formed a film over his eyes. He
cupped his hands around his nose and mouth so as not to swallow water,
then held a breath and bailed again.

But they needed the rain to live. During the night, they spread a sheet
of canvas to all corners, ducking beneath the thwarts until the canvas
sagged in the middle from the weight of the water. They punched a hole in
this spot to drain it into the cask. When dawn finally came, every stitch of
clothing on the boat was wet and each man battled chills, yet they'd succeeded in filling the 40-gallon cask and the four demijohns. For insurance,
they filled some of the watertight holds not taken by bread or food. One of
their greatest fears, dying of thirst, had been allayed for now.

In other ways the sea was not so kind. At 6:00 A.M., a southeast breeze
rose that kept them on their course but kicked up what Mitchell called a
"good deal of cobbling sea," his term for choppy water. With that sea came
problems. At noon, Mitchell drew the boats together to take a reading, an
exacting process in the best of times demanding precise instrumentation.
Fixing latitude was not difficult: a sighting was taken at noon by lining up
the sun in the mirror of a quadrant, then swinging the reflected image
down the arc until its lowest rim touched the horizon. Reading degrees of
arc gave a measurement of the sun's altitude; Mitchell then ran through a
series of calculations listed in the almanac for local noon and with that he
had latitude. There was a world of difference, however, between taking a
sextant reading on the steady deck of a ship and taking one down here in a
tiny boat bouncing on the waves. The swells were never so high on the
Hornet, but on the longboat they'd be in the valley of a trough at one
moment, with the horizon in their face, then atop a peak seconds later with
the horizon miles away. This soon convinced Mitchell that his readings
were inaccurate, so he made several readings and took the average.

Even more complicated was the process for fixing longitude, marked
off east and west from the prime meridian that ran through Greenwich,
England. Latitude sailing—the trick of following an invisible line to the

east or west—was easy. It was traveling north and south that crashed sailors onto rocks since they had no idea of their location. To fix longitude, one needed a precise knowledge of time, down to the second. Each of the 360 degrees in the earth's circular belt was divided into 60 minutes of arc, and each minute equaled one nautical mile, or 6,076 feet. Since the earth spun once every 24 hours, a heavenly body passed over 15 degrees of longitude every hour, or 15 minutes of longitude each minute. Using these constants, longitude could be calculated by comparing the time when a heavenly body appeared overhead to the known time when it appeared over Greenwich. The difference in time was converted to arc, which told the mariner how far to the east or west he was from the prime meridian.

Everything depended on accurate timekeeping, and Mitchell and his mates now realized that their chronometers had been damaged. Both had been calibrated before the disaster—now, neither of them showed the same time. This was more serious than anything else short of the fire. Being even a degree off in their calculations meant an error of 60 nautical, or 69 statute miles. That might not seem serious when headed toward something as big as a continent, but their lives now depended on finding islands no more than a mile or two wide.

Samuel and Henry did not immediately grasp the problem, but to Fred Clough and the other sailors the meaning was crystal clear. They could drift forever in this ocean, and without an accurate fix they'd never know which way to steer. Yet all was not lost. They still had "dead reckoning," a workable technique if an unfortunate choice of words. *Dead* was thought to have come from "de'ed," a contraction of *deduced*—and that's exactly what one did, deducing a new position from a previous fix by using measurements of time, speed, and distance. There was a rough elegance to this solution. One kept a record of the compass heading, then determined speed by throwing out a knotted piece of line with wood at the end, called a chip log, and counting the number of *knots* passing through one's fingers in a given time (thus the origin for the nautical term for speed). Time was measured in a "slow glass" or by counting seconds: speed and distance were transferred to a chart, from which the ship's estimated position could then be determined. In theory it worked, and ships' officers practiced the skill in case everything else failed, as was the case now. As with much else in life, where you had been determined where you might end.

It was comforting to know that the method had saved other shipwreck victims: although the odds were long, sailors considered life at sea a gamble. The most famous success was that of Lieutenant William Bligh aboard the *Bounty*'s launch in 1789. There were many similarities between the *Hornet*'s and *Bounty*'s castaways. Both Mitchell and Bligh set out from their ships with little preparation, though Bligh was forcibly ejected. Bligh's boat was 23 feet long and 6 feet wide, barely larger than the *Hornet*'s, and badly crowded with 18 men; there were two sails instead of one, so it had a slight motive advantage. Bligh's launch, like the longboat, was badly overloaded, frequently shipped water, and was kept afloat by constant bailing. Bligh had a Ramsden 10-inch sextant and quadrant, a compass, and navigation tables; he did not have a chronometer but *was* blessed with clear noon sightings. In the end, Bligh's men endured 41 days in the launch and sailed 3,618 miles from Tofua in the South Pacific to East Timor above Australia, covering up to 130 miles per day. It was a record in the annals of seamanship, and though each man lost an average of 56 pounds and some died afterward, Bligh got most of his men through.

Bligh's feat seemed the limit of the possible. Others had lasted longer on the ocean, but after a point their accounts degenerated from privation to something closer to hell. From November 7, 1765, to January 29, 1766, the sloop *Peggy* drifted mastless in the North Atlantic until all food ran out and the crew killed and ate a black slave. In 1811, the brig *Polly* was also dismasted, and the crew drifted for 191 days. Unlike the *Peggy*, the crew used the bodies of the dead for bait, not meat, and hooked a number of sharks on which they subsisted. The most famous disaster was the sinking of the whaleship *Essex*, rammed by an enraged sperm whale on November 20, 1820. Three whaleboats with 20 survivors sailed 1,500 miles to a deserted island, but after a week ashore all but three men returned to the boats in hopes of reaching South America. One boat disappeared at sea, while the other two covered approximately 4,500 miles after 95 days. Yet their rescue came at a price: only eight of the original 20 men survived, and they did so by cannibalizing several black crewmen and a cabin boy.

Obviously, the men of the *Hornet* didn't want to reach that point, but Bligh's voyage could give them hope even without trustworthy chronometers. Mitchell took a compass bearing and got under way as Clough, Thomas, and carpenter's apprentice Thomas Tate fashioned a chip log. Tate took a thin piece of oaken plank from his chest and sawed a small triangle, six inches per side; one face was weighted with sheet lead and a hole bored in each point. Mr. Thomas made a bridle of stout fishing line for the chip, then measured off 12 fathoms (at 6 feet per fathom) and marked the place with his thumb. Clough had been twisting bits of handkerchief; as Mr. Thomas held out the line, Clough rove a bit of the rag through the strands and knotted it fast. Then, with a carpenter's rule, he measured off 25 feet and knotted two bits of rag. He repeated this eight times and practiced counting the seconds as Mitchell watched his chronometer. When their count seemed accurate, he told them to heave the log.

Clough took the line in his right hand and paid it out freely, starting his count when the 12-fathom mark passed through his fingers. When Mr. Thomas counted 15 seconds, Clough grasped the line and cried, "Nearly five knots, sir." Mitchell made his calculations. They seemed to be at Lat. 4° N, Long. 111° 30' W, and had moved 120 miles north in the day and a half they'd been sailing. "Luck is with us, sir," Mr. Thomas said. But Mitchell didn't trust to luck where there shouldn't be any, and lowered the daily hardtack allowance for each man.

So they coasted north toward the shipping lanes. Every hour they cast the chip log; every noon they took a fix with the uncertain chronometers and checked their results by dead reckoning. They picked their way from point to point, but always with the suspicion that every reading was flawed and that they navigated blind.

SOON AFTER THE first noon reading, the luck Mr. Thomas said was with them changed. That afternoon, the wind stiffened to a strong breeze of 25 knots, erasing the long, easy swells advancing from the horizon and replacing them with dark blue, choppy waves crested with white foam. This was followed by a squall, visible from miles away. Henry was learning to read the sky like a sailor. If light showed under the cloud line, the storm wouldn't be too violent—it was the ones where clouds at the leading edge plunged like breakers and the sky from cloud to sea was nothing but inky black that he learned to fear. On land such storms were occasion for excitement or annoyance, but here the storms were more personal. He watched as the squall sped at them then passed miraculously to port and sighed with relief. It was as if the squalls sniffed out their positions. "God help us if they find us," Mr. Thomas said.

Eventually, one did. It boiled from the west, lighted underneath by a dull, leaden glow. The wind preceded it, kicking up oily swells and leaping from wave to wave, slicing off thin horsetails of spray. A frigate bird wheeled before it, great wings spread. Sometimes these birds traveled in pairs in such weather, scaring up shoals of fish, but this one rode the wind alone. It hovered over their boat for an instant, then tipped its wings and scudded off. "Stand by to heave to, boys," cried Mitchell, breaking the crew's silence. "Reduce sails!"

The men up front tied a rope around the sail's belly, giving it an hourglass effect that reduced the force by half. "Throw out the drag!" One of the men threw over the sea anchor while Fred Clough paid out the line. "Stand by your bailers!" Mitchell cried as the first blast hit them, shoving them sideways and enveloping the boat in gloom. The sea anchor acted as a brake, the canvas cone grabbing the water and keeping the boat's head into the wind. The bow rose up on a wave and wavered, then the dragline grew taut and the wave passed harmlessly beneath them. "It's working, Cap'n," Fred yelled, but he celebrated too soon. Even as the sea anchor kept them headed into the wind and water, the line tied to the quarter-boats behind them counteracted that force and created a shear like a pendulum. As Henry watched, the longboat heeled to windward, the gunwale within inches of the water. He leaned on instinct to the weather side with the others; the move counterbalanced the tilt but only for an instant, for the sea unerringly finds weakness and in this case that was the towline. The wind stiffened and the longboat leaped over 10-foot waves, pausing in mid-air before crashing down the other side. Henry held tight to keep from being tossed overboard. As the quarter-boats followed into the trough, the towline slackened, then sheered off hard as they climbed another crest, stiffening the line. Each time the line cracked and the longboat heeled over, its gunwale mere inches from the sea.

"Cut the line!" cried a sailor. Another screamed: "Cut it or they'll drag us down!!"

Samuel and Henry stared at Mitchell. "I won't do it," he cried back, as if arguing with himself. "They won't make it if I cut them loose now!"

But it wasn't the quarter-boats that were struggling. The smaller boats crested each wave with ease, leaping at the ends of their ropes like horses, while the longboat sailed like a chunk, burying its nose in each breaking wave. Henry bailed like crazy and wondered if Mitchell had gone mad. *Would he drown them all?* They were already knee-deep in water and as it deepened, the boat grew so heavy that he wondered whether they could rise over the next advancing swell.

Then, quickly as the squall had hit, it broke, the sky lightening in the southwest, the rain smoothing out the more dangerous waves. The reprieve helped them get ahead of the water and bail it out—a few minutes later there was a break in the clouds and Mitchell gave orders to haul in the drag and take the reef from the sail. They'd made it this time, just barely, and everyone wondered whether that towline would kill them all.

Henry could never remember the next two days without reliving some of that terror. The hours were one-two punches of wind and rain, ticking back and forth like a metronome under the endless dark sky. Nights were infinitely worse: they saw nothing, but heard everything. It must be what the condemned experienced as they were led, blindfolded, to the field of execution, Henry imagined, all senses heightened as they awaited the shock of a bullet or fall of an axe. The sky was uniformly dark except for the occasional stream of moonlight through a rent in the clouds, yet in that sudden light he could see walls of water that were frightful to behold. Their matches gave out, soaked through and useless, and Mitchell steered in the dark, guided only by the tingle of wind on his cheek or back of his neck, listening for the wind's heavy piping when it blew harder. Although Henry couldn't follow their passage up and down the wavecrests, he certainly felt it in his stomach. The stern sank low beneath him as the longboat struggled up the peak, then lifted up and he felt weightless as they dropped into the valley below. At times he could look back and spot the ghostly paleness of the two following sails.

On the morning of Sunday, May 6, the fourth day since the *Hornet* sank, they had a brief reprieve. The wind fell off and the officers passed out to each man the fragment of raw pork and moldy morsel of hardtack that made up his meal. Some ate theirs in one gulp, others daintily in small nibbles. They were getting less than a fifth of an ordinary meal for an entire day's ration: at this rate, Clough figured, they'd either pass out from weakness or attack each other for the remaining scraps. They stared in each other's faces or out to sea in search of a ship, but were too downhearted to talk beyond an absolute minimum.

That morning, after four days of tension and interrupted catnaps, Henry finally slept and dreamed. Samuel was glad that he did so: he'd noted how downcast his brother had become over the last two days. In later dreams, Henry seemed to be back home in Stamford, and there is a good chance that he dreamed the same now. He was coming out of church with his family. His mother pulled on her gloves as she walked down the weathered steps, bowing stiffly to social equals as they climbed into a waiting carriage. His father carried his whalebone cane with the burnished gold knob that he liked to take everywhere. Henry glanced across the street and spotted Josie Taylor; he tried to get her attention, but she didn't seem to hear.

"Doldrums," Henry wrote in his journal when he awoke, his only entry on that Sunday. It was the same and only entry that he'd make for the next five days.

That Sunday morning, Mitchell also dreamed. The lifeless tiller propped him up; he sat like stone, eyes growing heavy until his forehead drooped and he slipped away. He dreamed of somehow escaping alone to San Francisco and telling a friend of the disaster. Word of the *Hornet's* death had not yet made it back, and he was the first to bring the news. Mitchell and his friend walked alone on the headlands near the Presidio. The conversation worried him. How had he made it back when all the others were still in the boats? He'd done something terrible, but he didn't know what—he'd made some devil's bargain to insure his own survival. He felt a guilt sweep over him as cold and violent as the breakers, yet for the life of him, he couldn't remember details. But everyone else seemed to know of his decision, including his friend. "You can't blame yourself," he counseled, poking at a rock with his cane. "You've suffered horribly yourself." Mitchell glanced overhead as the man continued to talk and spotted the most magnificent golden eagle outlined against the sky. "Look there!" Mitchell cried, pointing as it wheeled then dipped out of sight, a disappearance that caused him a great sense of urgency. "We must go find the boats. They're depending on me." They climbed down the rocks to the beach and stared west, but in the vast expanse of ocean there were no boats, no sign of survivors, nothing. Just the endless swells of the Pacific, stretching as far as he could see.

THE DOLDRUMS

THE DREAM HAUNTED MITCHELL for a week, a period of daily "calms, burning suns, baffling airs, and rain drizzles" and nightly "torrents of rain, thunder, and lightning." As if Nature itself mimicked his state of mind. The days were interminable stretches of dead air filled with the faint but sickening odor of rotting vegetables. Many of the potatoes had spoiled, and the men plunked them over the side to gauge their speed. Those that didn't sink floated beside them, nibbled by minnows. They placed bets on which moved faster, the boats or spuds; the agitation caused by the fish pushed the spuds ahead. The sails hung limp; the boats rocked in oily swells. The men shipped the long oars called "sweeps" and rowed for an illusion of progress, what sailors called kicking up a "white ash breeze." Henry's mind drifted like the boat and he imagined them as tiny specks in the center of a vast round mirror. They rowed forever but never drew close to its edge.

This was not adventure. This was more like jail. Strange that open space could be confining, but it was true. "What is a ship but a prison?" wrote Robert Burton in *The Anatomy of Melancholy*. "There is in a gael, better air, better company, better convenience of every kind," said Samuel Johnson, "and a ship has the additional disadvantage of being in danger."

Henry closed his eyes and tried willing himself to another place and time. But sounds, or their absence, drew him back to reality. He hated the near-silence of mid-ocean, the faint creaking of oars upon the thole-pins, the monotonous lap of the waves. It grated worse on the sailors. They were used to the deep roar of the wind or its piping in the rigging. The main sounds in the boat were human: a cough or sigh as a man changed position, the groans of the sick, the mutters of dreams. A man was alone with his thoughts, and for many that was unnatural.

Their progress, or lack of it, grated most on Mitchell. The rain stayed with them until Sunday, May 6, then dried up as if shut off by a valve. Light breezes pushed them to all points of the compass, changing direction so often that it was impossible to maintain a heading. Sometime a strange mist rose from the water, obscuring the sun. By the noon reading, he realized they'd made less than 20 miles since May 5, a rate of less than one mile per hour.

From noon of May 5 throughout the next week, they averaged 22¼ miles a day. By the second day of this, Mitchell knew they'd never survive if this kept on. Fortunately, lack of water, the great killer after cold and drowning, was not yet a concern. The human body requires at least a pint of liquid daily to flush out waste: thanks to the torrents and drizzles, they'd kept their water casks filled. No, hunger was the growing concern. Although current U.S. Department of Agriculture guidelines recommend 2,200 calories daily for men and 1,600 for women, it was estimated that in the mid- to late-19th century sailors consumed 3,800 calories each day. On the very first day after the *Hornet* sank, they'd cut that back by two-thirds, to 1,300 calories. The *Hornet* seemed a well-provisioned ship and the men were well-nourished when she sank, but shipowners were notorious for scrimping on food to increase profits, and malnutrition was a common complaint on merchant vessels. In addition, the diet of hardtack and salt beef led to scurvy, dysentery, or other shipboard plagues. The outbreak of sickness just before the *Hornet* sank may have indicated such a problem, and by Day 5 of their ordeal, hunger cramped their bellies.

Mitchell prescribed chewing tobacco to quell the pain. Nicotine suppresses appetite: while some researchers believe it causes the liver to release glycogen, thus raising blood sugar, others suspect it blocks the body's pathway for carbohydrate storage and a third group thinks an unknown substance in tobacco controls weight. Sailors always had a quid of twist tobacco in their mouth—it has been estimated that a man could go through 70 to 80 pounds in a single voyage. They had 100 pounds in the three boats and chewed constantly.

By Day 5, Mitchell noticed signs of weakness in his men. They received 10 ounces of hardtack daily, providing less than 22½ percent of their energy needs. He'd calculated slightly less than 3¼ pounds of bread per man to last ten days, but the seemingly indestructible hardtack—baked to the consistency of mortar to prevent spoilage and so hard it could chip teeth—was going black and moldy in its canvas storage bag.

Among the longboat's sick—Antonio Possene, Neil Turner, John Campbell, and Samuel Ferguson—Mitchell already saw the pinched cheeks and bright eyes of starvation. The sick burned calories faster in their fever, and in two or three weeks even the healthiest among them would start to look consumptive. Hunger consumed their body fat, then their muscles and minds. An obsession with meals already filled their thoughts: Mitchell watched as Harry Morris stared at the hardtack in his palm with a look of injury and amazement, then clapped it to his mouth and rolled his eyes to heaven as if asking God to witness such indignities.

There *was* a solution, but one Mitchell was unwilling to consider. Their longboat had been towing the two smaller boats since leaving the *Hornet*. Their sails were smaller than the longboat's, too small to efficiently catch the light breezes of the doldrums, and an implicit promise existed that he would pull them through. Yet how many times had the towline nearly capsized them during the storms each night? How many times did the added weight hold them back when they needed all the spring they could get to hold the shifting airs? "The three boats still attached," Mitchell wrote on May 7, the first mention in his journal of a thought all had. To cut the quarter-boats adrift in these seas would be the same as murder, but if he continued to tow them he doubted they'd make land before exhausting their stores—thus killing them all.

There was another way, one that avoided this decision, and that was to change course for a pinprick on the map closer than Clarion. This was Clipperton Island, also known as Clipperton Rock, 300 miles to the northeast. Even if they missed it, the easterly course would put them more nearly in the highway of northbound ships and in a better position to strike for the Revilla Gigedo Islands. He told the men of his thoughts and they agreed that anything was better than this. At 10 o'clock that night, Mitchell steered east-northeast in hopes of finding land.

LAND OF ANY SORT sounds like paradise to castaways, but Clipperton Island was far from the Garden of Eden. *Bowditch* described it as a thoroughly inhospitable "speck of terrain," a place that actually existed a few minutes' difference in latitude and longitude from what was listed in the charts, making it possible to miss by just a few miles. Such an event would echo the island's history. Clipperton was discovered, forgotten, rediscovered, and claimed by several nations, then finally ignored. It was apparently first sighted in 1520 by Ferdinand Magellan, rediscovered in 1705 by British pirate John Clipperton, then found again in 1711 by French explorer Michel Bocage. Clipperton was a low-lying lagoon island, destitute of trees, its highest point a 62-foot cliff at the southern edge. At a distance of 15 miles, this great rock resembled a sail; closer up, an "immense castle." There were two openings into the central lagoon, both hard to spot in stormy weather; once these were negotiated, one then faced sharks. "They were very large, and literally swarmed," wrote British explorer Sir Edward Belcher in 1839. "In all probability they were attracted by a shoal of file . . . and other small fish" that fed on the copper sheathing of their hull.

Other hazards awaited. There were no fresh-water springs on the island, so they'd still have to depend on rain. Food was a problem, too. The island lay at the western edge of the Humboldt Current, the deep upwelling of cold water that flowed north from Antarctica along South America. This current was rich in phytoplankton, zooplankton, and krill, which meant the island was surrounded by all the things that fed on them, but very little of this abundance ventured on land. Belcher saw turtles, dolphin, and porpoise in the lagoon, but they were outnumbered by sharks. He reported nesting gannets, boobies, pelicans, and tern, but experience in other ecosystems showed their eggs were quickly depleted by hungry men.

More than anything else, there were land crabs. Clipperton swarmed with them, making life precarious. When the Oceanic Phosphate Company of San Francisco later mined the island from 1893 to 1898, workers were forced to elevate their wooden cabins on posts to prevent the crabs from attacking them in their sleep. The company sheathed the pilings in sheet metal to prevent the crabs from dismantling the buildings, splinter by splinter. They moved in red waves, clicking their claws and feasting on corpses, a scavenging army of crustaceans.

One thing in their favor was the fact that Clipperton was a guano island, and everyone wanted guano. Although Clipperton's deposits were not as nutrient-rich as those on islands lying closer to the Peruvian coast, it was still part of the guano frenzy. From 1856 to 1865, American entrepreneurs laid claim to every island, rock, or key sighted in the Pacific and Caribbean in hopes it contained guano; prospectors from rival countries would often lay claim to the same lonely islands, a scenario enacted at Clipperton. In 1858, Emperor Napoleon III of France awarded mining rights to a French firm and renamed the island *L'Ile de Passion*, but few paid heed. Americans landed on Clipperton in 1861, ignoring French claims. By 1866, a three-way tug-of-war existed between France, Mexico, and the United States; although individual prospectors visited and mined with pick and shovel, no one really settled there. Still, the greedy and hopeful drifted in and out, and Mitchell could hope that *someone* might be there.

THEY STEERED EAST-NORTHEAST, taking to the sweeps or catching a light breeze. By noon of May 8, they saw dolphin under the boat, but efforts to hook them failed. The sailors swore "dorado" were the ocean's tastiest fish, but Joe Williams, the *Hornet's* best fisherman, tried every lure imaginable. He fashioned one from the metal handle of a clasp knife and some strips of red cloth from his shirt, then trailed it behind the longboat at 40 to 50 yards. The fish was a powerful creature, a muscular wedge of aquamarine and yellow with a dorsal fin stretching along its back; several seemed intrigued by the lures, but at the end of a rush would veer away. "They're too smart," Williams swore. This was not sport but survival. "We need live bait," he concluded, telling the men in the bow to scoop up the small mullet-like fish crowding under the boat. They used their hats as nets but caught only water.

Still, the increasing number of dorado and baitfish gave them hope—a sign that they approached the western limits of the cold Antarctic stream. They were doing something other than drifting randomly. "Had both boats along side and had a good talk," Mitchell wrote on May 8. "Men cheerful." He watched as they began rowing and let them continue, but soon considered it futile. With the limited rations, their remaining energy was too precious to spend on a mile or two of progress that could be canceled by a contrary shift in the winds. "I see and feel no prospect" for rescue, he added.

Increasingly we see these two sides of Mitchell: the public opposed to the private, the stoic versus the doubt-ridden. Nineteenth- and twentieth-century biographers made much of the public Mitchell, an image Americans likened to themselves. He was James Fenimore Cooper's Pathfinder, Gary Cooper's Kane standing alone at high noon. He was paid not to have doubt, and especially not to show it: clipper captains were expected to be tougher than anyone else aboard. But underneath the surface calm roiled nagging uncertainty. "The prospect of being saved is small," he wrote on May 9. On May 11: "My own strength failing fast." May 14, the twelfth day out: "God is our only help. I pray continually."

Like Henry, he was trapped in private doldrums. As Stephen Crane later wrote in "The Open Boat," a semiautobiographical story from his own castaway experience off the Florida coast, he was lost in that "profound depression and indifference that comes to even the most enduring person when the business folds, the army capitulates, the ship goes down." Was it possible, Mitchell wondered, that he could spend a life on the ocean and still be killed so easily? Perhaps he should blame Mr. Hardy, but poor Hardy was ruined, and with him his wife and child. His shipmates might forgive him, knowing the doldrums made fools of every man. But the shipowners in New York would be less forgiving.

So they struggled on. Research suggests that within one week after abandoning the *Hornet*, the men in all three boats experienced an emotional and intellectual progression that would determine their survival. Generally, the response to disaster begins *before* a catastrophe occurs. There are efforts at prevention or preparation—drills and evacuations, requirements to upgrade equipment in the danger zones—and during this "threat phase," denial seems so common that psychiatrist Robert Jay Lifton in his study of Hiroshima survivors dubbed it a "consistent human adaptation." When disaster struck, this myth of personal invulnerability was the first victim, followed by a phase in which "individuals swing between feelings of terror and elation, invulnerability and helplessness, catastrophic abandonment and miraculous escape," observed psychologists Warren Kinston and Rachel Rosser. Survivors showed an "absence of emotion, inhibition of activity, docility, indecisiveness," and often granted to authority figures a honeymoon of unquestioning trust. But this soon evolved into a "recoil phase" marked by lifted spirits, a search for explanations—and a need to assign blame.

No one was more vulnerable at this moment than Sam Hardy, whose disobedience had landed them here. He never moved from the tiller, as if serving penance for what he had done. Every morning the first gray streaks of dawn would stretch along the eastern horizon, and taking shape in that light was the stone statue in the stern. When Henry glanced back at the mate's boat, the sight stirred up such melancholy that he had to look away. Something in Hardy's solitude touched a common nerve, as if, of everyone, God had marked him for doom.

Such fatalism resonated in sailors, expressed by the fear of Jonahs. Anyone could be a Jonah, given the right circumstances. Finns and cross-eyed men were Jonahs, as were clerics, since the devil sent storms to destroy them, and heretics, hated by God. The cruelest Jonah was the man who believed it of himself, who'd escaped death once but not its shadow, whose cursed survival rippled through the generations. The men on Hardy's boat looked on the first mate every morning and shuddered. They could do nothing to him that he was not doing to himself.

Each morning, as Hardy watched the dawn, he probably relived what psychologists call a "tormenting memory" of the fire. The first mate did not leave a journal to record his thoughts, but observations by the others and written accounts by men in similar situations suggest that he replayed Mitchell's order to bring up the cask of varnish and remembered his moment of empathy for his crew when he said they'd take a light down instead. He saw the lamp tip . . . tried to grab it . . . watched flames run like quicksilver. He panicked, calling for water rather than smothering the fire. For most survivors, repeated flashbacks have a healing effect, replacing scattered images of horror with an explanation. Owen Chase, first mate aboard the whaleship *Essex*, was gripped by such a memory until concluding that the whale that attacked them was guided by a "decided, calculating mischief." The psychologist William James, on surviving the 1906 San Francisco earthquake, realized that man's belief in God was more therapeutic to survivors than were the facts of science. Unable to make sense of disaster, victims invoked God or fate, giving it purpose and meaning. But Hardy denied himself that luxury. Neither God, nor fate, nor the doldrums burned his ship. It was his own disobedience and carelessness.

It is painful to imagine the hatred he felt for himself and the self-loathing he faced each morning. Almost surely, he wanted to die, calling up the guilt that formed a background chorus for the 19th century. Nathaniel Hawthorne saw familial guilt passing through generations; Herman Melville created an Ahab whose vengeance turned his men, like him, into monsters. Poe's fictions were saturated with death and guilt that no amount of penance could expunge. A century that began with vague stirrings of guilt over the continued slave traffic would explode into civil rebellion and dissolve finally into the extermination of the Indian and mutual destruction by labor and capital. How easy it was to feel guilt in this era; how easy to just let go and die. Like men in similar circumstances, Hardy no doubt imagined hurling himself over the gunwale—sailors knew that the human body was heavier than water and the head was the densest part. He'd sink headfirst into the darkness and plummet like a torpedo. He'd disappear entirely, taking his memories.

Rather than blame Hardy for their misfortune, an odd solicitousness sprang up in the sailors of his boat, as if they wanted to shield him from further pain. It was Hardy's luck that he was liked by the men. After a week in this furnace, the crew had sorted out what happened and would easily have killed a less respected man. They knew that Hardy had been careless, but his mistake was to save crewmen from backbreaking labor. Sam Hardy was a good example of a "fishy," or democratic mate, a counterweight to the captain, who was expected to be distant and authoritarian. Democratic mates instilled a spirit of cooperation in the men. There is no mention in any journal of grumbling over Hardy's mistake; Mitchell, who had most cause to despise him, was always kind. The men on Hardy's boat were especially protective: "The Mate's boat," wrote Samuel, "is careful and contented, recognizing the awful position we are in."

Hardy *was* fortunate in the makeup of his crew. Little is known about seamen George Whitworth, William Lintern, Joseph Frank, Joseph Collagan, or Charles Beale. All were rated as ordinary or able-bodied seamen: Lintern and Beale were from New York, Whitworth from London, and Frank and Collagan from Spain. No sick were aboard, as in the other two boats. They could have demanded a bottle of brandy from Samuel or exceeded their daily water ration, but maintained a strict self-discipline. Later commentators attributed this solely to Hardy's authority ("They were evidently under the eye of a *man*," Twain later wrote), but men in such conditions submit only as much as they choose. Something else bolstered their morale.

In addition to the common sailors, William Laing, Joe Washington, and Henry Chisling were aboard. Laing was sunk in a depression as deep as Henry Ferguson's. He wondered why he'd given up the comforts of home, why he'd succumbed to the romance of the sea. As Mitchell muttered on May 10, "All romance has long since vanished," but it had vanished earlier for William Laing. After little more than a week in the boat, his nightly visions were filled with food. He dreamed of the holiday when his father bought three ducks and the house was filled with the fragrance of duck pies. He saw white napkins, clean china, silver forks, smoking meats, steaming vegetables, and quivering aspics and jellies, all cocooned by laughter and a warm fire.

Joe Washington and Henry Chisling were the hidden glue holding together morale. Washington, the cook, led them in prayer. As historian William Jeffrey Bolster pointed out, white sailors looked to black sailors and their evangelical form of worship for spiritual strength when death was near. Up to a point, the black whalers in the *Essex*'s lifeboats had led white Quakers in prayer. In 1818, when a North Atlantic gale had threatened a whaleship, the captain had begged the black cook to pray. He "prayed out fervently to God to protect and save us," the captain later wrote, and to the amazement of all, the ship survived.

Although few of the *Hornet*'s men were profoundly religious, old sayings about the dearth of atheists in foxholes apply equally well to castaways. A psychiatric study of seven castaways from a 1973 shipwreck off Tasmania showed that six of them started praying immediately. "Oh, God, get me out of this," was the common approach. "If You get me out of this lot, I'll play ball." Said one survivor: "I sort of talked to Him in more or less as many words as I could remember out of a prayer and filled the rest up with my own."

Recounting survival tales was another form of hope, and the steward had survived not one disaster, but three. He'd "twice wrecked and once went down," Chisling had told Samuel aboard the *Hornet*: one wreck is not recorded, but the second was off the north coast of Iceland, where the icy waters of the Greenland Sea could kill a man in minutes from hypothermia. The sinking he mentioned was most likely that of the two-masted schooner *Nimrod* on August 26, 1858, on Lake Erie near Buffalo. The ship left Buffalo for Cleveland on August 25, loaded with 200 pounds of grindstone. A storm sprang up and it foundered in 75 feet of water west of Port

Stanley. By September 2, when no one in Buffalo or Cleveland had heard from the *Nimrod* all hands were listed as lost. But the crew had escaped safely in the longboat and rowed to shore.

Chisling had also survived the *Dreadnaught*, perhaps a greater challenge. If any clipper deserved the name of "Yankee hellship," it was the three-masted ship launched two years after the *Hornet*. Under notorious "driver" Samuel Samuels, she broke speed records but ran into things. The first collision occurred in 1853, when she hit the British ship *Eugenie*. In 1862, she struck and sank the *John Ennis*, with considerable damage to herself. In January 1863, she was five days out of Liverpool when a stiff gale snapped the rudder; Samuels' leg was broken and he nearly washed overboard. The only way to save the ship was to sail it stern-first into port; the captain who replaced Samuels died soon afterward of injuries brought on by another storm. The *Dreadnaught* still sailed in 1866, but not for long. Three years later she wrecked on the rocks off Tierra del Fuego, becoming another hulk to spook sailors as they rounded Cape Horn.

Surviving life aboard a hellship was a miracle in itself for blacks like Chisling. Hellship captains reserved their worst punishments for crimes like "wasting beef," "burning a pudding," and "boiling rotten eggs," all the bailiwick of black cooks and stewards. On July 13, 1851, Captain Robert Waterman of the *Sea Witch* attacked his steward for some unrecorded offense and sliced his scalp with a carving knife. A cook on another ship was force-fed a pudding made for the entire crew after scalding it; in 1852, the steward of the *Columbus* got drunk in port, a common offense, but was brought to the captain, who "stamped him and hammered him and then asked the mate for an ax." He continued the assault until the poor man was mutilated.

Washington's and Chisling's treatment aboard the *Hornet* never approached such abuse, but there was real irony that the sailors now looked to them for hope. Before 1840, seafaring was one of the few institutions where an African-American could "presume upon his equality" with whites and "feel like a man." This turned for the worst after that decade, when the idea of "whiteness" as a working-class value gained precedence and blacks were assigned less frequently to foremast stations and more often to the kitchen and pantry. In time, white sailors assumed these billets belonged to blacks because the jobs were considered menial. Common sailors condemned black shipmates for their "dirtiness" and discriminated against blacks in the same way their superiors discriminated against them.

Since a cook's and steward's place were lonely berths, it is not surprising that the two became good friends. They lived apart from the sailors and officers, and were called "idlers" because they did not keep a regular watch; the cook's power in rationing food and the steward's perceived relationship with the captain sparked further resentment. Cooks were especially disliked for making money from "slush," the grease used to lubricate masts and spars. That part left at the end of a voyage could be sold in port, and a cook's "slush fund" sometimes grew into a small fortune. British cooks were said to skim £50 in slush per voyage, while Melville said a cook made $30 to $40. Washington saved the money to give to his wife, hoping to open a restaurant in Five Points, the center of New York's black community.

Few details are known of Chisling and Washington, and mostly from the journals of the Fergusons. Both were older than the average white sailor, and seemed in their 30s or early 40s. Washington was darker-skinned than Chisling and contended with a prejudice against darkness found even among other blacks; at the same time, he was a family man and ambitious, so he would have been viewed as a stabilizing force in the developing urban Negro community. Both lived in Five Points, a half-mile district jammed with 8,000 black, Irish, Italian, East European, and English families, and home to nearly 270 saloons and even more whorehouses and dance halls. They'd lived there during the Draft Riots and knew the stories of white rioters attacking Negro victims. The mob had swarmed into the LaFarge mansion on Amity Street and beat the black servants; had burned the Orphan's Asylum and killed a little girl; had lynched William Jones as he defended his family from attack; had smashed the skull of another man named Williams with 20-pound rocks. Which was more dangerous, the sea or home?

Although neither left a journal, a contemporary did. Ship's steward Charles A. Benson kept a diary from 1862 to 1881, a rarity among black sailors. His days were filled with loneliness, and though he often hated the life, he kept at it to support his family. "Last night I dreamed of home," he wrote on May 13, 1862. "I feel homesick today . . . what a miserable life a seafaring life is." Most of Benson's free time was spent with the cook, Aaron Moses, his best friend on the bark *Glide*. The cook's galley was his second home, where he slept, read, talked about home, and spun yarns, and

Benson and Moses would be friends for life. Benson endured the taunts of sailors and sense of uselessness because, he told his wife, "You and the children must have things to eat and drink and wear." Yet even with such purpose, the idea of dying at sea haunted him. One night in 1862, he awoke to loud voices on deck—an alarm of someone crying for help from the sea. The watch heard the cry "three times, but it was dark and it blew half a gale. They could not tell for certain but the Mate says he thinks it was one clinging to something in the water."

Now Chisling and Washington were lost in the dark, alone. All they had were those in this boat: white sailors once distant or abusive, the morose young gentleman sailor, the silent mate contemplating his ruin. Both knew such camaraderie would vanish the minute of rescue, but from the last boat in the chain came a reminder of what awaited should they abandon even the most temporary alliances.

There was no accord on Mr. Parr's boat. The despised second mate had lost all authority. The tins of meat were eaten up, every drop of water in the demijohns sucked down. By the morning of May 10, after one week in this furnace, shouts came over the water:

"Give us more water! We're dying of thirst!"

"Give us more food! You have no right to keep all the stores!"

CHIMERAS

THUS THE SOUNDS of discord rose in the doldrums. "This is the 8th day" since the *Hornet* sank, Mitchell wrote—Thursday, May 10. "Men begin to look famished and dispairing [*sic*], almost out of resources for encouraging them. The diet beginning to affect us all. 2nd Mate's boat very improvident and troublesome." Samuel was more detailed. "Rather a bad spirit is beginning to develop itself in the 3rd boat. . . . They are not at all provident and having eaten up all the cooked meats, etc., brought from the ship, they now are discontented."

There was little warning of this storm. Samuel had not noticed problems two days earlier when he entered Parr's boat to read to the men from his Book of Common Prayer. Parr and the carpenter, Ben Laarson, grumbled in the best of times, but they were countered by the stolid Germans and Scandinavians. Peter Paulson, the sick man, thanked him for the reading, and Jimmy Cox announced that he planned to sell the tale of his adventures to the highest bidder once saved. Their high spirits continued the next day when they took the lead in rowing and made sail when a breeze arose. A race to nowhere ensued. "Catch 'em, boys," urged Mitchell. "It's a soldier's breeze, Captain," Fred Clough laughed, referring to a beam wind by which even a landlubber could sail. Their larger sail worked in their favor and they soon took the lead.

They'd been fortunate in other ways also. Joe Williams landed not one dorado, but two. It had become a war of nerves between Williams and the fish: they nudged the lure then sped off, turning on their sides as they flashed beneath the boat as if mocking those above. The average dolphin measured three to four feet and weighed 20 to 30 pounds, though Williams told of one off Cape Verde that was six feet and 60 pounds. Such a fish could knock a boat to pieces if dragged inside. This was a smaller one that struck the hook, but Williams didn't want to take a chance: he pressed his thumb and middle finger in the eye sockets and the fish was paralyzed. The deep blue sheen of scales turned gold, then back to a silvery blue. There was richness in its death, a wealth of nutrients soon theirs. As Williams cleaned the fish, even the little gamecock grew excited; Williams removed the organs and fed the little bird a strand of intestine.

By now the bird had earned a name: Richard the Lionheart, or simply Richard, and was almost considered an equal. Every morning at four he hopped on the sternsheets and crowed at the sun. At six each evening, he repeated the challenge. They'd feel heartsick watching the sun rise or set when suddenly Richard would crow like a maniac as if cursing God for leaving them this way. The whole boat started laughing, even Mitchell, who laughed very little anymore.

Williams chopped off the dorado's head and tail, plucked out the eyes, and cut the meat into strips as Charlie Kaartman built a tiny fire from salvaged wood. Kaartman stuck the strips of meat on his knife; although the fire was scarcely large enough to warm the meat, the thought of eating made Henry's mouth water. The boats were called together and the dolphin divided 31 ways. The meat tasted better to Henry than any dish at Delmonico's, the finest restaurant in New York; he slowly sucked the juices before nibbling the strip of flesh. It was heartbreaking how quickly he finished, yet even as he ate his body revived. Except for a few shreds of salt pork, this was his first protein in days. Kaartman said they had wood for only one more fire; after that, they'd eat fish raw. Henry had never eaten raw meat and wondered if he could do it, but realized he'd have to adopt the ways of the savage who had little choice in selecting or rejecting food. If raw fish was offered, he'd eat it. If a seabird landed on their boat, it didn't stand a chance. It was a miracle the rooster hadn't been devoured. Some objected when Williams jabbed his hook through the dolphin's tail and tossed it over the side, but within minutes a second dorado struck, smaller than the first. They dried the strips across the thwarts, provisions for a less bountiful tomorrow.

Maybe it was this brief jolt of protein that gave Parr's men energy to rebel. A week of little food but adequate water produces in the body a balancing act between the old metabolism and a new one wrought by hunger. Studies have shown that a weight loss of 10 percent is the point at which humans can no longer work efficiently; at 20 percent, many find it hard to move. The men on the boats had lost between 4 and 8 percent of their weight, mostly in body fat and water loss, or about 7 to 13½ pounds apiece. They dozed often and felt weak when awake, but were still capable of brief spurts of energy when called upon to row or reef sail.

In some ways it was remarkable they'd remained even-tempered so long. The torture of starvation is markedly different from that of thirst, a slow, insidious diminishment often compared to the guttering of a candle from lack of fuel. During the first couple of days in the boats, Henry and the others experienced dull, pounding headaches; these disappeared by the third day, replaced by stomach cramps. In some men, this brought vomiting, but the most common reactions were waves of painful peristalsis in the gut, accompanied by *tenesmus*, a desire, but inability, to use the bathroom. During that first week, two or three men might be on the gunwales at any moment, straining but unable to have a bowel movement. Mitchell experienced this, but from Henry and Samuel there is no word. Henry, especially, was too embarrassed to leave such details to posterity. He was mortified by the boat's public nature. The castaway stories he'd read emphasized privation, determination, madness, and murder—never the strong smell of his urine, the rank smell of their bodies, the indignity of hanging over the sea for a bowel movement as tiny fish flashed beneath him, or the white pimples and red rash from constant exposure to salt water that enveloped him like a second skin.

Samuel may not have noted *tenesmus* because there was nothing to report. Every available nutrient was consumed by the tuberculosis burning inside. He noted other changes, though—a blurring of his vision, a dimming of brighter colors, and most dramatically, a greater susceptibility to dizziness and sunstroke than the others'. His vision doubled when staring at something with both eyes; the line of the horizon became a blue X, corrected only when he closed one eye. At the very worst moments, his head felt crushed by a heavy weight and his field of vision filled with a bluish haze. He dipped a rag in seawater and wore it as a cooling turban, then lay in the shade of the sail for long periods of time.

More than anything else, the men experienced a growing lassitude. Black depression is a companion of starvation, a state observed among

London's unemployed during the hard winter of 1837–1838. "The first indications of a deficiency of food," wrote an attending physician, "are languor, exhaustion, and general debility, with a distressing feel of faintness and . . . chilliness, vertigo." Time took a physical form. In the 374 years following Columbus's voyage to the New World, shipwreck narratives had become the most popular print genre in Europe and America, and the accumulation of days at sea was always advertised as a defining characteristic. Mitchell already counted. People in meditation who've experienced a slowing of brain waves and heart rate report that "time stands still." Clinical depression is marked by the "molasses-like feeling of being stuck in endless time." Starvation time is the same. The body and time wind down together, every day the same as the last, entrapped in an endless present.

Even in normal voyages, time is one of man's greatest enemies. Studies of fishing crews subject to isolation show that a period exists when ships and sailors are particularly vulnerable—a period defined simply by the accumulation of days. A 1973 study of crewmen aboard deep-water fishing trawlers showed that in the first two months response time to emergencies and relationships between sailors were at an optimal level and productivity was high. But after three months, from Days 61 to 80, the accident rate rose from 35 to 45 mishaps per 100 cruises. After Day 81, the accident rate plummeted to 28.5 per 100 cruises, as if a learning curve kicked in. But just when a captain might breathe a sigh of relief, the mean rate of fights tripled in Days 91 to 120, accompanied by a rise in injuries attributed to anger and aggression—black eyes, cut hands, broken jaws, concussions, cracked skulls, and first- and second-degree burns. Crewmen also suffered a number of emotional complaints: difficulty in concentrating, nightmares, insomnia, homesickness, nervous exhaustion, and low-grade physical ailments like headaches and upset stomachs. The *Hornet* had been 108 days at sea when she burned, putting her crew within this window of anger.

One difference in the last boat was the presence of John Parr. The second mate was a difficult man. Samuel and Henry didn't like him, Mr. Thomas didn't like him, and neither, it seems, did Mitchell. Mr. Parr was a classic example of a "bucko" mate partial to the *colt*, the single-coiled whip used to beat careless crewmen. Although Mitchell didn't condone such treatment, a certain violence on any clipper was assumed.

Instead, Parr resorted to free rein of his temper, much like his famous predecessor William Bligh. By the standards of the day, Bligh was less physically violent than other captains, but his language was more abusive. He would go into towering rages at any indiscretion, and his ability to humiliate men was so infamous that he was court-martialed for bad language in 1805, long after the *Bounty* mutiny. Bligh taunted men with their fears, shook a fist in their faces, stuck a pistol to a man's head, threatened to make men jump overboard, and promised to make them eat grass like cows. In the tight spaces of a ship, humiliation was resented more than flogging. Now, on the third boat, similar rebellion festered. When Parr told his men to limit their water, they ignored him and drank it all. Their taste of dolphin fueled their hunger and they attacked the tins of food. When Parr ordered them to stop, they told him to go to hell.

That afternoon of May 10, Williams caught his third dolphin, and they chanced upon a sea turtle, two bits of luck that Mitchell hoped would quiet the anger on Parr's boat. A man on watch called attention to a small dark object; any change was welcome in this sameness, and every eye bent that way. When they drew close, it was a sleeping green turtle rising and falling on the swells. The stupid things were known to bump into boats in search of mates, but this one was insensitive to their presence and they sculled up slowly, careful not to raise the sweeps lest drops of water announce their position. Williams bent forward in the bow, directing Mitchell with hand signals; Mitchell whispered instructions to Fred Clough at the oars. Williams held up his hand, then pounced, grabbing one flipper and then another as he heaved the turtle aboard.

Williams flipped the turtle on its back, where it thrashed in the bottom of the boat until settling down. Some men wanted to butcher it immediately, but Mitchell said to save it. They guessed the thing weighed 50 pounds at least, which set off rounds of yarns about turtles so huge you could use the shells for a boat. Henry half-listened to their stories: he stared into its bulging eyes set above a nasty-looking beak. The turtle scrutinized him with a cold, unblinking stare.

Such fortune would not hold. That night a northwest breeze sprang up, pleasant at first with a cool drizzle, but this proved deceptive when the breeze pushed them off course. By the morning of May 11, they were three-tenths of a degree farther south than they'd been on the previous day. The men in Parr's boat raged. "Second mate's boat again wants water today, showing they overdid their allowance," Samuel wrote. "Captain spoke pretty straight to them."

Thomas said later that he was pleased by the sharpness with which his captain, who rarely raised his voice, addressed Parr. If Mr. Parr could not keep his men under control, Mitchell said icily, then he would cut them loose and they'd die of thirst if that's what they desired. He'd publicly humiliated the second mate as Parr had done to others, but more important than that, the men heard plainly that their lives lay in their own hands. Mitchell had no sympathy for men without discipline. The exchange left a bad taste, and he put into words the thought he'd avoided all week. "Shall be obliged to separate the boats, all very crowded."

Samuel wondered if they were reverting to a primitive state. They'd been adrift for nine days, and one boat seemed poised for murder. Nineteenth-century Western civilization was obsessed with man's primacy in an age of science, yet right beneath the surface lurked questions of man's true nature. The Civil War and its savagery put the lie to moral certainty: behind the high ideals lay age-old brutal dreams. Even the definition of truth was changing: once thought transcendent and objective, philosophers now asserted that it now changed "pragmatically" with society and the times. Right meant might. Truth belonged to the strong.

There were times when Samuel felt lost, philosophically and physically. He felt like an anachronism. He looked at the rabble in the street and in the forecastle, and feared their numbers and growing power. The moral certainty of those born to a privileged class slipped away. It seemed to him a vision of the future, where order fled and chaos reigned.

Samuel's despair was part and parcel of a 200-year debate on the heart of man. Suddenly the *Hornet* was transformed into a natural laboratory for competing philosophies. To 17th-century thinkers Thomas Hobbes and John Locke, the world adhered to well-defined causal laws, but beyond that they disagreed. In a world stripped of comfort and pretense, how did man "naturally" behave? Was nature a state of "every man, against every man," as Hobbes presumed, where "the life of man [would be] solitary, nasty, brutish, and short?" Or was it characterized by reason, as Locke envisioned, a state where common sense dictated respect for "life, health, liberty, or possessions?" Locke's point of view, outlined in *Two Treatises of Government*, was called liberal and optimistic, while Hobbes's, developed in

Leviathan, was believed pessimistic and authoritarian. In Hobbes's world, men lived in a natural state of war, a good description of what was developing in Parr's boat. In Locke's universe, men settled into a self-adjusting state where government's main purpose was to deal with emergencies and stabilize their needs—a picture of life aboard the boat of Sam Hardy.

And there was a third way, characterized by the *Social Contract* of Jean-Jacques Rousseau, where government existed through the consent of the governed and law codified their customs. It was the philosophy adopted by the Founding Fathers, yet in a place like the doldrums, what was the law of the boat? If their welfare hinged on standards so savage that they violated everything Samuel had come to consider just, what was his obligation?

HENRY ROSE FROM his depression on May 12 by making a compact with God. "Please God, [if] we are saved, we will all have an awful lesson against carelessness," he wrote. "If we do not live better lives than we have . . . we deserve worse than we have now."

But God was not in a bargaining mood. He indulged instead in a catlike cruelty. Deep sleep, for one thing, was withheld from them: the effects were most fully pronounced in Mitchell, who rarely relinquished the tiller. Most human societies adopt a single, "monophasic" sleep, but deep-water sailors work best under shorter, uninterrupted "polyphasic" periods ranging from 30 minutes to two hours. *Uninterrupted* was the operative word, and the boats experienced too many interruptions for deep sleep to occur. "Captain pretty much worn out," Henry wrote, but only Mitchell knew the extent of his exhaustion. For the past few days he'd heard a "strange music," which he seemed afraid to describe. It was most likely a thin, pipe-organ wailing, high up in the wind. Auditory hallucinations can be so relentless that they drive victims mad: some sufferers hear bells, whistles and horns, while others hear voices.

Although auditory hallucinations seemed confined to Mitchell, visual hallucinations affected them all. Mirages appeared without warning in the sea's flat emptiness. Mariners have told of sailing toward the sky or into a hole in the sea; of the sudden appearance of inverted icebergs floating on the horizon; of watching buildings and mountains emerge from the surface. The most frequent illusions in the longboat were visions of ships and sails. "The horizon," wrote Samuel, "is filled with little stand-up clouds that look very much like ships." On the evening that Henry rose from his funk, a sailor stood in the bow and pointed to the north. "Light ho!" he cried.

It looked like the glimmer of a ship's lantern rising above the curve of the sea. All of them rose in their excitement and nearly upset the boat as they waved their arms. For breathless seconds they stared, eyes straining to discern the speck of a ship, hoping that Mitchell's promises weren't empty and they'd drifted into the sea lanes. But the light mounted higher . . . higher than any ship's lantern could possibly reach . . . until they finally realized it was the evening star.

"It was a bitter disappointment," wrote Henry. "Chances dark," Mitchell said.

Dashed hopes and isolation do unfathomable things to those at sea. Deep-water sailors vow that not everything they've encountered is an illusion, and that strange beings do ride the waves. George Harbo and Frank Samuelson, two men who rowed across the Atlantic in 1896, swore they saw a black, shaggy beast resting on the surface. Its snout was pointed like a Newfoundland hound's; its eyes were intelligent and aware. As they approached, the creature examined them, then slipped beneath the waves. Some enigmas weren't flesh and blood. Joshua Slocum, the first man to sail solo around the globe, wrote of a ghostly stranger sitting in the helm of his boat. Lyn Robertson, floating in the same stretch of doldrums, saw a person sitting behind her husband who helped guide them through a long and dangerous storm.

But no such guardian angels watched over Mitchell and his crew. That Sunday, May 13, was their second Sunday in the boats, and they were expected in San Francisco a week from now. "Have thought much of all the loved ones at home," Samuel wrote, "and the disappointment next Sunday of the not hearing from us" by telegram. They reduced their rations by half, convinced that help might never come. For breakfast they limited themselves to one-quarter hardtack biscuit, one-half pint water, and one ounce ham; for lunch, each man got the same amount of bread and water, and four tiny tinned oysters or clams; for supper, the same bread and water, and 12 large or 14 small raisins. This cut their daily intake from about 1,270 to 635 calories, but they hoped to supplement this by harvesting the sea. And luck seemed with them—in quick succession they caught another dolphin, and Mr. Hardy's boat landed a second turtle.

On that day and through most of the next, a good breeze sprang from the south and they sailed directly toward Clipperton. But on the afternoon of Monday, May 14, the wind changed again, bringing with it "the biggest rain squall I ever saw," Henry said. The southern horizon was blacked out by a great wall of clouds. The sun glowed pale, with no warmth; the advancing swells were lit by a dull red glow. Moaning sped before the storm like the bellowing of beasts, and before they knew it, they were overtaken.

It continued all night, the winds shifting and searching, until by next morning they had no idea of their location. Mitchell took a reading of longitude, but the noon of May 15 was too cloudy to fix latitude. Then a sign appeared. Some blue-footed boobies circled the boats and the bravest lit on their yardarm. It cocked its head and surveyed the emaciated creatures spread beneath it. After a minute, it snapped open its wings and flapped into the sky.

"Boobies are land birds," Clough cried in hope. "They don't fly far over open water."

"Clipperton must be close," said Mr. Thomas. "Keep your eyes peeled, boys."

They looked but saw nothing, and later that afternoon Mitchell called the boats together again. He wanted to test their seaworthiness, he said. Parr and Hardy knew he played with the idea of cutting them loose, but neither spoke his fears. The night had brought a new moon and with it the first hint of a trade wind; one week earlier, during similar tests, Mitchell's boat had beaten the others, but this time Parr's boat outdistanced the rest and Hardy's lagged behind. The effects of starvation were showing on the first mate's crew: they were weak as babies, fumbling like green hands as they tried to reef the sail. A storm was brewing and Mitchell signaled Parr to heave to until they all caught up and tied together. A cold rain hit them, filling the water barrel but turning the men into shivering heaps. The rain continued with little letup until 2:00 P.M. of the next day, May 16—exactly two weeks after the *Hornet* went down.

Mitchell looked at his men. They were weak, but still able to put out when needed, their spirits still high. They still had the turtle and hoped to catch more dorado. Each day Richard the Lionheart crowed at sunrise and sunset, but had grown too weak to mount the gunwale, so splashed around in the bottom of the boat. The bird's condition seemed to speak for them all.

Mitchell took a reading: Lat. 10° 40' N, Long. 109° 30' W. They must be near Clipperton, but he didn't know how close. In fact, they were heart-breakingly close, a mere 21 miles north and 17 miles west, but they might as well have been a thousand miles away. The breath of trade wind they'd felt on the previous night was growing stronger by the minute. They'd gotten what they'd prayed for and were finally escaping the doldrums.

But the wind pushed them west, deeper into the ocean. This moment would be the closest they ever got to Clipperton. The rock upon which they'd placed their hope was the cruelest illusion of all.

THE STALKING SEA

HENRY'S REALIZATION that they'd missed Clipperton Rock brought a new bitterness. Nature did not concern herself with his survival, and could dispose of him with a shrug. "Tell me the truth, what are our chances?" he asked Mitchell on May 16, their second week in the boat. "Our only chance now is Clarion," Mitchell sighed, then looked squarely at his young passenger. "I think there's barely a shadow of a chance for our rescue."

Panic rose in Henry: his lip quivered, but rather than show emotion, he stared out to sea. "I'm sorry," he said when finally able to speak. "I just thought how I might not see my college mates again." Samuel laid his hand on Henry's arm, but remained silent. Mitchell studied the brothers, sitting together like a still life. The two were made of good grit after all.

Henry stared east toward Clipperton, humbled by Samuel's touch. He'd gone West to comfort Samuel, but his dying brother comforted him. The world made no sense in this place, and he cast for the first time a cold eye on his degeneration. In his fourteen days adrift, he'd eaten little more than three pounds of food. His stomach was in knots; his ribs poked through his scanty flesh; most body fat was gone and his muscles would soon feed upon themselves. The red patches of rash were beginning to connect: they burned like fire, turning from pimples to pus-filled abscesses. Every movement was tiring. Visions of food snapped from his dreams like faces in the dark.

It didn't seem fair, but fairness had no meaning here. He imagined the boat as a speck seen from high above. A storm was building in the east and swells marched before it with awesome solemnity. He wondered if this was the iron face of God. If so, no wonder the ancients feared looking in His face. They knew they'd find no kindness there.

But such thoughts were apostasy. If his life was snuffed out, it had to mean *something*. Samuel recognized Henry's dilemma as the same he'd experienced when sentenced to death by TB. He'd been stunned, staring at the marble grandeur of Wall Street, repeating, *Is it possible?* like some poor imbecile. It seemed that all good things must end with him: perhaps an individual had to feel that his death was nature's last gasp, but when he tried explaining this one night to the lovely Miss Snow, she laughed nervously and said it was not healthy to be so *morbid.* He lingered on the porch after she left and bitterly laughed, thinking how fortunate it was that she was not a witness. He stared at a high blue star and its loneliness seemed to mirror his own.

One embraced despair or hope, no matter how frail. "Today we have been two weeks in these egg-shells and it certainly seems as if we are to be saved," Samuel wrote. "God grant us an end to our captivity." His meaning was ambiguous. A ship, or death, could bring that end.

By 8:00 or 9:00 P.M., the storm was finally on them. It had a strange glow as it approached: a wall of cloud crested by scarlet foam, like a huge wave about to break upon the world. To the west, a ferrous sun sank behind a flat red haze. In the north, flecks of rose-tinted cloud rode high in the sky: the entire northern sea was rose-hued, light glinting off the wavetops like pale fire. The swells advancing from the south looked like darkened hills. There seemed a cosmic rhythm to the swells, a periodicity like a clock stroke, and Henry measured the time from crest to crest as roughly the count to ten. Mitchell guessed they were 100 yards apart, which meant the sea moved at about 25 knots. The greater the wave length, the faster the wave. Wave lengths of 200 yards were not unusual in the Central Pacific; waves that long traveled about 35 knots and were as tall as five- or six-story buildings. They could not hope to survive the slopes of such waves in these tiny boats. Wavetops breaking from such monsters had the concussive effect of ten or more tons.

So night fell. Henry could still see shapes as the sea reared its back against the starlight and swept toward them. He hated this anxiety of waiting. A cold blast struck them from the starboard side and Mitchell struggled with the rudder to keep the boat pointed into the wind. The blast passed and there was brief silence, then the air above them filled with constant roar.

For the next few hours, they were enveloped by the storm. "The most anxious night I ever passed, dark as Erebus," wrote Mitchell. "Passed a most awful night," Henry echoed: "We went in every direction . . . . It rained five times as hard as I ever saw it anywhere else." And Samuel: "A most uncomfortable set of wretches one can imagine."

They were lucky to survive, for Mitchell's notes suggest they were in a strong gale. Seas build to more than 25 feet in such storms, with wind speed averaging 44 knots and gusts even higher, possibly a Beaufort Force 8 or 9. Storm reporting was never accurate, inspired more by terror than science, with waves described as "monstrous," "prodigious," and "gray-backed beasts," and wind speed determined by the destruction. In an attempt to make some sense of Nature, Sir Francis Beaufort of the British Royal Navy drew up in 1805 a scale linking wind strength to sea conditions. It was officially adopted 25 years later. Yet there comes a point where words no longer have meaning, and on the Beaufort Scale, that point is manifested by a Force 12 storm. In such a tempest, winds are lumped together as 70 knots or greater, and waves called "phenomenal," as if oceanographers threw up their hands in despair. It is very hard for an adult to walk upright in a 70-knot wind: water driven by such force stings like buckshot and can permanently damage the eyes. Those who've lived through it say the sea seems bent on murder.

All depends on perspective. Most Beaufort readings are taken from the decks or superstructures of ships, towering 25 to 40 feet above the sea. In Henry's boat, there was no such separation between them and the thing being measured. From their perspective, the waves looked maleficent and measured off the scale. At 25 feet, crests begin to break apart: the air is filled with long strands of spindrift that burn like white phosphorus; the sea growls like an ill-tempered animal. But even amid the chaos, Henry discerned patterns. The largest waves came in groups of three to five; their crests curled up, then broke from the force of the wind. "Keep bailing!" Mr. Thomas shouted, though no one needed to be told. All night Henry and Fred Clough knelt together in the bottom of the boat, bailing until their backs locked up and their hands grew numb. He and Fred cursed together the fact that their task never seemed to end. Even King Sisyphus got a break in Hell when his boulder rolled away, but in bailing there was no such breather, for if they stopped, they drowned. A longboat swamped in such a storm would float dead in the water and turn sideways to the sea. A swell would catch them and they'd roll over.

Yet even as Henry fought for his life, he felt a strange exhilaration. Researchers have noted that the body does not differentiate between emotions: the autonomic nervous system releases comparable doses of adrenaline and dopamine, the brain chemical linked to pleasure, for situations we interpret as either terrifying or exciting. Psychologist Michael Apter labeled the interpretation of such chemical signals a "protective frame," a fortress built up by previous experience that says we'll survive. When the frame collapses, panic ensues.

Mitchell saw the storm as a problem. "These three boats together," he lamented. "If I had but this one it would not be so hard. But I cannot cast them off." He could not risk running before the seas since he ran so slow and risked being "pooped," or swamped by a wave breaking over his stern. Facing directly into the waves would beat his little boat to death. He lay to again with the sea anchor, bow to the wind, yet the lateral force of the towline caused his boat to sheer from side to side. He hung to the tiller all night, steering a sinuous course up and over the crests to minimize the forces coming at him, then bearing off to compensate when down in the troughs.

The morning of May 17 broke slowly, their fifteenth day at sea. The water changed at dawn from slate to green. Their hair stood up like madmens', stiff from wind and salt; two-week beards covered their faces; their eyes were locked in thousand-yard stares. Their daily ration of a tablespoon of Samuel's brandy ran out on this day, a comforting ritual that reminded them of better times. The rain slacked up at 6:00 A.M. and settled in as drizzle that would last the next few hours. The storm had blown them fifty to a hundred miles west of Clipperton, and too far north to even glimpse the Rock from afar. Joe Williams felt a tug on his line and dragged in a midsized dolphin; Peter Smith, a quiet, blonde-headed sailor who seemed strangely regal to Henry, knelt uncomplainingly at his job as bailer. Samuel lay asleep in the sloshing water in the bottom of the boat. The little gamecock, too weak to hop upon a thwart, stepped around his inert body.

"Shall I take over, Captain?" Mr. Thomas asked. Mitchell only shook his head. Two men in the bow glanced at each other, then looked away. The brief glance seemed ominous to Henry, though he could not say why. He worried about Mitchell, too. Their captain had rarely left the tiller since entering the boat, and although the work of bailing, rowing, and trimming sails was exhausting, at least it warmed the blood. The Old Man sat like a statue, the leaden light sharpening his face. He seemed alert, but could not suppress shudders from the cold.

"What's that?" cried Harry Morris, pointing off the port beam. "Over there."

Less than a mile away two squalls met head-on and the ocean beneath their impact seemed thrown into the air. A black cloud bellied down until its center tapered to a tentacle; this searched for a footing until it met the sea. A column of foam and froth lifted up, then coalesced into a spinning funnel.

"Waterspout!" Mitchell cried. "We're in for it if it heads our way." He told Peter Smith, their strongest oarsman, to take the port-side sweep, and ordered Fred to the starboard side. Mr. Thomas yelled at the stern boats to get their own men at the oars and trim their sails. "Which way is it going?" Mitchell muttered: the funnel grew in width and turned from dark green to black as more water was sucked up. The cloud grew bloated and blacker, its edges spreading until it resembled a hideous balloon whose tail spun through the water.

Henry froze. He'd wanted a sign of some sort from heaven and now one dropped in their laps, a whirling maelstrom of 100-knot or faster winds that could shatter their boat if the vortex even nicked them. At first the tail seemed locked in place, but then twisted in small ellipses. He heard a hiss of spinning water, followed by strange sighs. Slowly, the funnel began to grow.

Mitchell saw it, too. "She's headed for us," he snapped, ordering Peter Smith and Fred Clough to row at right angles to its path, and do so fast as hell. Thomas waved directions to the other boats. "Row, boys," Thomas urged tensely. "Don't look over at it, just row."

As oceangoing ships have become steel fortresses, waterspouts have been portrayed as pallid cousins of the tornado. No such arrogance existed in the Age of Sail. Called *prester* by the Greeks, *typhoon* by the Romans, *timmins* by the Persians, and *dragons de mer* by the French, waterspouts annihilated ships and massacred sailors. "A great black dragon is seen to come from the clouds, and puts its head into the water, and its tail seems as

though it were fixed in the sky," wrote medieval chronicler John of Brompton. "The dragon drinks up the waters so greedily, that it swallows up
along with this any ships that might come in the way, along with their
crews and cargo." The dragon put a face on the fatality that stalked seamen, a manifestation of the monsters perched at the edge of old maps with
the legend *hic sunt dracones*: "Here be dragons."

All witnesses struggled to express that radical sense of otherness they
felt divorced from normal life, a dread translating into religious awe. Sev-
enteenth-century buccaneer William Dampier saw a huge waterspout in
Indonesia that raged for half an hour and yet from which a bird emerged
unharmed. It seemed a glimpse of the divine, but one best glimpsed from a
distance. He cited the 300-ton British frigate *Blessing*, which strayed too
close to one in 1674 and sank off the coast of Guinea. A waterspout sank
five ships in Charleston Harbor on May 4, 1761. Captain Cook saw six
huge waterspouts, each 60 to 80 steps in diameter, move slowly across his
path off New Zealand in 1775. William Bligh's longboat was stalked by a
waterspout in 1789.

Nothing seemed to stop them, though plenty of mariners tried. Asian
seamen beat drums to frighten them away; in the 1800s, captains "shot the
dragon" with four-pound brass signal cannons in an attempt to "jar the
waterspout down." Medieval sailors knelt at the mainmast, made the sign
of the cross, and slashed the air with swords as if to cut the funnel to
shreds.

Today scientists classify waterspouts as "tornadic" or "fair-weather,"
based on their formation. Tornadic spouts start over land as true tornadoes, then swirl into the sea. They drop from thunderstorms, squall lines,
and the leading edge of cold fronts, and can be as huge and destructive as
anything experienced on land. A famous Black Sea spout of July 1924 was
certainly tornadic: it lifted a rowboat and canoe into the air, as well as the
terrified fishermen in them, then flung three shepherd boys to their deaths
when it hit land. The spout responsible for one of Britain's worst bridge
disasters, the 1879 collapse of the span across the River Tay, was most certainly tornadic, too. Although a severe gale was blowing, a witness
attested that it was waterspouts, more than 260 feet high, that triggered
the collapse, sending the Edinburgh mail train plunging into the river and
killing 75 passengers.

"Fair-weather" spouts are smaller and only form over water; they often start at sea level and climb skyward like an Indian rope trick. The name, however, is a misnomer, since they develop in all kinds of weather, dry and humid, fair-weather and foul, and for small vessels like the longboat, they are still quite deadly. Their rotating winds have been clocked up to 200 knots; the sudden pressure reduction explodes confined spaces; when the funnel breaks apart, tons of water come down. Although tornadic spouts last longer than their fair-weather cousins—thirty minutes to an hour, as compared to 10 to 20 minutes—there's also a better chance of getting out of their way. Tornadic funnels churn along at a ponderous five knots or less, while fair-weather funnels dance and zip nervously at speeds of 45 to 70 knots, changing course without warning, and endowed with the unexplained habit of being drawn to vessels.

To add to the confusion, there are hybrid spouts that show attributes of both. Considering its size, longevity and behavior, this seemed the case now. This was no ponderous spout, like Captain Cook's, but one bearing down quickly. All three boats sailed a broad reach at right angles to the spout, yet within minutes it swirled within 500 yards. It seemed sentient, drawn by a predatory sense, and the hair rose on Henry's neck. "It might have been a fine sight from the solid deck of a ship," he wrote, but not in a flimsy boat tossed by the waves. The voice of the funnel changed from sighs and hisses to groans and howls; a sulfur smell permeated the air.

Mitchell couldn't afford the luxury of religious awe. "To the sheets!" he cried as the sails began to slat. "Trim 'em flat!" They changed direction not a moment too soon. The cloud was overhead and black as night; they'd sailed a hundred feet when the green column passed astern. The sea churned at its base with such loud roaring that conversation ceased—the funnel rose up hundreds of feet and was thicker than an oak, yet spun like a top and looked clear as glass inside. Jimmy Cox cheered when it missed them, but it changed direction and looped back again. Possene screamed in Portuguese and crossed himself; Henry wondered what they'd done to deserve such a visitor. "It's coming back!" Mitchell shouted, watching the funnel dance close. "Pull for all you're worth, boys! Now!!"

This time it headed straight for them. The winds shrieked around the vortex; the cascade around the base rose up a hundred meters; the funnel changed colors, now stark white against the gray clouds, so white it seemed to glow with an inner fire. It probably *was* glowing, since subtropical spouts are known to lift tons of water filled with billions of phosphorescent microorganisms that blaze green and white when agitated. The funnel writhed in the overhead winds as it strode across the water, glowing with a pale, pure light like the tallest ghost in the world. They'd been stalked for 15 minutes and it showed no sign of diminishing. "This thing hates us," a sailor chattered, and Possene screamed again. Yet even as he did, the funnel grew thin and ropelike as it marched close; the strand swayed hypnotically with the prevailing winds. The tube stretched out, thin as pulled taffy; it sagged in the middle like a rope of glass, then snapped. A cascade of water splashed somewhere nearby.

"We made it," Mitchell gasped.

"You can stop rowing, boys," Thomas sighed to Smith and Clough, who leaned over their oars. A nervous sob rose up front. A keening passed above them that softened into whispers.

It rained until 2:00 P.M. They drifted with the backward current, drained of life by their close call. Henry wondered what new monsters would appear. Until the encounter with the waterspout, Henry's greatest fear had been of sharks: several times already he'd seen a torpedo shape glide silently underwater, barely glimpsed shadows waiting for scraps or the clumsy sailor fallen overboard. A few well-placed oar-thrusts seemed to keep them at bay.

But it wasn't a shark that found them now. In mid afternoon, a shoal of flying fish exploded to their right: they skipped across the water, wings banking, tails flickering like tiny propellers. As they dropped into the water, Henry caught a shadow from the corner of his eye.

Something moved beneath the surface on the port side. He bent over the stern and spotted a long, streamlined fish with blue bands on its body and a tail like a crescent moon. It swam a few inches from the rudder in perfect parallel; he motioned to Mitchell, who called it a bonito and wondered why it acted so oddly. It matched every turn of the rudder; even when their shadows fell across the water, the bonito would not dive. When Mr. Thomas came back with the gaff, he, too, was intrigued. "It's like it's hiding from something that scares it more than our shadows."

The next moment, they saw what that was. The men up front shouted and Mitchell told everyone not to move. A giant swordfish swam off their bow, circling around the longboat from starboard to port. As it circled,

Henry saw the bonito switch to the opposite side of the rudder, blending again into its shadow and swimming inches away. "It's after the fish," he said.

The swordfish looked more sinister than the sharks, and Henry suddenly realized that not a single shark was around. Its sword alone was five feet long, a sharp and bony projection thrusting from the upper jaw. Behind that rippled 500 pounds of sleek and shiny muscle, the biological equivalent of a lethal weapon. Its dorsal fin raked back as it cut through the water. Its eye was huge and black, round as a dinner plate.

When the fish surfaced and stared, unblinking, Fred Clough flinched. He'd seen what these things could do. They were indiscriminate killers and in the Central Pacific were feared. Off the Mexican coast, he'd seen a monster like this rise up from the water among a shoal of mackerel and fall flat with such concussion that stunned mackerel floated to the top. Then it raked right and left with that sword. Fish parts were strewn across the water, while others writhed in circles, spines snapped like twigs. He saw one big mackerel float up with a hole punched through it as the swordfish threshed among the dead and wounded and swallowed fish whole. Fred could believe anything of such beasts. They killed for the joy of it, not just to feed.

There was little they could do on the boat but freeze or pray. If they gaffed the bonito, the swordfish might attack; if they pushed the bonito away from the rudder, they'd be in the path when the swordfish spotted the fish and lunged for its meal. Their mouths watered at the thought of swordfish steaks, a feast that would stave off hunger for a week, but molesting such a monster would just ensure their doom. Attacks on boats were frequent and well-documented, and everywhere man and swordfish met, an armed conflict ensued.

The myth of the monster's origin even sprang from war. When Achilles voyaged to Troy, he went as leader of the Myrmidons; when he was killed by Paris, his loyal followers rushed to kill the Trojans, who wisely stayed inside their walls. In a blind fury, the Myrmidons threw themselves into the sea. The gods took pity on such loyalty and turned them into fish; they were allowed to keep their swords, which grew as long spikes from their jaws. Warriors in myth; killers through antiquity. *Xiphia gladius*, scientists called them: the Greek and Latin for sword.

One great risk faced by the castaways was the monster's fabled capriciousness, especially toward large objects: swordfish were famous for rushing and impaling boats, ships, and whales. Captains noted in their logs that schools of oceanic fishes liked to shelter beneath their slow-going ships, thus bringing the vessel in line when a swordfish rushed upon its prey. Whales were said to suffer a similar fate, though this was unsubstantiated. Anything floating on the surface was an island, and out here islands were like an oasis, drawing life like a sponge.

The longboat was no different. If Henry ducked his head beneath the wooden hull, he'd see weeds and gooseneck barnacles growing on its bottom, a nursery for the phyto- and zooplankton at the base of the food chain. The two-week-old barnacles measured about one-third inch and had not grown their hard adult shells. They attracted sardines and anchovies, which attracted flying fish and mackerel, which attracted dolphin, bonito, shark—and swordfish. An island could be anything and anywhere.

Not surprisingly, large predators were attracted to such floating buffets. In 1817, the *Foxhound* felt an impact and found the sword of a *Xiphia gladius* protruding through its bow. In 1847, a gentleman naturalist presented the Royal College of Surgeons of England with a portion of the whaler *Fawn* that had been pierced by a South Seas swordfish, the sword penetrating "the copper sheathing, the felt, the deal, and the hard oak timbers to the depth of 14 inches." The *New York Herald* of May 11, 1871, reported that the English ship *Queensbury* was "penetrated to a depth of 30 inches, causing a leak which necessitated the discharge of the cargo."

Mariners were terrified of swordfish, and the *Hornet*'s men were no exception. A writer in 1854 said the fish possessed one of the foulest tempers in the animal kingdom, and was "neither to be trusted or trifled with." Later observers spoke of the swordfish's "choleric disposition": the fish was so instantly eruptive that "the pugnacity of the Swordfish has become a byword." Witnesses wondered whether the fish was possessed by a kind of temporary insanity, but this one's actions were cold and calculating. It lurked behind the stern, waiting for the bonito to leave the rudder, but its prey never strayed. Whenever the swordfish shifted position, the bonito passed beneath the rudder to stay concealed. As the cat and mouse game continued, the swordfish grew frustrated, darting at the boat with a loud rushing sound, then would break off suddenly or pass beneath the keel. When he rushed, his body changed color from dull brown to a beautiful azure. They tried to scare him off by raising the sweeps and screaming, but this did little good. Sometimes the men saw the monster disappear beneath the surface only to see the lunate fin rise behind the stern.

Death by impalement was not unknown with such a fish, and although they stood a better chance of drowning should the fish tear their boat to splinters, every man imagined himself skewered by its sword. The first recorded impalement occurred in 1813 when a man was pierced through the stomach while swimming off the coast of Massachusetts. In 1876, South Seas missionary William Wyatt Gill wrote that native fishermen were stabbed in the wrist, hip, knee, and foot when their boats were run through: "It not unfrequently happens that, in chasing flying fish at night, the course of the sword-fish is arrested by the stout outrigger of a canoe."

The best-documented account of impalement would not occur for another twenty years. On August 9, 1886, Captain F.D. Langford sailed out of Lanesville, Massachusetts, in the 12-ton fishing schooner *Venus* with a crew of three. They were hunting swordfish, and at 11:00 A.M., one was spotted basking in Ipswich Bay. They rowed after the fish and harpooned it in the side. What happened next was told by one of Langford's men:

"It quickly turned and rushed at and under the boat, thrusting its sword up through the bottom . . . 23 inches." The captain fell on his back . . . "and while he was in the act of rising the sword came piercing through the boat and into his body. At this time another swordfish was in sight near by, and the captain, excited and anxious to secure both, raised himself up, not knowing he was wounded. Seeing the sword, he seized it, exclaiming, 'We've got *him*, any way!' He lay in the bottom of the dory, holding fast to the sword, until his vessel came alongside, while the fish, being under the boat, could not be reached. Soon the captain said, 'I think I am hurt, and quite badly.' When the vessel arrived, he went on board, took a few steps, and fell, never rising again.

The *Hornet*'s men were luckier than the unfortunate Captain Langford. The swordfish lurked around the boat, circling and feinting, but disappeared as unexpectedly as it had materialized. They held their breaths, waiting, watching . . . but the fish did not return.

The bonito, for its part, was not so lucky that day. Once certain that the swordfish had departed, Mr. Thomas gaffed it and dragged it aboard. That night, Henry ate raw dolphin; the next morning, raw bonito. He savored the fatty belly meat and the crunchy skin. The space between vertebrae held water; his teeth crushed squirts of liquid from the eyes. He laughed at his former squeamishness: nothing went to waste. Once he would have felt guilt for eating the bonito after its escape, but no longer. Sentiment was a luxury. Alliances shift quickly at sea.

It was eat or be eaten out here.

———◦◦◦———

THE FIRST PARTING

THE NEXT MORNING, on May 18, Richard the Lionheart died. They'd known his death was imminent, but this did not make his passing easier. Even when no longer able to mount the stern sheets, he'd borne up bravely and received his portion of bread crumbs without complaint; the last couple of days he'd slopped around weakly in the bottom of the boat, and the men cradled him up so he could gaze over the side. It was strange to watch the tenderness they bestowed upon the little cockerel, but sailors grew attached to the oddest things. Roosters, like sailors, tended to crow about themselves and were brave, and they were charmed by their reflection. There was pain in their voices when at 4:00 A.M. Richard did not rise from his spot by the water cask. By then, he'd started to stiffen and seemed little more than feathers: a breeze would blow him away.

The eyes of Harry Morris and the other sailors teared up and they looked away. They were funny like that, Henry thought: tough, yet sentimental. "You grabbed him and jumped overboard with flames licking your pinfeathers, remember, Harry?" Fred Clough said. They laughed as the Frenchman recalled how Richard crowed as if he'd take on the fire alone.

Death seemed much closer now. It was Day 16 in the boats and Richard was the first to go: it was as if their luck had run out, an old superstition that mascots must be rescued or a crew's fate was sealed. Their own battle for survival was reflected in Richard's plight, and with his death they read a portent. Any death on ship was like losing a part of oneself, Dana wrote years earlier. "It is like losing a limb."

Their grief extended to disposing of the body. They couldn't leave him to rot; they couldn't drop him overboard to the sharks; considering their hunger, it's a wonder they didn't eat him themselves. But there was a horror at that solution, as if someone suggested cannibalism. They wouldn't touch that subject yet—at least not aloud. Instead they sewed Richard in a burial shroud and handed him over to Mr. Hardy's boat. The sailors there could do as they pleased.

Sewing up a corpse was one of the most macabre rites of sea. Sailmakers performed the honors, sewing the corpse into canvas then passing the last hitch through the nose to insure that he was really dead before dropping him overboard. If not, he might come back at night to walk the planks in revenge. There were practical reasons, too. Corpses that were not tightly secured and weighted down with shot showed a tendency to bob along in a ship's wake, pulled by the suction. Like the cook and his "slush," the sailmaker received a fee for his work: in the British navy, for example, the man who "sewed the corpse" pocketed a guinea.

It grew very quiet in the longboat after Richard's death, each man alone with his thoughts. "Sailors are almost all believers," Dana noted, "but their notions and opinions are unfixed and at loose ends." Fred Clough was a prime example. He called himself a Christian but never attended church, and his idea of an afterlife rested on a concept of fairness. Like most sailors, he hoped that his hard treatment on earth would count for something at the pearly gates. "To work hard, live hard, die hard and go to hell after all, would be hard indeed," many sailors said.

Mitchell steered north, avoiding thoughts of justice or fairness. "God in his goodness has preserved us another day. . . . Boats still together." The postscript hinted at the decision he'd soon make. Whatever he did might be just—but for at least half the crew, it wouldn't be fair.

If Mitchell could not make that decision, others already had. The waterspout decided the question for them. Just when they'd needed speed and maneuverability to outrun the funnel, the towline slowed them down. "Expect we will separate soon as there will be more chance for some of us to reach safety," Henry wrote. Samuel hardened himself against the inevitable: "We talk of separating and must soon do so. We can take one boat in tow, but not two. It seems too bad, but it must be done for the safety of the whole."

But doing so meant playing God, since cutting the cord could mean a death sentence for some of the men. As long as they remained in these doldrums, even here at its northern limits, the small sails of the quarter-boats were useless for catching the light, mocking breeze. A separated boat would be stranded without the larger boat to pull it, condemned to slow death by thirst and starvation. But in the two-and-a-half weeks that they'd been afloat, they'd barely succeeded in moving 40 miles a day, and at this rate, they'd die.

How could Mitchell judge one boat worthy of life and tell another it was their lot to die? His dilemma echoed battlefield ethics, but in some ways the rule of the sea was far harsher. The sailor's rule was simple: no ship had a legal duty to help another, since rescue attempts jeopardized both saviors and saved. Rescuing people from a dinghy or derelict ship was a dangerous operation: sails must be taken in, a vessel hove to, the boat put overboard, and the ship moved to leeward. In heavy seas, both vessels stood a good chance of sinking, and many captains attempted rescues only in calms. Yet such pragmatism had horrendous consequences, the most famous that of the American brig *Polly*, which sailed from Boston on December 12, 1811. Three days later, it sprang a leak and capsized during a gale. For the next 191 days, the *Polly* drifted 2,000 miles and passed more than a dozen ships, yet not one stopped to help. Only two of the original nine crew members survived.

In admiralty law, the needs of the ship were paramount. Survival meant everything. Each of the *Hornet*'s boats had adopted that principle. On the morning of Richard's death, the two stern boats slaughtered and cooked Mr. Hardy's turtle, but did not share the meat with Mitchell's crew. It was understood that the longboat would do the same when they butchered theirs. Parr's boat did not share the birds they caught, while Mitchell's men split raw dorado and the ill-fated bonito only among themselves. Battlefield ethics dictated that soldiers operating as a unit make every effort to preserve a fellow soldier's life, yet the sea complicated such norms. While the men in Mitchell's boat depended on each other for survival but not on those in the following boats, the quarter-boats depended on Mitchell to drag them through this windless hell.

This conflict of responsibility, of the self against the group, was as old as civilized man. At what point did social ties break down? The harsh rule of mariners echoed the principle in Jewish law that one's life was more precious than another's. According to the Talmud, "His life is no less valuable than your own," echoed elsewhere by the question, "What makes you think his blood is more red than yours?" The 16th-century scholar Rabbi David ben Zimra said that anyone who put his life in jeopardy to save a friend was a *chassidshoteh,* or "pious fool."

Some men in the longboat already thought that of Mitchell. He was hanging them by the towline; just one more storm would kill them. Mitchell could be a martyr to his conscience if he wanted, but must they be, too? Yet there was a practical reason to separate the boats. They'd stand a better chance to hail a ship if spread out than if linked together. Henry and Samuel could sense the captain's struggle, but thought he should compromise—cut one boat loose, if not two.

Still, Henry could not help but feel sorry for Hardy's men when their boat pulled up later that afternoon. Everyone's weight had fallen drastically, but in Hardy's boat the effects of starvation shook them all. Henry Chisling and Joe Washington fared worst. They were probably in poorer health than their white counterparts when they shipped aboard the *Hornet*: in New York City, tuberculosis killed twice as many blacks as whites, a reflection of poor health care and adverse living conditions. A recent study comparing body fat among ethnic groups found that black Americans seem to have less than Caucasians. Once a starvation victim exhausts his or her fat, the body consumes muscle, leading to organ damage and death. The initially lower fat ratio in Chisling and Washington meant they may have already exhausted that reserve.

William Laing wasn't much better. Although in better health before the voyage due to his higher standard of living, his frostbite injuries were black with infection and he'd lost the will to live. The study of seven survivors aboard the cargo vessel *Southern Star* emphasized "the need to refuse to accept death, to be determined not to die and to hold to the belief that one was not meant to die." Those who made no effort dropped like flies. Laing was one of these.

The two boats tied together and Hardy came aboard. How long he and the captain talked is not recorded, yet a certain peace descended.

Mr. Parr sat alone in the last boat, excluded from decision-making. "What you think they're talking about, Mr. Parr?" asked one of his men.

"I'm sure we'll find out," Parr replied. But he could guess, and in his mind he damned them all.

THAT NIGHT, SAMUEL DREAMED. Although this had been rare in the past, "[I] now hardly shut my eyes for a cat-nap without conjuring up something . . . [a state] accounted for by weakness, I suppose." He envisioned the waterspout, the swordfish, home. More than anything else, he dreamed of food. All starvation victims reach that point, their dreams almost excruciating. The words of an Arctic survivor were typical: "At first my thoughts dwell with fond recollections upon all sorts of dishes, but gradually they concentrate themselves upon sandwiches—Danish sandwiches, with no top slice, very different from the dull, dry things one gets in England." The sight and smell of his dream feasts were so real that Samuel's mouth watered, and he snapped back into the conscious world. If he thought of this as a holy fast, perhaps it would be easier. Hermits sought enlightenment in the early years of Christianity by turning starvation into a spiritual act: "You can't humble the soul if you don't ration the bread," one Desert Father said. Adam and Eve had been expelled from Paradise for breaking a kind of fast; Father Tertullian of the early Church declared that "an emaciated body will more readily pass the narrow gate" of Paradise. Such thinking seemed to help: Samuel woke to a serene sea in the cold lunar light, a wilderness as alien to human experience as the moon.

On the morning of May 19, Mitchell did the thing he'd dreaded for so long.

It did not go well. Shortly after dawn, he steeled himself and called over the quarter-boats. A dead calm settled around them, "the deadest and flattest that I have seen yet," Henry wrote. Every sound was magnified in the silence: the dip of the oars as the two boats approached; the feverish breathing of Peter Paulson; the creak of Mitchell's voice as he said without preamble, "We're going to have to separate. One of you will have to go off on your own hook. I can continue to tow one boat, but not two." He paused and looked at both mates. "These calms are killing us and if we do not get a breeze, we all will perish. Separating doubles our chances of running against another ship." He took a deep breath. "Mr. Parr, will you cast off your line?"

"I will not," Parr said.

The blunt refusal took Mitchell by surprise. "You won't do as I ask?"

All night Parr had anticipated this moment, and grew inflamed. "I will not. Why me?"

To those in the longboat, the answer was obvious. Parr's boat had constantly overeaten its rations during their seventeen days afloat. The men showed no sign of discipline; Parr, no sign of cracking down. Their profligacy threatened everyone. The captain pointed out that Parr had a more reliable nautical compass than Mr. Hardy, who only had the small pocket compass loaned to him by Samuel. Parr's boat had proven the most seaworthy when the three raced.

But Parr would not budge. He'd watched the conference of his captain and first mate and imagined their conspiracy. Mitchell's request confirmed his fears. He was the odd man among the officers, the despised English sailor in a cast of Yankees, and he refused to be sacrificed to their transparent nationalism. History bolstered such suspicions. Outsiders had the odds stacked against them, always first to be thrown overboard or cannibalized for the greater good. In the unhappy *Essex*, black sailors had died first; in the wreck of the *William Brown*, which hit an iceberg on April 19, 1841, crewmen had jettisoned passengers from the longboat to ease overcrowding. "In general," wrote Lewis Petrinovich in his study of shipwreck disaster, "the order of survival is for the captain and officers to be favored over the crew, next passengers, with women and children favored over male passengers, men with family favored over boys, foreigners being in jeopardy and slaves [or blacks] being thrown over just after animals, which go first."

On the longboat, such sides were already forming. At this point, most rancor focused on Antonio Possene, the despised "Portyghee." He'd stuffed himself with bread when the ship was sinking; his feverish rambling in his native tongue maddened them all. His abscesses ran with pus and stank. He was useless in his debility, and no more than an extra mouth to feed. Mr. Thomas was not circumspect in his hate, and if not for Possene's countrymen, he might already have been cast overboard. Years later, the prejudice lingered and was passed on to posterity. "After thirty-two years I find my prejudice against this 'Portyghee' reviving," Mark Twain wrote in a 1900 article about the *Hornet*. "His very looks have long since passed out of meaning; but . . . I am coming to hate him as religiously as ever."

It doesn't take long in extreme circumstances for an outsider to be perceived as the cause of all hardship; it was a mere baby step from annoyance
and dislike to threats and murder. One of the most detailed records of
exclusion occurred in the account of Dougal Robertson, whose 43-foot
schooner was sunk by killer whales in June 1972. He piled into a raft with
his wife, three children and 22-year old Welsh graduate student Robin
Williams; for the next 38 days they took the same route through the doldrums as the *Hornet's* men. Other survivors have hailed Robertson's
account of ordeal and rescue as a modern survival Bible, but a forgotten
subtext was the attitude change toward the one non-family member on the
raft as time dragged on.

From the beginning, Robertson cast their plight in a Darwinian context: the short-term goal was daily survival, but the long-term goal was
continuing his gene pool—that is, the survival of his children. Anything
standing between him and that goal was cast as the enemy. His account of
the ordeal, *Survive the Savage Sea*, is a chronicle of hardship and disappointment, where rage against the elements became his psychic shield.
Nothing would beat him, not even Nature, a classic illustration of the will
to survive. Yet rage finds a scapegoat, and his was Robin Williams.

When he first met Williams in Panama, "his smiling visage and adventurous spirit made him stand out," Robertson said. Yet as the castaway
voyage continued, Robertson grew intolerant of the young outsider. Nothing Williams did was right: at one point, Robertson threatened to kill him
if he disobeyed an order. Even his sleep was criticized. Williams is seldom
heard, yet one suspects he saw his position as increasingly perilous. He was
called to his face a drain on the resources, like the *Hornet's* despised
"Portyghee." "Left to your own devices, you would be dead already,"
Robertson told him. Williams objected and Robertson added, "If any one
of us dies because you don't feel like doing what you're told, I'll kill you!"

The most dangerous moment for Williams occurred on Day 35 when
he reached for a turtle and missed after Robertson yelled for him to move
away. When Robertson struck him with an open palm, Williams snapped
that it was lucky they weren't on a rugby field or "it'd be a different story,"
apparently the only time he returned the older man's aggression. In
answer, Robertson grabbed the paddle and said, "If you disobey an order
again, I'll hit you with this!"

Empathy was no longer possible for Robertson—just blind rage and evolutionary imperative. This illustrates how rage demands a victim, a need filled by the outsider. By now, the once-liked student had been demonized. Given more provocation, he might have lunged for Robertson, but doing so would have upset the small raft and probably killed them all. Instead he backed off, and since the castaways were rescued three days later, the standoff went no further. But when Robin Williams made his exit, one gets the idea he felt lucky to escape, realizing perhaps that he'd come closer to death at the hands of a shipmate than by the vagaries of the sea.

Mr. Parr, for his part, was not as quiet or calm as Robin Williams, and refused to be a scapegoat. The master and second mate faced off. Mitchell's authority was being challenged, while John H. Parr would not go gladly to his death, even for his captain.

At this point, a noble and tragic act occurred. "I will go," someone said. It took a moment for the voice to register, then they realized that Mr. Hardy had volunteered. His face was pale and strained, for he knew this probably meant his death. His men looked stunned, too. Whether he acted from a sense of gallantry or guilt is something we do not know, for Hardy left no record, yet he and everyone else knew whose carelessness had put them here.

In exchange for casting off, he wanted Mr. Parr's more seaworthy boat, as well as the second mate's more reliable compass. One imagines he made these requests with a cold disdain: Hardy's offer humiliated the second mate, and Parr quietly complied. They made the transfer easily: there is some confusion in the accounts, but Hardy took eight men with him, including Henry Chisling, Joe Washington, and William Laing. Two members of Parr's crew, disgusted with their mate's behavior, volunteered to take the place of Hardy's weakest men. Jimmy Cox, the youngest, stayed with Mr. Parr. All were silent as they changed places; Mitchell divided the stores equally among the boats, despite the fact that there were more men in his own. This left his men with two-thirds of a ham, one-fourth a box of raisins, half a bucket of biscuit crumbs, fourteen gallons of water, and three cans of beef bouillon, or what the sailors called "soup and bully." They still had their sea turtle, which rocked weakly against the wooden hull.

Now it was time to go. "Speak well of me to my wife, Captain," Hardy requested, and Mitchell grabbed his hand. William Laing gave his parents' address to Henry and asked him to contact them. Joe Williams gave

Mitchell the address of the Catherine Lane mansion where his wife worked as a servant. It was as if they all knew they were going to die; as if they were already dead. Mitchell tried to keep their spirits up by telling Hardy he was still on course for Clarion. Above all else, "follow the dictates of your judgment," he said.

At 11:00 A.M., they separated. "God bless, boys," cried Mitchell, refusing to look back at John Parr. "Goodbye," said Hardy and the others with him. The sea spread out as smooth as a satin sheet; the distance between the two boats widened. By 3:00 P.M., Hardy's boat had dwindled to a small white spot on the windward horizon; an hour later, she dipped beneath the earth's red rim. Once or twice they spotted the peak of the sail as the boat lifted on a swell. They waited for more, but Mr. Hardy's boat had gone.

"DEATH IS AT ALL TIMES SOLEMN, but never so much at sea," said Richard Henry Dana, and partings, perhaps, were the same. There was a suddenness in both events that seemed unreal. A man falls overboard like a disappearing act; a small boat is swallowed up by the horizon as if sucked into the sea. "In an instant he is gone, and nothing but a *vacancy* shows his loss," continued Dana, as if nothing is ever permanent, and man's existence just a dream.

Every parting is a little death, a time to reassess one's life, and Samuel faced his own survival odds. "Must admit that this life is telling pretty severely on my strength," he wrote, a chink appearing in his optimistic armor. "Water now will be a scarce article, for as we get out of the doldrums we only now and then get showers in the Trades." He believed it was a toss-up who would die first—the "Portyghee," or him. If he were a gambler, he'd lay odds on Possene's survival. The fire inside burned Samuel a little more each day.

Tuberculosis and malnutrition have been linked since the disease was identified. It was common knowledge by the 19th century that TB increased in frequency and virulence during famine; it progressed most rapidly in malnourished patients, and simple measures of rest and wholesome food magically arrested its spread. As Samuel sat in the longboat, his digestive tract grew smaller and the muscle fiber in his heart grew dangerously thin.

Researchers have noted an inverse correlation between TB and the consumption of milk and meat: proteins are the essential elements of the immune system's antibodies, and proteins, especially of animal origin, seem essential in fighting the disease. The current recommended dietary allowance for protein is .36 grams per pound of body weight daily, or about 54 grams for a 150-pound man. The men in the lifeboat were getting a fraction of that. Even a moderate protein deficiency of long-term duration can profoundly impair the production of T-lymphocyte antibodies, rendering a malnourished animal less able to fight infection by the tubercle bacilli. The lack of protein was not only killing Samuel, it was turning him into an even greater threat than ever for those nearby.

Mitchell, like Samuel, was worried about infection, but of a different kind. The open rift with Parr chipped at his authority: the sailors in both boats had watched the second mate's refusal to obey his captain with unfeigned surprise. They were institutional men, conditioned to deference, yet the nature of control between rich and poor, owners and workers, rulers and ruled was changing. As Greg Dening points out in his study of the *Bounty*, power and authority onship was as much a function of ceremony and symbol as it was of force and law. The power of officers continued because it was allowed by those who believed themselves powerless. A captain's prescribed power was "public, independent, dependent on rituals of reification and signs of distance," while his individual authority, a far more subtle force, was "private, personal, dependent on interpretive wisdom and signs of adaptability."

Without personal authority, many hellship captains flogged and terrorized their crews into submission. Mitchell did not rely on this. On the *Hornet* and here in the boats, his men deferred to his authority as well as to his legal power. They trusted his wisdom and sense of fairness to get them through. The hazards of the sea were so great, the need for instant efficiency so obvious, that sailors easily deferred to controls they trusted since they felt it made for a safer ship. Yet Parr had challenged that wisdom, implying that he no longer trusted the captain to keep them alive.

Parr's rebelliousness was even supported by admiralty law. Once a crew was cast adrift, they were no longer under legal obligation to obey their officers. Authority was determined by personal traits. The sea and disaster spawned a harsh democracy.

Decisions, once reached, take on a life of their own. If one boat was cast off, why not the other, too? What Parr did that morning was not quite mutiny, but insubordination, unchecked, could plant a seed, especially as the food stores dwindled and suffering intensified. The most famous mutinies in history have to some extent been hunger strikes. In the great rebellion at Opis, the soldiers of Alexander the Great placed the lack of wine and Greek oil first on their list of grievances. The dissolution of Lee's army in 1865 was fueled by lack of food. The opening act of the *Potemkin* revolt sprang from the crew's refusal to eat spoiled beef; the French mutinies of 1917 were blamed on starvation; the end of Ludendorff's army one year later was due to a dearth of food. Hunger aboard the longboat would only get worse. Parr's example was a threat unless he drifted far enough away to be nothing but a memory.

Perhaps Parr's influence was already felt that afternoon when the men butchered their turtle, abandoning further rationing for immediate need. They grabbed the rear carapace and flippers; Joe Williams put a foot on each front flipper, held the beak, and plunged his knife deep through the leathery neck into the spinal cord. The turtle thrashed in agony and hissed as Williams severed the main artery to the head with quick outward strokes. As blood spurted into the bottom of the boat, the men collected it in a tin cup. Sharks circled and swarmed as blood splashed into the ocean; they bumped the sides of the boat in their excitement. Three or four pints of blood can be expected from a 65- to 75-pound turtle, and the men drank it warm since blood coagulates if left too long.

Butchering a turtle of that size takes one-and-a-half hours of work, sawing with the knife to remove the belly plate, hacking and cutting at tendon, bone, and shell. Turtles have a poor "killing-out ratio" of 25 to 30 percent meat, and the joints seem inaccessible. It took Williams an extra hour to hack out the shoulder meat and that around the flippers. He cut the meat into strips and passed it out; passed out bones, which were sucked and licked clean of bittersweet marrow. When the job was finished, they had 20 pounds of meat and bone. They ate half and saved the rest for tomorrow, boiling a soup of entrails and bone inside the shell.

The food worked on them like a drug. It broke down the starvation discipline they'd imposed on themselves, making them hungry for more. Gone were signs of fastidiousness in Samuel or Henry, both of whom deemed the repast "excellent" and "very good." After 17 days of eating little more than hardtack, they tore at the flesh with their fingers and teeth, grunting with pleasure and laughing. An average-sized turtle would produce two or three pounds of meat and an additional half-cup to cup of fat and blood for each man. They ate the organs quickly, savoring the vitamin-rich liver and heart. Altogether, the feast totaled 4,000 to 4,500 calories apiece—the caloric equivalent of a holiday meal. If any experienced pain as their shrunken stomachs labored to digest the sudden load of nutrients, no one mentioned the fact. They ate their fill, then fell asleep. Parr's crew heard the sounds of feasting, but were not asked to share.

That night, for once, Henry felt strength flood through him, lifting him from the disappointment and depression of the past few days. He felt a cheer that resembled abandon—it was amazing what happiness a little blood could bring. If he was a savage, so be it: in survival, there is no apology. There was even beauty, aided by being well-fed. "There was the finest rainbow and most beautiful sunset I ever saw," he wrote, wrapping up a day of greater emotional swings than any he'd ever experienced. He slept that night in contentment, remembering a line from Sophocles: "One must wait until the evening to see how splendid the day has been."

THE NEXT TWO DAYS passed in a dull blur. They finished off the turtle on the morning of May 20; this revived them temporarily, but then they drifted into another dead calm. The blue stretched around them, little cats-paws of wind cross-hatching the water like diamonds before they instantly died. "Oh, how glorious, if one could be anywhere else," Mitchell exclaimed. "A lovely day, but oh what a place to pass it in." There were no signs of Hardy's boat; no sign of any passing ship. "Very little hope, I am getting weak," he said.

More than anything else, they wondered at the continued absence of the Northeast Trades. "It is very strange we do not get the Trades, which usually come at 8° or 10°," Samuel said. Instead, that afternoon, a two-knot breeze sprang up, which cooled their parched skin and gently drove them north, still in line with the Revilla Gigedos and Clarion. It was their eighteenth day in the boat, their third Sunday, and at Mitchell's suggestion Samuel began reading regular morning and evening services from his Book of Common Prayer. "When not a sparrow falls to the ground without our Heavenly Father's knowledge," he croaked, "He will certainly take care of us." Henry tried to be attentive, but a strange scene unfolded in the boat behind him. A blue-footed booby, an odd-looking bird "as large as a wild duck," had landed on Parr's yardarm. These were comical birds: he'd watched one booby float beside them and peer underwater as a shark crept up. But instead of breaking into flight, it waited until the shark was almost on him, then pecked four or five times at its nose before flapping away.

This one showed the same disdain for peril. It perched nonchalantly, preening its feathers and gazing over the sea. As its plumage puffed out, Jimmy Cox thrust out his arm. The bird's wings spread wide, but were a half-second slower; Jimmy's fingers closed around its straw-like legs. The booby squawked and snapped its wings for lift; when that didn't work, it pecked savagely at Jimmy's hand. Another sailor leaped up, placed his huge fist around the bird's head and neck, and twisted. The head flopped loosely on its stalk, wrenched completely around.

Henry no longer quailed at such scenes. As with the sparrow of the Scriptures, God watched over that booby but did nothing to stop its death. Life was based on death, a fact preachers forgot in church. God might not forget life's brutal truth, but He certainly looked the other way.

The coming of death to the world was man's basic mythology: it was not a very great leap from tales told around the campfires of primitives to the sacred texts Samuel now read. "The world lives on death," mused the folklorist Joseph Campbell: "The necessity of killing—killing and eating . . . this deeply moving, emotionally disturbing glimpse of death as the life of the living" was the heart of religion and all things civilized. It was not a comforting sight, watching Parr tear the dead booby apart and hand the red morsels to his men, but it was the basis of life. Parr was his boat's priest, distributing the bird like the host.

The next day, on May 21, they hit another squall-line, but one Mitchell recognized as the border between the doldrums and the Northeast Trades. They were able to partially replenish the water cask, but the seas were confused and the longboat pitched and rolled in heavy cross-seas. Their small boat was thrown around like a toy until it finally happened: with a sudden twist, the mast was violently swung about, breaking just below the step and sending a balloon of sail down upon those in the stern. The boat bucked violently, its center of gravity suddenly changed. Mr. Thomas grabbed the hatchet and cut away the rigging; Mitchell steered the boat downwind of the trailing mast, maneuvering so the waves didn't drive the mast into the hull. For once, Nature was with them. The masts and sail served as a sea anchor, stabilizing pitch and roll. The weakened men, fueled by fear, adrenaline, and the recent infusion of protein, cut and trimmed the mast from the fracture and reset it in its step. The studding sail, its extraordinary size once an aid in capturing scant breezes in the doldrums, was a hindrance in the stronger trade winds, so they cut that down, too. The work completed and the squall past, they collapsed. "Our rigging, like ourselves, is rather weak," Samuel said.

That night the trades finally grabbed them, shifting at first but then remaining steady well into the morning. The sun rose at 5:30 A.M. and at that moment a man in the bow cried, "Sail ho!" They'd been through this before, fooled at dawn by little "stand-up" clouds, but as they stared it became apparent this was not another hallucination. The spot of white grew larger, dead ahead. They cast off the line to the second mate's boat and set sail to catch the distant spot, cheered on by Parr and his men.

They all bent forward, faces into the spray, urging the longboat forward with their bodies. Never before had Henry felt so alive. A sail, no doubt about it! It wasn't another trick! Samuel pounded him on the back and they started laughing. They'd done it—they'd survived this ocean! What a tale to tell their family—how Henry would terrify the girls in Stamford and regale his pals in Trinity. Samuel's faith in Providence had been justified.

But ten minutes later, the laughter stopped.

The sail was real, all right, but far smaller than they'd thought. Once again, the light and lack of perspective on a flat ocean played cruel tricks with their minds. They'd caught up with a boat—but it was Mr. Hardy's boat, which had disappeared over the horizon three days ago.

THE SECOND PARTING

HOW DOES ONE RESPOND when salvation becomes a mockery of hope, and the mockery is by one's friends? *Disappointment* rings out in all three journals: "bitter" disappointment in Mitchell's, "great" disappointment to Samuel, "dreadful disappointment and sickness of heart," to Henry. The longboat came abreast and "spoke" the quarter-boat. "Ship ahoy, Mr. Hardy," called Mitchell. "How goes it?"

"Like you, Captain," the chief mate answered. "All's well."

A grim joke that few found humorous, though some may have grinned. If so, they looked quite mad: eyes bright, lips peeling from the teeth, faces shrinking around the skull. Washington and Chisling resembled stick fig-ures, rags hanging from their bones, skin gray and ashen from sickness and dried salt dusting them like powder. William Laing looked insane.

Mitchell and Hardy talked wind and waves. It was evident by now that they were almost in the zone of the steady Northeast Trades. Yesterday's reading was Lat. 13° N, Long. 111° 40' W; today's was Lat. 13°20' N, Long. 112°35' W. Each day brought a few minutes of northing, but their western course gained by more than a degree, or sixty nautical miles. With the trades blowing strongly from the north-northeast, the chance of landing on Clarion did not look hopeful since that island was almost due north. They feared they'd pass it to the west as they had Clipperton. A better chance lay in following the nautical road: they hoped to hit the Great Cir-cle Route, the 4,433-mile track plied by steamships on a regular run from Panama to Honolulu.

Mitchell and his first mate talked for twenty minutes, then separated again. "I'll see you in Frisco, Captain," Mr. Hardy called, a brave attempt to be cheerful as his crew unfurled the sail. The canvas filled with wind and they moved off as Mitchell's boat waited for Parr.

Suddenly, a thought sprang up in everyone. They recalled the speed with which they'd chased Hardy, cut loose from the towline. How could they hope to catch a steamship if held back by that line? When they looked at one another, no words were needed. "Throw over the line, Captain, and we'll make fast," Parr called as every man on the longboat stared at Mitchell. A vertigo gripped him: it was as if the moral ground beneath him shifted. He looked out to sea after Hardy. He cleared his throat and told Parr that they wouldn't be towing him anymore.

What exactly happened next is speculation. It was too unpleasant for any but Samuel to report, and even he seemed shaken. A "good deal of unpleasantness was done," he wrote, nearly leaving it at that, yet the crew's silence was never absolute and in time details emerged. At first there was a dumb hush, as if all lost the use of their vocal cords. As shock turned to comprehension, Parr's boat exploded with rage. The second mate saw in an instant that once again Mitchell and Hardy made life-and-death decisions without him; once again he was deemed expendable for the greater good.

"This is murder!" Parr shouted, a cry taken up by others in his quarter-boat. Even Mitchell knew this was a betrayal of trust. On May 19, when the decision was made to cast off the first boat, it was understood that the longboat would tow Parr for the rest of the voyage. It was with this understanding that Parr gave his faster boat and superior compass to Sam Hardy. Now, with a chunk of a boat and a useless toy compass, his chances alone on the sea were laughable.

At this point, the anger of Parr's men turned to panic and they tried to board the longboat. "2nd Mate wanted to all get aboard the boat and cast the other adrift," wrote Samuel, but doing so would doom everyone. After everything else—the waterspout, swordfish, storms and deadly calms—they'd sink under their own weight, and Hardy could do nothing but stay clear and watch them drown. "Stop them, boys!" Thomas shouted, but the crew didn't need to be told. This was a fight to the death if Parr's men didn't back off: they held off their friends with the sweeps, unfastened their jack knives, threatened to cut any man who came aboard. In all probability, Samuel drew his revolver and aimed it at Parr. The pistol's appearance galvanized everyone. Before May 22, no sailor in the longboat knew of Samuel's revolver. After this day, none could forget.

Through it all, Henry heard the shrill voice of Jimmy Cox. More than anything else, those cries made him feel like a murderer. This was the moment he'd anticipated, when man became a savage. Now the moment had come, and he was ashamed.

Jimmy's pleas affected Mitchell, too. He was supposed to be the boy's protector, but shifting crews would turn man against man. Yet if Jimmy were left on the boat, he'd be the first sacrifice when the stores ran dry. Leaving Jimmy on the boat was a death sentence, but any other choice would condemn another man. "Captain, don't leave us," cried Jimmy. In that moment, Mitchell wished the funnel would return and tear him limb from limb.

Then the uproar passed, madness replaced by realization of what they'd nearly done. "You win, Mitchell," spat the defeated Parr. Mitchell's guilt was overwhelming and Parr wouldn't do a thing to alleviate it; Parr wasn't one to reprieve those who cut his throat for the common good. In a sudden fit of pique, Mitchell ordered that the stores be divided equally among the two boats; when Mr. Thomas reminded him that they'd done that once already, Mitchell snapped, by God, they'd do it again. The men on the longboat stared aghast at their captain: this sudden decision seemed almost as suicidal as letting Parr's crew climb aboard. They threw half the remaining supplies into the smaller boat, leaving themselves three small cans of oysters, one can of beef-bouillon soup, two-thirds of a ham, six quarts of bread crumbs and one-quarter box of raisins. They divided the remaining water, gingerly passing over casks filled with the precious fluid.

They drifted apart and Jimmy Cox began to scream. These were animal cries of terror: the boy struggled as the others tried to hold him back; it seemed to Henry that he meant to jump into the sea and swim over, but what would happen then? Perhaps Jimmy realized the not-uncommon fate of cabin boys in castaway boats; perhaps he just panicked and reached for Mitchell, the closest father figure in over a thousand miles. Though no one knew it, upon this single moment hinged the fate of the longboat, and the captain's response was pivotal.

Mitchell hung his head. This was murder heaped on murder—first the exchange of good men who'd trusted him for the survival of his boat, now the sacrifice of a boy. He couldn't take it anymore. Cox would make fifteen in their boat, one more mouth on already strained rations, but he was not a monster. He could not look into the eyes of Jimmy's parents and lie that he'd done everything he could for their son. These were choices no sane man should have to make, but sanity had followed the *Hornet* to the bottom of the sea.

"Shut up, you pup," snarled Parr. "He don't care about your precious hide." Mitchell thought of his own son. He glanced up and saw that Parr had raised his hand as if to strike the boy. "He'll kill Jimmy in that boat," Mr. Thomas whispered. "Captain, please," Fred pleaded. "One more mouth won't make a difference. He's pretty small, you know."

Mitchell stood in the stern, propping himself against the tiller so he wouldn't fall. "Send the boy over," he said. "You'll stand a better chance with one fewer mouth."

"You're a saint, Captain," Parr replied.

The sarcasm was not lost, but Jimmy did not care. He leaped the space between the boats, landing near the water cask and holding tight as the boat swayed. "That was a fool thing to do," said Mr. Thomas, but there was only relief that nothing worse had happened. "God speed to you, Mr. Parr," Mitchell said as Peter Smith dipped the sweeps into the water to put distance between the boats. Parr stared back at his captain in contempt. "God speed to you, too, *sir*," he said.

Cox sank amidships beside the third mate, and he was trembling. "I'm sorry how I acted," Jimmy said to Mr. Thomas. "I know it was shameful, but I saw myself dead if I stayed there."

"Don't thank me, boy," Mr. Thomas answered. "It was the captain who saved your skin."

The boy crawled back to Mitchell like a wounded animal. "Why did you let me come over, Captain?" he asked. "It's not like I'd make things easier."

Mitchell gazed at the boy, and the look on the older man's face was heart-wrenching. He seemed to struggle for an answer. "I couldn't leave you on that boat," he finally said.

"Thank you, sir," Jimmy answered. "You saved my life. I won't forget it."

The wind filled the sails; the longboat caught up to Hardy's boat and pulled ahead. Henry looked back at Parr and shuddered at what might have been. A commotion began as they pulled off: enraged voices drifted across the water; men faced Parr, who stood threateningly in the stern. The anger in that boat had reached its boiling point, but the wind carried them off and none would have to watch as the sins of the bucko mate finally caught up to him.

THEY FELT UNCLEAN AFTER THAT. "What's to become of us?" wrote Mitchell. "God in His wisdom knows."

If anything, they wanted to leave the past behind, and the wind obliged. By leaving the doldrums, they entered a belt of winds existing on a planetary scale. Trade winds were a manifestation of the anticyclonic high-pressure zones located 30 degrees north and south of the equator; the zones were permanent, spinning clockwise in the Northern Hemisphere and counterclockwise in the Southern, and the trades trailed "downwind" of the earth's rotation. Air is a fluid, like water, and the trades were the constant flow of fluid from the high-pressure zones to the low-pressure doldrums; this occurred along the pressure slope, or gradient, an avalanche of air we call the wind. Speeds are determined by the steepness of the slope, and *katabatic*, or downslope, winds like these were the most constant winds on earth, their constancy measuring as high as 80 percent with speeds averaging 11 to 19 knots. These winds would push them west, away from California, thousands of miles across the ocean to the Sandwich Islands or beyond. "From San Francisco to the [Sandwich Islands]," said Maury, "the way is plain."

They also entered one of the least understood crucibles of life on the globe. These were the latitudes affected by El Niño, the vast, Pacificwide oscillation of air mass and ocean temperature that flowed east along the equator until bumping up against the coasts of Ecuador and Peru. The shift in precipitation brought floods to South America, drought to Asia and Africa, fish kills to the guano coasts, and changes to life everywhere. In coastal Peru, unprecedented rains in 1877 changed the landscape so extraordinarily that witnesses believed they hallucinated or stood in the presence of a miracle. Yet the same equatorial plane that served as this vast engine of destruction also abounded with life, a tongue of phytoplankton extending west along the equator past Hawaii. Oceanic deserts stretched on either side, but life thrives in the presence of nutrients, and in this equatorial swath organic material was brought to the surface by the constant rise and fall of warm and cold water, a mix-cycle of life conducive to all levels of the food chain.

In the days that followed, the men saw life all around them, tantalizingly close but rarely close enough to reach out and snare. After the torture of the doldrums, it was as if they'd drifted into a new reality that wasn't meant for them. The first signs of change could be seen at night. They were surrounded by green trails of phosphorescence as sea life darted by. Henry could see, deep down, large blurs of light chase after swift dots of green fire. Scattered areas burned with color; sometimes he saw dorado in the moonlight, patrolling near the boat, scales like shining silver. He glimpsed pale ghosts gliding beneath them, green shadows as big as leviathans.

The change was in the air. Pairs of frigate birds appeared from nowhere: flying fish, their favorite food, shoaled in cloudy weather, and a frigate bird would dive and panic the shoal toward its partner. There were more fluttering storm petrels than ever, dipping their feet in the water as they picked off food. The sailors called it "Little Peter," since, like the Apostle Peter, the petrel appeared to walk on water.

There were whales here, too, more than Henry had seen than at any other time in the voyage. The long column of their spout, expelled as high as 20 feet, was visible for miles. These were mostly right and gray whales, 60- to 80-foot monsters with eyes so human it seemed a shame to hunt them, Mr. Thomas said. One afternoon a pair surfaced a hundred yards away; Henry watched their black backs emerge from the deep, their triangular dorsal fins sliding through the water, their white undersides that seemed to cut them in two. They coasted on the surface, blowing fine rain around them, then dove lazily. "It's just as well they're gone," Mr. Thomas said. The tales of attacking cetaceans were too numerous for comfort: in addition to the *Essex* and accounts of orcas attacking small boats, the Nantucket whaler *Union* accidentally rammed a whale in 1807 and sank immediately. The fear of the whale was ancient, its huge belly believed one locus for Hell. Hell or no, most men on the boat saw wisdom in the saying, "If you don't touch the whale, he won't touch you."

More than anything else, they saw flying fish, though few obliged the hungry men by flying aboard. So many things preyed on the silver fish it seemed a wonder any survived. Bonito, frigate birds, and especially dorado cut swaths through their shoals. A few powerful tail strokes sent them out of the water, their bodies pointed up, only the lower lobe of the tail submerged. The tail seemed the secret of its flight: its blades formed a V, the bottom blade nearly twice as long as the top. As the fish gained speed, the tail would leave the water until with a final flip the fish skimmed above the surface, turning whichever way it pleased. Yet for all this grace, they might just be the strangest fish Henry had ever seen. The translucent wings seemed gossamer fantasies pinned to a creature with the face of a gnome. But most important, the flesh was sweet, soft, and pinkish-white, while the eyes and spaces between the vertebrae held fresh water.

But the shoals of fish did not fly into their laps, and they sadly watched the airborne banquet from afar. Wednesday, May 23, was Day 21 of their ordeal. Three weeks of starvation is the point at which the body becomes treacherous and the mind unreliable. Henry watched himself turn into his diseased brother Samuel. All the plumpness Samuel used to kid him about had vanished, his body withering from a lack of starches, vitamins, and sugars. His well-padded rump disappeared first, replaced by hollows of flesh rimmed with sharp bone. His arms and legs atrophied, hanging from his shoulders and hips like limp string with knots for his elbows and knees. His hair fell out in tiny clumps. The lenses of his eyes had grown cloudy, while the pressure in the eyeballs had decreased. The whites of his eyes took on a strange bluish tint. His eyes sank in their sockets; his cheekbones protruded.

They all looked that way. Hunger turns us into carbon copies of one another, all wearing masks of lethargy. Hunger's benchmark study was conducted during World War II at the University of Minnesota's Laboratory of Physiological Hygiene under the supervision of Dr. Ancel Keys, immortalized forever by having K rations named for him. The participants, all conscientious objectors, agreed to lose 25 percent of their body weight over six months by eating carefully measured rations of root vegetables, macaroni, and dark bread. A goal of the study was to help the Allied armies cope with concentration-camp internees, refugees, and prisoners of war who would flood hospitals and refugee centers at the end of hostilities, and their diet was designed to resemble what refugees might scavenge during and after the war. The men never suffered from thirst, always knew that another meal was coming, and were never in danger of violent death. Nevertheless, they soon began to suffer the same mental and physical distress experienced by the castaways, and found it hard to recover once the study was over. Just like the men in the boat, those in Keys's study became lethargic in body and spirit, could not concentrate on simple tasks, and lacked strength and coordination. Sexual desire disappeared, as did all sense of intellectual activity and creativity. They sank within themselves, were easily irritated, and seemed overly sensitive to cold. More than anything else, they felt as if they were "growing old."

These changes added up to a behavioral adaptation to stress Keys called "starvation neurosis," a state strongly resembling the "war neurosis" and "shell shock" which in the 1940s psychiatrists were only beginning to understand. Its onset in so many settings and situations suggested the fragility of the personality, or the soul. Keys cited a witness to the Russian famine of 1918–22 who was impressed by the "unusual vindictiveness" of long-term starvation victims. Suffering, whether by war or disaster, reduced "all individuals to a common denominator . . . the *combat* personality," Keys said.

Yet within the sameness of suffering, individual torments remained. Perhaps the castaways' carefully husbanded agonies helped them retain some sense of individuality. For Henry, hunger pangs were not as great as the pain of his salt-water sores. Starting as stinging pimples on his hands, feet, arms, legs, and buttocks—anywhere that came in constant contact with seawater or the salt crust on his clothing—these turned to small slits that never healed. Scar tissue formed around the wounds with raw pits in the center; these burst open and pus burned deep into the skin. By the third week, they clustered thick on his hips and ankles; the pain in his buttocks was constant; the skin on his nose and back of his hands burned black from exposure. The corrosive effect of salt water softened ruts in his fingers and made them leak blood. He'd become a battleground of boils and raw flesh, and his prayer for relief was that they might dry. They'd still be infected, but at least they wouldn't spread.

Samuel tended to faint, so spent most of his time flat in the bottom of the boat. These fainting spells probably resulted from his body's shutdown of all but its most essential systems, a diminished state resembling that of a hibernating animal. In such a state, systolic blood pressure is unnaturally low, while diastolic pressure remains more or less normal. Because the loss of body mass outstrips loss of blood volume, there is relatively more blood in the body than during heathier times, which can have fatal consequences. The heart rate increases, since the poorly nourished cardiac muscle works harder to pump blood through the body: whenever Samuel sat or stood upright, he felt lightheaded and his heart raced dangerously. An "intoxicating blindness" like death overcame him and he either sat back or fell. For his own safety he learned to take things slowly, and wisely stayed supine.

Jimmy Cox lay curled in a fetal ball. Though he never seemed to sleep, he always seemed to dream, existing in a near-constant state of stupefaction in which three-quarters of his faculties were awake and a crucial one-quarter was numb. He dreamed of feasts . . . of bread, fowl, and meat . . . everything piled high on a table before him. He sat down, seized upon the first dish within reach, brought it to his lips. Then he woke and looked around. He saw the same starving companions, the same vacant sky and sea. The only thing to ever change was their rations, and this always for the worse, reduced by now to five tiny oysters apiece, three spoonfuls of juice, an eighth of a hardtack biscuit and less than an ounce of water.

Mitchell worried that he'd never see his family again. Something was changing in his body that he feared could never be repaired. The trades had cooled the air, so the days were not as hot and languid; he'd say things to buck up the men's spirits, such as getting them to talk about preposterous feasts they'd have once ashore. "What about you, Captain?" they asked. "Plain bread and butter will be good enough for me all the days of my life if I can only get it," he laughed, shaking his head. In his gut he felt solid lumps—"tough balls," he called them—and imagined stopping up like a cork until toxins filled his blood.

The wind blew hard and steady through May 23 and 24, raising a heavy sea. They continued on their northwest course, still west of Clarion. As the boat weaved its way over the blue crests, it seemed to Henry that he lived through moments of poetry. The swoop and dip of the little boat and swash of the bow wave were exhilarating. Flying fish broke the iridescence, their wings glittering in the swept-back spray. Each time the boat was flung aloft he'd gape over miles of angry water and hear its roar. The sunset glowed with mares tails strung out in a mackerel sky; the moon glowed white, surrounded by a ghostly halo.

Its message, however, was anything but poetic. "Storm moving in," Mitchell said. That night, the seas were so high that their sail hung slack when they fell in a trough, then filled with a bang when they were raised aloft on a crest. Lightning cracked, and water poured in on the weather side. Mitchell crouched at the tiller with a frozen face, glancing back as each new sea reared up to overtake them. One false move on his part and the boat would broach and fill. All hands bailed: they bailed all night, using tin cups, hats, hands. Every minute passed like an hour; after several hours, time lost meaning. Henry felt displaced from his body, as if his soul were elsewhere.

It occurred to him several times that night that he might die. Although fearing the brief agony of death, he was so weary that he almost welcomed the end. Victorians had a strange fascination with death by drowning: burial at sea was a return to the primal soup; there was a belief that those about to die were consumed by a "preternatural calm" in which all truths were revealed. James Lowson, a Scottish doctor who nearly drowned off Sri Lanka in 1892, remembered great pain with the first gulp of water. But as he lost consciousness, he found himself in a "pleasant dream" of home and friends. There is nothing pleasant about what happens next. If thrashing near the surface, a victim sucks in enough air to create a foam barrier, triggering vomiting that is then sucked into the windpipe. In about 10 percent of people, the muscles around the larynx contract violently when touched by water, a condition called laryngospasm, or "dry drowning," that leads to suffocation. But in most victims, water floods the lungs. In fresh water, circulation absorbs the water, diluting the blood until red blood cells are destroyed; this releases potassium, which poisons the heart and induces fibrillation. In salt-water drowning, the reverse occurs. Water leaves the bloodstream and enters the lungs' alveoli to dilute the salt, leading to pulmonary edema. Like Dr. Lowson, the drowning victim experiences a fading consciousness; he grows too weak to fight and gives in. The heart beats erratically from low levels of oxygen. Metabolism slows until only faint electrical activity is left in the brain, then that too fades.

For all the bodily violence, there seems to be a psychological element accompanying death that some call as seductive as the sea. "An immense energy pulls at my mind, as if I am imploding with my body," wrote Steven Callahan of his own castaway experiences. "Darkness widens, closing in. How many eyes have seen like mine? I feel them, all around me, millions of faces, whispering, crowding in, calling, 'Come, it is time.'" One of the best-known examples in Victoriana of tranquil resignation was the 1844 experience of the Scottish explorer David Livingstone in Africa. One day as he tried to protect tribesmen in his party from a lion's attack, the beast seized him in its jaws and shook him "as a terrier dog does a rat." Livingstone had the weird sense of drifting in "a sort of dreaminess, in which there was no sense of pain nor feeling of terror." To Livingstone, this was a spiritual moment, a "merciful provision" from God.

Lowson and Livingstone both experienced the so-called Lazarus syndrome, the much discussed phenomenon of "coming-back-from-the-dead." When psychologist Kenneth Long interviewed 102 survivors of life-threatening illness or injury, he found a basic sequence: peace and a sense of well-being; separation from the body; entering darkness, then seeing and entering a light. Other, less frequent occurrences included meeting deceased loved ones or a godly "presence," watching one's life pass in montage, and deciding to return to the world of the living. Although those who lived through such moments cited them as proof of an afterlife, Dr. Sherwin B. Nuland in *How We Die* called them natural indicators of a biochemically induced end-game that is not yet understood. Yet physiological causes did not preclude hope. "Nothing would please me more than proof of His existence," said Nuland, "and of a blissful afterlife, too."

Mitchell didn't want to test the possibility of an afterlife, but the time might be getting near. In such cross-seas, he feared a rogue wave. Instead of marching in well-defined rows before the wind, waves in cross-seas merged into freaks that were two or more times the usual height and seemed to appear from nowhere; such waves inspired terror in the few minutes they existed, rearing up above other waves then breaking in all directions. Mitchell released Clough and Thomas from bailing to keep an eye out behind him and to the sides for the approach of such a monster. He'd been on square-riggers where a canvas shield was rigged behind the helmsman for no other reason than so he couldn't look back and see such a rogue bearing down.

No one knows how high such rogues can climb. Oceanographers estimate the maximum theoretical height for wind-driven waves at 198 feet: a wave like that resembles a skyscraper, a moving mountain of water generating pressures greater than six tons per square inch. The highest wave ever reliably recorded was 120 feet high and was recorded south of Cape Horn in the Southern Ocean, an area not surprisingly called the "Dead Men's Road." When Sir Ernest Shackleton crossed the Southern Ocean in a 22-foot boat, he was almost killed by such a wave. It came out of nowhere, a wall of water so high that he mistook the foam at its crest for a cloud glowing in the moon. "Hang on, boys, it's got us!" he screamed before it broke, but amazingly they did not founder. The approach of such monsters is unmistakable: witnesses compare their breaking to the passage of freight trains. "It's terrible, Oh God in Thy mercy, send us relief," Mitchell wrote the next morning after his night-long battle. "Oh my dear wife and loved ones, pray ever."

They survived that night, but another boat did not. After noon they spotted a single lonely spar, shaped to form a mast, floating on the waves. They dared not come too close lest the sea pitch it through their hull like a javelin. No one said a word, but they all had the same thought. It was all that remained of one of the quarter-boats, and of their former friends.

ALONE

WHOSE SPAR WAS IT? Which boat had gone down? Was it Parr's, with its tendency to turn beam-to in a heavy sea and its hole in the side? Or Hardy's, which would have been closer to their position during the storm? Samuel edged close to voicing their fears when he wrote, "I am afraid for the other two boats, for the sea we had Thursday and Friday was very hard for them."

The silence spoke of their guilt, the knowledge of complicity in something like murder isolating each man. Just when the men on the boat needed each other most, they sank into themselves.

Over the next four days, their physical environment grew more tolerable. The drizzle died out and the sun was haloed in white; a booby and three flying fish delivered themselves for a needed shot of protein. The trade winds strengthened, staving off thirst by cooling their skin. On May 26, Mitchell's reading placed them at Lat. 15°50' N and Long. 115° W. They'd traveled 270 miles north and 400 miles west since May 18, at an average rate of 80 miles a day.

Yet during this time their minds closed off, each man sinking into his own pit of guilt, obsession, or despair. Such despair can change a man. Commodore Richard Byrd, trapped alone for five months in 1934 during the frigid Antarctic winter, sank into a disillusionment he barely believed possible. He wrote: "The dark side of a man's mind seems to be a sort of antenna tuned to catch gloomy thoughts from all directions." His mind lingered on "the fine and comforting things of the world that had seemed irretrievably lost," and loss became the core of days.

Of all the castaways, Henry and Samuel fared best for having each other. "Henry and I have quiet little chats which are of great comfort and consolation to us," wrote Samuel, "even if on very painful subjects." They studied family photographs as if peering at images from a forgotten age. "Henry bears up and keeps strength the best of any aboard, I think," Samuel said. He, too, tried to bear up, but at times his legs refused to function. On Sunday, May 27, I "tried this A.M. to read the full service to myself with the communion, but found it too much." Unable to give the words his full attention, "I abandoned half until this P.M."

It was hard to explain to others how insubstantial he felt, as if mind and body both drifted away. It was a lightness of being he'd never experienced, coupled to an appreciation for each moment unshackled by pain or delirium. During these periods his vision of God became almost pantheistic: he felt God's breath in the trade winds and saw God's face on the waves. He understood Captain Mitchell now, and spent long periods gazing at the sky. When he stared like that, Henry worried for his sanity. He'd nudge him from his reverie when he stared at the sun.

Too often, however, bitterness crept into Samuel's world. He wondered if their prayers were heard, yet such thoughts could not be condoned and he tried to blot them out with an assertion that he did not "feel despondent at all, for I fully trust that the Almighty will hear our and the Home Prayers, and He who suffers not a sparrow to fall sees and cares for us, His creatures." He caustically described the reason for the ship's fire as carelessness, yet did not mention Hardy's name, realizing that his journal was for posterity . . . as if his better angels still prevailed.

On the night of May 27 to 28, the brothers talked quietly of what would pass should one or both of them die. The sea was calm and quiet, the moon full. "I'm not sure I'll make it," Samuel said. "The consumption is killing me. We should have spotted *some* other ship by now." He stared at the sea in that strange way that frightened Henry. "Yet, when we left the ship, we only had provisions for 10 to 15 days, and here it is the twenty-sixth. That's a kind of miracle, don't you think?" He hoped that by "rigid economy" they could make the stores last another week. "It's like that story in the Bible about the widow."

"The widow of Larepta," prompted Henry, who prided himself on being the better scholar of the two. Unfortunately, there is no Lareptan widow in the Bible—either hunger muddled Henry's thoughts, or he missed that day in school. There *is* a widow of Zarephath, who fed the prophet Elijah at the well. At first she was reluctant to help: the widow was so poor that handing over her few scraps of bread could mean death for her and her son, but Elijah calmed her fears. "The jar of meal will not be emptied, and the jug of oil will not fail," he said.

Surrender everything and you'll be saved. Henry'd heard the commandment echoed from the pulpit, but found it hard to believe. With this brief, mistaken journal entry, we see something in Henry begin to change. He'd emerged from his self-pitying doldrums and was stronger for it; now he began to question accepted wisdom in ways he'd never dared. There was another starving widow in the Bible, more troubling than the first, and Henry would have remembered that story, too. This widow was observed by Jesus just a few days before his death as he sat opposite the Temple and watched the rich pour sacks of money into its coffers. The poor woman deposited two copper coins, and as they rattled down the treasury box, Jesus knew that this was all she had. With this final act of surrender, she would starve and die. Christ was fascinated, perhaps more than by any other act recounted in his parables. Hers was an act of both surrender and tragedy, since she surrendered everything to a corrupt system whose *raison d'être* was power and greed.

Samuel voiced his own skepticism as they talked. "I'm not afraid of dying. What bothers me is that I cannot bring myself to view death and the judgment as I know I should." He'd give anything for one more talk with Dr. Braithwaite, pastor at St. Andrews Episcopal Church in Stamford, or Dr. Henry Coit, rector of St. Paul's preparatory school in Concord, New Hampshire, which Henry had attended before Trinity. Henry echoed Samuel's doubts, but what in the idea of death did both brothers find hard to believe?

The importance of religion in the daily life of the 1860s insured that death held a prominent position. Its arrival was brutal and quick, so one learned early how to mourn. American churchmen painted images of life on earth as a "battleground for the soul of man," and death should hold no terrors for the faithful: dying was merely a transition to a "home beyond the skies." But something was wrong with the picture and doubt was creeping in. The old truths no longer answered everything. Many city dwellers, ensnared by crime, poverty, and disease, questioned God's benevolence; the established religions were in tatters, sundered by slavery and the war. Methodists and Baptists, the nation's largest denominations, had split into north and south conventions in the 1840s and remained apart. Episcopalians, splitting in 1861 but lacking two decades of bad blood between them, rejoined in 1865. Both sides had claimed God for their own.

Others said God was out of the picture entirely, a fear given wings by the 1859 publication of Charles Darwin's *On the Origin of Species.* More than any other single book, this sparked a war of belief giving rise to the modern age. "Evolution" had existed before Darwin, the belief in the "Great Chain of Being," where lower beings evolved into higher, on up to humans, seen as evidence of a divinely guided plan. Darwin's heresy was to introduce a mechanism by which species responded to the environment, not to purpose or design. In Darwin's cosmos, life did not improve with time. God did not have consciousness. Existence was random and chancy.

In the presence of such doubt, God was silent. Maybe Darwin was right after all. Would a just and reasoning God plague those in the longboat for no reason? Or maybe there was a pattern, an evil one, and He toyed with them like a child tortures a bug. Henry had entered such debates in class, but never dreamed he'd put them to the test. It made his head spin.

Ever since St. Augustine, shipwreck had been the moral lesson of the West. Travel symbolized life's journey. Adam's fall exiled him from the Garden, and his purpose was to make it home. Failure was the traveler's fault, no matter what the reason: weather, icebergs, fire, mutiny, pirates, starvation, or thirst. Failures were found wanting in the eyes of God, yet these very failures drew the greatest audience. Individual tales of shipwreck emerged in 16th-century Portugal as "string literature," or *literature de cordel,* cheap pamphlets strung on a cord in the doors of shops in Lisbon. Most were self-published, as if survivors needed to broadcast their suffering, but in 1735 the first popular anthology of these tales was collected in Bernardo Gomes de Brito's *Historia Tragico-maritima.* Similar collections followed in other languages.

By the 19th century, shipwreck accounts were the literary equivalent of gold. Most titles appeared in England, followed closely by America, but the most lurid tales received worldwide attention. They always focused on the physical: on suffering, endurance, cannibalism, the drinking of blood, until they eventually sounded the same. Yet such similarity may be due more to human limitation than to failed imagination. Physicians and writers alike have noted that the worst pain is hardest to detail. "Physical pain does not simply resist language but actively destroys it, bringing about an immediate reversion to a state anterior to language, to the sounds and cries a human being makes before language is learned."

Others on the longboat were changing, too. The gap between the men in the front and the back grew wider and deeper. A sullen silence divided aft and forward. The men seemed "callous to their condition," wrote Samuel: "Thank God there is no complaining nor swearing aboard." Even Mr. Thomas came in for censure: "Third Mate's disposition I like least, but he is quiet now and does not oppose the Captain."

The friction point between Thomas and his admired superior was apparently the third mate's obsession with Possene, the hated "Portyghee." On Day 27, Tuesday, May 29, the daily rations were cut from three meals to two, a loss felt keenly. Now they were reduced to a teaspoonful of bread crumbs and an ounce of ham for breakfast, a spoonful of crumbs for supper, and an ounce of water three times a day. "Going without [lunch] is very well when you have a good supper to look forward to," said Henry, "but here I find you feel pretty hungry." To Mr. Thomas, however, the further rationing called up a bitter memory of how Possene had lain sick on the *Hornet,* raising a whole "family of abscesses" to escape work, "but when the ship took fire [he] turned out as lively as any one." He remembered again how Possene ate several loaves of bread before he was discovered, and his hunger made the memory worse. He calculated that under the current regimen, the devoured bread would have lasted another three weeks, and when Mitchell passed rations to Possene, Thomas could not control his anger. "He shouldn't get none," he snapped. Mitchell didn't immediately respond. Such dangerous thoughts could lead to murder. There'd already been death enough. "Every man eats," Mitchell replied.

"He already ate," Thomas answered.

"*Every man eats!*" Mitchell hissed with a viciousness that turned the third mate pale. Mitchell glared at the men up front, daring them to say anything. He poured the spoonful of bread crumbs into Possene's shaking hands.

Silence fell over the boat, interrupted by a "tremendous big" swordfish chasing a small albacore tuna. Henry could not tell if it was the same one that had menaced them earlier, but he was "not at all sorry to have him go away, as with his sword he was not a pleasant neighbor." Once rid of the fish, the men remembered their grievances and silence descended again.

After Possene, Samuel sparked the most resentment among the men. Samuel, with his cultured and haughty demeanor, his imperious insistence on morning and evening devotions; Samuel, who reminded the forward crew of all the real and imagined injustices endured at the hands of their "betters." The only crewman Samuel seemed to like was Peter Smith, the best man at the oars. There was a reason for this, based on class. "We have here a man who might have been a Duke had not political troubles banished him from Denmark," said Samuel. "He is one of our best men and . . . have today quite enjoyed a chat with him."

A banished Danish duke, signed on as Smith and pulling at the sweeps like any common sailor—the romance of the situation clearly impressed Samuel, though Henry and Fred Clough never mentioned him in their own recollections, and Mitchell only said that he was their best man at the oars. Twain, their chronicler, would exclaim, "Isn't the situation romantic enough?"

No. Providence added a startling detail; pulling an oar in the boat, for a common seaman's wages, was a *banished duke*—Danish. We hear no more of him; just that mention, that is all, with the simple remark that "he is one of our best men"—a high enough compliment for a duke or any other man in these manhood testing circumstances. With that little glimpse of him at his oar, and that fine word of praise, he vanishes out of our knowledge for all time. For all time, unless he should chance upon this note and reveal himself.

But Peter Smith never revealed himself, preferring anonymity.

Tales of banished royalty (as well as of pretenders) push up through the wars, revolution, and fallen kingdoms of the modern era like exotic buds through the hothouse soil. They too are castaways, stripped of home and title, blown by historical tides or political winds. In times of such upheaval, tales of outcast or endangered royalty proved irresistible to Western writers: Twain had his *Prince and the Pauper* and *Huckleberry Finn*'s Duke and Dauphin; Dumas had his *Man in the Iron Mask*; Anthony Hope, his *Prisoner of Zenda*. And there was the real-life "dauphin," son of Louis XVI and Marie Antoinette who was imprisoned during the French Revolution and died at age 10. Yet rumors persisted of his escape, and claimants rose throughout the 1800s, one so convincing that the Dutch government allowed him to be buried with the title "Dauphin" on his tombstone in 1843.

The presence of a banished duke on the boat seems too perfect—a political castaway, twice-bereft of home. Yet timing was on Smith's side. The 1864 "Schleswig-Holstein question," a brief conflict fought over two duchies claimed by the Danes but coveted by Otto von Bismarck as an early prize in the pan-Germanic movement, would be a precursor to the 1914 sweep through Belgium and 1939 blitz of Czechoslovakia. When the Austro-Prussian army stormed the duchies, the tiny Danish army caved quickly and the "war" was over as soon as it began. The Treaty of Vienna ceded Schleswig-Holstein to Prussia and Austria, and Danish dukes like Peter Smith packed their bags.

The longboat was marked by a strange class line, but Peter Smith straddled it well. If he was a former member of royalty, he understood the sense of privilege assumed by men like Samuel Ferguson, as well as their fear of the growing power of the mob. Yet he'd lived in the forecastle with that mob and was accepted by them. The fact that he admitted his origins on the longboat, without comment from the others, suggests they'd already heard the story. Although the "total institution" of a ship resembled medieval fiefdoms, forecastles could be as egalitarian as later legends of the French Foreign Legion or of the American West, and as in both, identity was as fluid as the sea. We do not know the aliases for Peter Smith, but Antonio Possene was variously listed as Posini, Passaic, and Cassero. Charles Kaartman was also known as Charly Irons.

If Smith were a duke, he would have been literate, which raises intriguing questions. An educated man would be aware of Darwin and fascinated by questions of which shipmates were most likely to survive. He knew through experience that adversity bred strength. His forecastle mates lived and thrived in what sociobiologist E.O. Wilson later called a "marginal environment," the harsher habitat with limited food, water, and other resources. In social terms, these were the slums and waterfronts where no one willingly chose to live. Marginal environments are "nature's flophouses for the outcast," but are important because the conditions force species to adapt quickly or die. Wilson studied the ant, another social creature, and noticed that when marginal colonies grew tough enough, they invaded the lush world of the privileged ants, killing them off or driving them into exile, turning the old guard into castaways.

As Smith watched the old, familiar anger rise among his shipmates, he heard murmurs rise against the captain, too—not at Mitchell, the man, but at Mitchell the symbol of power ruling their lives. In times of rage, symbols channel the mind. Historians believe that America's first labor movement began among sailors, a rudimentary "proto-movement" during the colonial period that expressed itself in riots "stirred up by impressment gangs and sporadic economic stringency," said labor historian Richard Maxwell Brown. Beginning on November 17, 1747, several thousand people participated in three days of riots in Boston that followed a nighttime impressment sweep. As one witness said, "the lower class were beyond measure enraged." Though press riots increased after the French and Indian War, by the 19th century the nature of protest had changed largely to work stoppage on individual vessels.

Mitchell could feel the discord, too. Good captains developed a sixth sense for such things, and his best defense lay in his navigation skills. Unless the entire boat turned mad, the men knew they were lost without him.

He still had the trust of the crew, but he didn't know how much he trusted himself, a fear he didn't dare reveal. Something was wrong with his readings . . . the instruments or maps . . . his own skill and judgment . . . he simply couldn't tell. "Got a chronometer sight putting us in longitude 118°30'," he wrote on Sunday, May 27, a day of pleasant winds and calm seas. "Can't be right, I judge 115°." In fact, later estimates put them miles from both at Lat. 16°06' N, Long. 117°24' W. Such uncertainty unnerved him and he could not keep it from his journal: "O how many thousands are worshiping God this fine day, and how utterly wretched are we."

Mitchell studied his map and charts like sacred texts, searching for answers. Clipperton was a thing of the past; Clarion Island was slipping past; the Pacific spread before him like a dark wilderness. According to his charts, a slim hope lay to the west-northwest in the form of another tiny speck—Henderson's Island, listed at Lat. 24°, Long. 128°.

But Henderson's Island wasn't at these coordinates. It lay elsewhere.

The subject of mythical and misplaced islands pops up throughout the history of men at sea. Their existence fascinated armchair sailors, but for those on borrowed time, they meant lost chances. It was as if they vanished when approached, and sailors' belief in disappearing islands was an ancient one. The trick was in the finding. One fairy island off Ireland's west coast was thought to solidify if sailors shook embers onto the phantom soil.

Legends include the islands of El Dorado and Atlantis, but most sinister was Satanaxio, or the Hand of Satan. Appearing only in fogs and dirty weather in the North Atlantic, Satanaxio was thought to be the hand of a huge undersea demon that reached from the depths and plucked away boats and men.

Most mythical islands of 15th-, 16th-, and 17th-century origin were deleted by 18th- and 19th-century mapmakers when more accurate means of navigation became available. Yet cartographers were a conservative bunch, tending to leave doubtful islands rather than risk allowing a shipwreck. Such was the case with Henderson, which appeared both in the Imray charts and on Maury's "Wind and Current Chart of 1852." The 1860 *Bowditch* located Henderson Island at 24°12' N, 128°06' W, with an alternative latitude given of 24°26' N, putting it close to the mythical Cooper's Island listed in Samuel's diary. Unfortunately, the real Henderson Island lay nowhere near the castaways. The real Henderson Island lay in the Southern Hemisphere, though in virtually identical coordinates (Lat. 24°25' S, Long. 128°19' W), an error corrected in 1870, four years too late for Mitchell. How Henderson managed to be transported bodily across the equator is a mystery, especially since the real Henderson figured into the *Essex* tragedy, which all American mariners knew and feared.

Did Mitchell know he was supposedly sailing for that same place? If he did, he held his tongue. "Want to live as long as possible," was all he said. The true Henderson Island was a 5-mile-long coral island "raised by some subterraneous convolution" with cliffs 30 to 35 feet above the water and a dry fossil lagoon, and was covered with shrubs. The *Essex's* three whaleboats reached Henderson on December 20, 1820, after sailing 1,500 miles; they stayed there a few days, exhausting its resources, then all but three of the men sailed east in hopes of reaching Easter Island. But others had been there before. Mate Owen Chase said his men found the name of a ship, *Elizabeth*, carved into the bark of a stunted tree, and charts give the real Henderson and its fictive counterpart the alternative name of Elizabeth Isle. The *Essex* crewmen found eight human skeletons in a cave behind the beach: later medical examinations showed that they were Caucasian and had died of thirst, and one was 3 to 5 years old. In all probability, they included a family of castaways, identities forever lost at sea.

OF ALL THOSE on the longboat, Mitchell was the most fragile emotion-ally. This is surprising, considering who and what he was, but of all the men he felt most alone. Not only did he feel guilt over the fate of the quar-ter-boats, doubt his navigational talents, and sense growing anger around him, but he was convinced that he'd betrayed his family. "Oh my dear Wife and children," he wrote on May 28, "if your father has ever given you offence, forgive him as he hopes to be forgiven. Oh could I but see you once more."

Although the Fergusons had the comfort of looking at rescued photos, there is no indication that Mitchell saved any of his. If so, he'd have studied images of one son and three daughters, all with dark, serious eyes and thick, unruly hair, like his. He'd spent most of his life away from them and felt it keenly now. Harry, age 26, had dressed in sailor suits as a boy and gone to sea with his father, but now in his 20s wavered between following the nauti-cal life and pursuing his own California dreams of riches. "I have no Harry to talk to now," Mitchell once wrote when his son stayed behind: "[I] never felt the absence of any person so much in my long experience of partings and leave-takings." Mary, at 23 the oldest daughter, journeyed to Bristol, England, with her father in February 1861; as a clipper captain's daughter, she felt herself "courted, flattered, caressed" by the English, but her voyage over was spent seasick in her cabin when "halfway over, we had a perfect hurricane." Sarah Abbie, age 19, was too interested in boys for Mitchell's comfort; Susan Flora, the baby at 10, was the merriest of the four. Mitchell had hoped to take Sarah Abbie and young "Flo" with him, first to visit Harry in San Francisco, then on to China, England, and home. Few girls in that day and age were such travelers, yet the suddenness of the *Hornet's* sailing negated their plans. In that way, at least, he was fortunate. How would he have stood it if his girls had died of hunger or thirst before his eyes?

But it was to wife Susan that he apologized most. "Sometimes I think I ought not to have come away at all," he wrote in 1850, "but on the whole I believe I did right on coming—if not, I hope to be forgiven." Eleven years later, with the *Hornet* tied up in Bristol, Mary in a European finishing school, and British visitors marveling at the size of his ship, Mitchell ended a letter with, "I only wish, My Dear Wife, that you were here to be with Mary and to give me the pleasure of your society."

But Susan never went to sea. She never accompanied her husband around the world, as did other captains' wives. Sometimes his irritation showed. In the same letter from Bristol, he said of Mary's tutor that she was "the most remarkable lady I have ever met," then almost pettishly added, "But I think you must be tired of our reception at Bristol."

These days their lives were distant, even when together. But it had not always been that way. The sea and Susan were his two great loves, harder to reconcile as he grew older. Before either there was Freeport, which acted as the polestar of his existence, a certainty he would always have a home. Freeport in the 1800s specialized in vessels of 400 to 500 tons, some cruising as far as the West Indies; his father, "Squire" Mitchell, was a prominent attorney, wealthy by the standards of the day. City records show he owned two barns, a horse, carriage, one or two cows, a two-story house with a hip roof on the town's Main Street, all located on a 25-acre parcel with a garden and orchard. Young Josiah had everything but a mother, who died on the day he was born. Perhaps her death was the cause of distance between son and father; perhaps this accounts for a sadness that dogged his childhood. He was not a healthy lad, not particularly studious, and seemed without direction until shipping to the Antilles with "Captain Maxwell" when he succumbed, like young contemporary Richard Henry Dana, to the "witchery of the sea."

A letter written on that first voyage to his father and stepmother was an eye opener for all:

Havannah, Dec. 29, 1829.

Dear Parents:

Supposing you feel some anxiety concerning me I will endeavor to write you a few lines. In the first place you must all excuse me for not bidding you Good Bye. But how could I?—my feelings wouldn't let me do it. When Pomeroy brought me the dollar I could not say good bye.

I was rather homesick the first day or two, and come to turn in at night how I felt! Then it was I thought of home, tears supplied the place of sleep, but soon these feelings wore away. I was seasick but very little. We had very pleasant weather until the Sunday after we came out crossing the gulf stream—in about two hours before when the mate called the Captain and told him it was blowing very heavy—I went upon deck. The seas were running mountain high. At one moment the ship would ride upon the top of the waves and the next plunge into the abyss beneath. The scene was awful but grand.

Every few minutes the sea would break over her, it carried away a barrel of new cider and a half barrel of tongues and rounds lashed strong to the deck, and if the pigs hadn't known how to swim they would have been gone too. Then I would have given anything to be at home, but I must say that I like the sea fully as well as I expected.

We arrived here Christmas Day after a passage of sixteen days. I ate my last apple yesterday, my cakes I have some of them yet. Captain Maxwell, the mates and likewise have all been very kind to me.

There is now in this place two frigates and about six men of war ships. I should like to have you hear the music they make. They play every morning and evening, it is delightful. They all fire a gun at sunrise and sunset and every flag in the harbor lowers at once. I wish you all a merry Christmas and a Happy New Year. Give my love to all my brothers and sisters and likewise inquiring friends. Kiss Su for me. Excuse my writing, it is dark, my pen is poor and I have no knife to mend it.

> From your affectionate son, Josiah A. Mitchell
> Tuesday evening.

P.S.—I must tell you again that I like the sea very well, think I shall follow it for a living if my health continues good.

> Good Night Adieu,
> I should like to see you.

He was 16 when he wrote that letter, and he followed the sea as warned, advancing steadily "up the hawse-hole" until by his midtwenties he was a staunch young ship's officer soon to make captain. The one thing that drew him back was Susan Kelsey, a lively girl from nearby Guilford whose presence brought rare grace to rougher Freeport. By 1836, she was one of the town's most sought-after belles, presenting the colors from the Ladies of Freeport to the local militia, admonishing them that "while its graceful

folds float amidst the slaughter . . . may the recollection that it was presented by those whose weakness leads them to look to you for protection
and safety, be your strongest incentive to courage and glory." Such senti-
ments in that day and age were guaranteed to fire young men's blood.

In 1838, Josiah and Susan married; five years later, Mitchell was made
master of the bark *Josephine*. Other appointments followed: carrying grain
and gold prospectors to California, wheat to Chile, immigrants to the New
World. In the 1850s, he was given command of the *City of Brooklyn*, a clipper called one of the "great white racehorses of the sea," and by 1859 was
regularly called upon to captain the *Hornet*.

It was an honor for Susan to be a clipper captain's wife, and though
never rich, the Mitchells were well-to-do. They kept two houses: Josiah's
birthplace in Freeport, which Susan apparently ran as a summer boarding
house, and a house in Brooklyn, which she preferred. Mitchell had some
connection with the Naval Shipyard in Brooklyn, while Susan had brothers and sisters in the New York area. Although she felt the country life was
better for her children's health, she felt incredibly lonely in Freeport when
Josiah was at sea.

It is hard to determine which took the greatest toll on Susan—loneliness, ill health, or worry. The last must always be considered. In 1840,
when son Harry was an infant, they were certain he would die of fever:
"The poor little fellow is all gone, wasted away," Mitchell wrote his father:
"He cannot live long, there is not the smallest chance of hope." Although
the boy lived, Susan was never as merry and secure again. She worried
constantly about Harry's health and was stiflingly overprotective: "God
grant that he may live and be a blessing to us all," she wrote in 1846,
"though I sometimes think I am too anxious about him to have him spared
me long." In 1847, the delivery of their third child, Sarah Abbie, nearly
killed her. Eight years passed before their last child was born. Josiah was
away when that happened—but Josiah was always away.

Even more than frail health, loneliness was her greatest foe.
Researchers believe that the greatest common crisis shared by sailors'
wives is the development of a "capacity to be alone." Like many "Cape
Horn widows," Susan never developed this defense and became emotion-
ally bereft when Josiah left on a new voyage. As another wife exclaimed in
her diary, Susan was "doomed to sad thoughts": the uncertainty of know-

ing whether she'd ever see him again was too much to handle. As one wife said: "To have a seaman's chest carried out of the house for its three year cruise was a sorrow almost as harrowing as if it had been a coffin."

Two excerpts remain from Susan's journals: July–September of 1854, then brief passages in 1864–66. The 1854 entries show a Susan who is religious and enraptured by nature; she seems impatient with the mechanics of writing, but is meticulous in preserving emotional and physical details. If anything, she falls prey to incredible highs and lows, some so pronounced one suspects she suffered from bipolar disorder, then included in the generalized female catch-all "neurasthenia." On the morning of Friday, July 28, 1854, she sat at her window "with feelings so excited and wrought upon by the exquisite beauty of the scene before me that ... [I] wept till I felt depressed, then wrote to my husband." Always she "felt isolated," in need of a "warm hearted sympathetic friend." Two days later she wrote, "Josiah, how much you would love this moonlight—I could sit ... with you all night." When he returns the following week, she fears he grieves to see the "rushing away of his wife's flesh and strength. I try to convince him all is well but the deep meaning seen through the window of the soul tells me he is not satisfied."

The only time Susan seems happy in these diaries is when Mitchell comes home. To Victorian women like Susan, sex was the great unmentionable, but a calm sensuality suffused her writing whenever he returned. In 1854, when Susan was 28 and Josiah 31, they were still very much in love. "We lay awake long that night talking," she wrote on August 19: she aspires, she says, to a pure spirituality, yet says unashamedly that "while we exist in the flesh" happiness is expressed through "physical love." At the same time, she feels such thoughts are scandalous and keeps them to herself. She convinced herself that a united family was all that she needed for happiness, and a gladness entered her voice when her brood was together. At such times for Susan, time seemed to stand still.

An image also crept into her voice during this time of her life—the image of the Garden, "where the thirsty soul may ever drink" and cares were washed clean. Nineteenth-century women often thought their role on earth was to be "uniquely pious," said historian Lisa Norling: since they were assumed and expected to be loving, feeling and sensitive, they were thought susceptible to a heightened spiritual influence in which marriage and motherhood were sacred duties. A woman's love for family reflected

God's love for mankind. Susan fastened to this self-image like a true believer, yet traps lay in wait. Mitchell said in his journal that he looked the world over for a Garden of Eden where he and Susan could retire and "be as children again," but sometimes for Susan the imagery of the Garden turned threatening. One morning she was out hunting for blackberries when:

> my eyes were for some reason attracted to the trees directly in front of me there, (I shudder while I think of it), on the dead branches of an old tree lay coiled in an oval shape a long large gray snake with his venomous head pointed directly at me, he seemed to be lying in ambush waiting for his prey, I felt that I was silenced, I think I made no noise but ran through the thicket as fast as my fear would let me, did not dare look back for I felt that his awful head was working its way through the brake I stopt at the first open space to breath freely, and cried out for the first time, O dear me, what shall I do!

Five days later, she had returned to the blackberry patch "to get some ripe fruit for Josiah" when she saw a "large black snake." This time she did not run in panic, but moved off slowly and returned by a different route, concluding that snakes "seem to be strongly attracted to me."

Ten years later, the exuberance, girlish joy, highs and lows—all were gone. Loneliness had won out; Susan Mitchell was tired. Harry and Mary, the two oldest children, had started their own lives and families. Sarah was nearly 20, attending boarding school, and boy-crazy in her father's eyes. Only the youngest remained at home. Josiah was no longer mentioned in her journals, and only once did she allude to her marriage. On February 27, 1864, she found her old diaries and read over the accounts of "some of the most useful and pleasant days of my married life." She lived them again, "forgetting the cloud and seeing only the sunshine."

These days, however, Susan Mitchell seemed inexpressively sad—so sad, in fact, that one wonders if clinical depression had not set in. She'd accepted the Victorian wisdom that suffering and self-sacrifice was a woman's lot: she believed such suffering was the "crucible of female strength," as described by Sarah Josepha Hale, editor of *Godey's Ladies' Book* and a major force in this domestic ideology. Susan, like Sarah Hale, defined a woman's heroism as "the calm endurance of affliction." Suffering to a woman occupied "the place of labor to a man, giving it a breadth, depth and fullness, not otherwise attained." A woman's work was to suffer for her family, and Susan gave herself to suffering heart and soul.

Not everyone accepted this view. An article titled "The Mariner's Wife" in the July 1838 *Sailors Magazine* said: "We can scarcely conceive a situation more wretched than that of the wife of an active sailor from the time she weds until the scene of life is closed. The anxiety which her husband subjects her to, will prey upon and finally destroy the finest constitution." The fear and sorrow caused by constant parting and anxiety were "poisonous to her existence, and sink too deeply into the breast to be eradicated," the author wrote.

Susan acknowledged as much and seemed to feel her life was coming to an end. "I am older now in my fiftieth year," she wrote on November 12, 1865, two months before Josiah set out on the *Hornet* for the last time. "What the record in God's book of accounts has been I know not, so little do we know ourselves. Last year was chequered with lights and shadows, the shadows resting longest; my health was not good, consequently my mind was not clear and hopeful." She often felt worn out, "a diseased and sensitive spirit" chafed by the "common events of life," and feared that "I become dissipated and live faster than my strength will admit." Although there were fleeting moments of happiness, these were like "the poor fledgling when it attempts to fly, some . . . greedy boring cat will suddenly put his paw upon it and 'tis lost."

Now she was in the Lake District around Detroit, visiting Mary and her family with young Susan Flora in tow. Excursions into Nature were the only things that brought her peace: every entry contained an idyllic vision of green. Sometimes, Susan thought, it would be easier to die and leave this earth for that more perfect heaven. Josiah feared that if she heard the *Hornet* was missing, the news would surely kill her.

And if that happened, he'd truly be alone.

THE THEFT

ON NOON OF MAY 30, the men reassessed their chances. They lay at Lat. 17°17' N, Long. 121° W, north of the equator and 200 miles west of Clarion and the Revilla Gigedos. It was impossible to beat back to windward against the Northeast Trades. Neither could they beat northward fast enough reach the listed position of Henderson Island—a lucky break for them. They had one can of oysters left, three pints of raisins, a can of beef soup and less than half a ham. Their bread was down to three pints of dry crumbs, kept in a canvas sack tied with a drawstring. Thirst did not yet torture them like hunger, partly due to the constant cooling winds. But like everything else on this ocean, a blessing was a curse, for as that wind picked up, there'd be less rain for drinking.

They headed west on a suicide course—but the winds left no alternative. They assured themselves that a ship would cross their path, yet they'd seen no other sails. It was easy to imagine they were the last of humankind. Meanwhile, Samuel had begun insisting that this fast was good for them: "We are all wonderfully well and strong," he said, a conclusion met with quiet derision. Thomas Tate gnawed on his clenched fist each night; Samuel had shrunk to the size of a stick; Possene was convulsed by sweats and fevers. Mitchell felt infected by a creeping weakness. "No exercise," he wrote. "Blood stagnant."

There was one "forlorn hope," as Henry called it, a group of islands reported in *Bowditch* at Lat. 16°–17° N, Long. 133°–136° W, a new heading that would require another course change. Mitchell figured they were about 650 miles due east of these islands, and at their current daily rate of

120 miles, they'd reach them by June 5—but just barely. Their scanty stores would be used up on that same day. They'd stretched their food and water as far as possible, and the only other landfall in their path now was the Sandwich Islands, over 2,200 miles away.

This hope was called in *Bowditch* the American Group, a group of five islets given, in various maps and charts, seven different names: Misipi [*sic*] Roca Coral, Bocca Perda, Eclipse, Sultan, Bunker, and New. Such confusion reflected the greater one: no one knew whether the islands really existed at all. They were listed in *Bowditch's* Table LIV, which was Mitchell's sacred script, yet *Bowditch* just had tables of positions. The only map on the boat was Samuel's Imray pocket version, which listed these islands as "American Group, doubtful." Although old shipping charts showed the islands originally attributed to Spanish authorities, three successive explorations did not confirm their location. In 1827, Captain F. W. Beechy aboard the HMS *Blossom* had found nary a ripple or rock, followed in 1837 by Sir Edward Belcher and a ship detached in 1839 from the Wilkes Expedition. If these islands existed, they rose, sank, or drifted all over the map like the legend of Satanaxio, playing havoc with sailors' charts and minds.

No one even knew how the islands came to be called "American." America was big, loud, and obvious, not ghostly and insubstantial like this seaborne phantom. A footnote in Findlay's *Directory for the Navigation of the North Pacific Ocean* speculated that Fanning Island, a coral atoll discovered in 1798 at Lat. 3°50' N, Long. 159°20' W, "may be the American Isles ... discovered by Captain Mather of the *American* in 1814." If so, such second- and third-hand information was a thin hook on which to hang survival.

Of greater concern was the fear that the American Group might be shoals instead of islands, a possibility that could explain its confusing history of sightings. This was worse than nonexistence, for the bottom of the longboat could be torn out on the sharp coral. Bligh happened on such a shoal during his ordeal in the *Bounty's* launch: the sea was deep when suddenly they saw the bottom less than a fathom beneath them, so close that they could pick out details. Its suddenness was frightening: flat as a table, strewn with dead coral, stretching a mile on either side. As night fell, they reached its end. It dropped off abruptly, a welcome return to deep water.

There was also the possibility that the American Group was the final resting place of the U.S. sloop *Levant*, which had sailed due east from Honolulu and into mystery in 1860. The *Levant* figured in Edward Everett Hale's *The Man Without a Country*, a novel in which Lieutenant Philip Nolan, charged with a minor part in the 1806 Aaron Burr conspiracy to allegedly create a separate republic in the Southwest, declared "Damn the United States! I wish I may never hear of the United States again!" The presiding officer of court granted his wish and sentenced him to perpetual exile on U.S. naval vessels, ordering those charged with his care never to mention the United States in his presence and to excise all reference of his former nation from books and papers. Nolan shuttled from ship to ship until dying of old age aboard the *Levant*. Hale's novel was published in 1863 as a piece of wartime propaganda, and he chose the *Levant* for the setting because the ship and crew had completely disappeared. Like the Flying Dutchman or the banished duke, Lieutenant Nolan was an eternal castaway.

One man insisted that the American Group did exist, and this was Captain John DeGreaves of Honolulu. DeGreaves, too, was a perpetual wanderer, though some called him an "island bum." He preferred to call himself King Kamehameha's science advisor. His account was just another part of Honolulu's local color until 1902, when the steamship *Australia* would report passing through shoal water in the American Group's position. Solving the mystery of the islands was imperative, since a regular steamship route between Tahiti and Frisco regularly traversed the area. Like the American Group itself, John DeGreaves surfaced in the news.

He'd been everywhere, he said: born on the Isle of Jersey, served in the British Navy during the Great Sepoy Mutiny of 1857, drifted to the Australian goldfields after discharge, served as first mate on Pacific ships, then landed in the Sandwich Islands to advise His Hawaiian Majesty on claiming and mining guano islands. DeGreaves swore that in 1859 he picnicked ashore on a small island in the American Group with the famous courtesan Lola Montez, then returning home from a stage tour of Australia. De Greaves spotted guano deposits on the island and said he'd filed a claim, a statement soon discredited. No such claim existed, and Montez had steamed home via India, the opposite direction. Acquaintances called him a con man, but DeGreaves said his memory was failing: he'd dined there, but with the dancer Kitty Hayes.

Now the *Hornet*'s boat entered the babble over the lost islands. "[I] f we can live so long and they are really there, we have a tolerable certainty of fetching them," Henry said. Samuel echoed: "Somehow I feel much encouraged by this change."

Mitchell was more subdued. One more dashed hope might be all it took to spell their end. He dared not even think about what would happen if the islands were chimeras. He looked at the full moon that night and wondered if he'd live to see another. "In Him we trust," he briefly said.

THURSDAY, MAY 31, dawned gently. The night had been cold, with a cloud cover so thick that at times all moonlight was shuttered off and they were plunged into darkness so absolute Henry could not see his brother beside him. The morning came like a benediction: the winds were sure and pleasant, the sea smooth, the clouds high and thick enough to screen the sun. On such a day as this, the men could believe that a ship would run across their path and speculated whether their rescuer would be a whaler, an Australian ship, or a man-of-war. They looked hard, but saw nothing. Instead, shortly before breakfast, they realized that the canvas bag had been opened during the night and a thief had stolen some bread.

Outrage exploded on the boat unlike anything thus far. Mitchell stayed quiet at first, focused instead on a detailed accounting of their remaining stores. He seemed almost disabled by the news. The theft, of about a handful of crumbs, threw his rationing into disarray, and he no longer was certain whether their food would last until they made the "uncertain islands" ahead. Henry and Samuel were less reticent. "One would not suppose that anyone claiming the name of man would rob his fellow-sufferers in such a time as this," Henry said. "We have thought before that [the food] went fast," but now they knew that "some of the pork went the same way." Samuel was just as disgusted. "We hate to suspect anyone of such a rascally act, but such is the case. Two days will certainly finish the remaining morsels."

Mitchell neglected to record the theft, but he interrogated every man. "Did you take the bread?" he asked. Each man denied it. The timing was abysmal: in addition to cramps, weight loss, and rheumatic pains due to Vitamin C deficiency, the pain in their bowels was much crueler, caused by a hardening of the feces due to the lack of fiber. Still, the denials were a relief to Mitchell, saving him the onerous duty of executing judgment on the guilty man.

The sea was never kind to thieves. In a place as public as a ship, theft destroys the communal trust that makes living possible. The traditional punishment for "stealing" was the whip, officially sanctioned in the Articles of War of both the American and British navies; it was one of the few punishments where harsh discipline seemed welcomed by the men. Here on the longboat, there was no room or energy for flogging, but the presence of a thief endangered everyone's survival. The ultimate punishment was to throw him overboard.

It is said that starving men lose all sense of morality: in the grip of hunger, those who pride themselves on integrity commit the most heinous crimes and still deny guilt, no matter how damning the evidence. Each individual shrinks to a private universe when the object of life is narrowed to finding food. "The most conspicuous psychological abnormality" noted by doctors of survivors of POW and concentration camps during World War II was their "increasing selfishness" in the face of starvation; even those who reached only a semistarved state—POWs protected by the Geneva Convention, compared to Holocaust victims—were consumed. A British aristocrat known in her prewar life for personal generosity said that as hunger increased, "Nothing else counted but that I wanted to live. I would have stolen from husband, child, parent or friend, in order to accomplish this. . . . I would remain close to those who were too far gone and too weak to eat their meager ration of ersatz coffee or soup, and instead of pressing them to eat so that they might exist, I would eagerly take it from them."

Tony Possene and Samuel Ferguson were advertisements of what awaited the others, their conditions accelerated by fever. They spent their time in a dreamlike state, screaming at night and dozing fitfully by day. Their difference lay in trust. Samuel, hailing from a privileged background, trusted death to open a door to a more perfect existence. Possene, whose life was hard scrabble, knew nothing came easy, not even the afterlife.

Theft placed individual needs above the common good, an abrogation of nautical life where no man can run a ship alone. It was not only an organizational threat, but a philosophical one. It mirrored the basic tension between man and society, its presence so real that captains often suspected theft even when it hadn't occurred. Bligh's problems aboard the *Bounty* were precipitated by his rage over allegedly stolen coconuts, and he was even plagued by theft aboard his castaway boat when one night someone stole a two-pound piece of pork unobserved. Since everyone was bailing water when the theft took place, it could have been anyone. No one confessed, and all Bligh could do was keep the pork by his side for the rest of the voyage.

Thievery also occurred in the *Essex*'s ordeal, springing from a surprising source. When Richard Peterson, an old black man who'd led the others in prayer, was accused of stealing bread in the night, Mate Owen Chase leaped up with his pistol and vowed to shoot the old man on the spot if he didn't hand over the bread. Peterson immediately returned the stolen loaves, pleading that he'd been unable to resist hunger. Chase felt an example must be made, but like everyone else on his boat, liked Peterson and felt sorry for his suffering. He was merciful that day, but warned the old man that it would cost his life should he steal again.

Very little mercy was evident among the *Hornet*'s men. Without evidence, they blamed Possene, citing his gluttony when the ship burned. Mr. Thomas led the blame: "We'd have 22 more days' bread rations if not for the Portyghee," he shouted. "His past actions damn him." Others agreed. Possene's eyes grew wide with fear as he gabbled his innocence; his English failed him just when he needed it most, and he lapsed into Portuguese, a damning lapse in others' eyes. He was dying, he pleaded, to which someone responded, "Them that're about to die better be quick about it and leave their food for others." Only the intercession of his countrymen John Ferris and Joe Williams saved Possene, yet even they were growing tired of the man. "God help you if you stole it," snapped Williams. "I'll throw you off myself." Someone said Possene should be the first to pay the price when they reached the point where one must die so others might live.

Surprise and shock cut short the attacks on Possene. There, it was out. The necessity of cannibalism. The taboo they'd avoided until now. The tally of wrecks and survivors who turned to it at last spoke of its reality— the *Peggy, Essex, George, Euxine, Jane Black, Cospatrick, Sallie M. Steelman, Caledonia, Frances Mary, Lady Frances, Granicus, Tiger, Nottingham Galley, Dolphin, Mary, Dalusia, Lucy, Earl Kellie, Leader, Blake, Anna Maria, Earl Moira, Jane Lowdon, Turley, Elizabeth Rashleigh, Hannah, Earnmoor, Home, Nautilus,* and *Medusa,* inspiration for the famous painting by Gericault. Cannibalism horrified and titillated the 19th-century mind. The captain's wife of the *Francis Mary,* wrecked en route to Liverpool in 1826, said after dining on the brains of an apprentice that it was "the most delicious thing" she'd ever tasted. Such statements were a delicacy in the world of cheap thrills.

There'd been precedents: Montaigne's "Of Cannibalism"; Robinson Crusoe, who watched cannibals eat human flesh "with undeniable enjoyment"; Jonathan Swift's bitter "Modest Proposal" for ending the Irish famine. But the 19th century raised the subject to new heights: Flaubert's *Salammbo* had a feast in which 40,000 soldiers dined on each other "with delight," and Poe's *A. Gordon Pym* feasted on his friend. Of all, Dickens gloried in the theme. In *Tale of Two Cities*, ogres relish young mothers and their children; in *Pickwick Papers*, Fat Boy leans toward Mary, plunges his knife into a meat pie and says, "I say, how nice you look"; in *David Copperfield*, David was so taken with Dora that during dinner, "my impression is that I dined off Dora, entirely." One ate what one loved; protein was *eros* and *agape*.

But cannibalism was just one small part of an imagination that struggled to make sense of a blood-soaked world. Civil war, revolution, extermination or enslavement of indigenous peoples in the name of progress—all bloomed like Baudelaire's "flowers of evil." This was the century giving birth to the literary vampire, the Jekyll and Hyde behind the civilized face, the Frankenstein's monster in every discovery. This was the age of a killer that ripped through London's East End and laughed as he did, the century that saw Poe and others fall in love with death—incestuous, premature, cannibalistic, and mad.

Henry's plight was not an excess of imagination. His was what 17th-century courts ruled an "inevitable necessity," but such necessity terrified. Henry had not trained in school for this; no formal education could train anyone. When the sailors declared that those who were dying "better be quick about it," they looked at Possene, but meant Samuel, too. "[I]f it be His will that we shall perish," prayed Henry, "preserve us from embittering our ends."

That night, Samuel dreamed of food. "Really, it is most marvelous how that every morsel that passes our lips is blessed for us," he wrote. "It makes me think daily of the miracle of the loaves and fishes." What a wonderful dream . . . bread and fish eternal . . . an endless cornucopia, as if Jesus appeared on the stern sheets and made daily rations. All that night, his giddy thoughts changed with the winds. At times he saw the men as rever-

ent; at others, as a curse. He saw Mitchell as Christlike, dividing bread and
fish between them. "He is a real good man and has been most kind to us,
almost fatherly," Samuel said. He mumbled as he wrote, unaware that he
spoke his thoughts aloud. Henry worried about such aimless drift: he tied
a damp handkerchief around his head to cool his burning brain.

That night, the cannibal's choice was laid on a plate for Jimmy Cox, and
he was asked to choose. Jack Campbell leaned close and whispered, "What
would you do, Jimmy, if it came down to it and someone died? Would you
eat human flesh, or starve?"

"I'd starve," Jimmy said, unconsciously backing away from the shadow.

Jack Campbell grunted in disgust. "Then you're a fool and would
deserve to die."

With this, Jimmy Cox's role in the boat began to change. He found himself positioned strangely in the boat's geography. He sat amidships, near
Mr. Thomas and the water cask, but even more important, between the
battle lines. As a young boy in the 1800s, he was neither child nor adult; as
cabin boy and apprentice, he was neither foremast hand nor part of the
aftercabin. All that mattered were his loyalties, but he was liked by everyone and he'd always felt the same about them. Now, suddenly, he was being
told to choose. He was everywhere and nowhere, made privy to all secrets,
yet never considered a threat. Jimmy was the perfect fly on the wall.

None of this was spoken loudly, but Mitchell heard muttering and
could imagine what was said. The Pandora's box of horrors had been
opened with the theft and threat of cannibalism. The clear line between
good and evil was blurred that morning, and Mitchell realized that their
ordeal had disintegrated into a voyage of the damned.

That night he mentally composed a letter, which he scribbled in the
back of his journal next morning. It was a last will and testament, a plea
for forgiveness, a final declaration of love:

> June 1st.
> My Dear Wife and Darling Girls and greatly beloved Son:
>   Could I but see you once more and ask forgiveness of you all for
> my seeming pettishness at times. God knows how dearly I love
> you. I hope and trust with the goodness of God you will be able to
> get along. If I could impart advice to you, what a comfort 'twould
> be to me before departing hence where there is no return. May

peace, plenty and harmony prevail in your councils, helping and loving one another. Your Father's loss you all will feel, but if it's Thy Father's wish, I am resigned. He knows what is best. Put your trust in Him and make a friend of Jesus our Lord and may your lives be happy and your end peace.

He was wise to write, for a desperation had entered the boat that could not be cast out. Nothing would be the same.

THE AMERICAN GROUP

THE DAWN OF JUNE 1 marked one month in the boat, an anniversary few chose to celebrate. "God has preserved us to the beginning of another month [which] none of us would have dared hope for when we left the ship," Henry wrote. "I have great confidence that in His great mercy He will send us deliverance soon." Mitchell was not as quick to sing God's praise. "Can't write, all very weak, particularly myself," he wrote. "30 days in the boat and no sail gladdens us."

Thirty days . . . 720 interminable hours punctuated by sudden terror . . . 43,200 eternal minutes . . . 2,592,000 lost seconds as the men floated outside of time. Time is the great enemy in survival extremes, yet no one agrees on its form. Plato considered space and time as part of the World of Ideas; Spinoza saw them as attributes of God; Kant believed they were constructs invented by man to order experience. Space and time physically existed to Einstein, but only as a pair—take away one, the other disappeared. The two flowed together in tides as shifting and observable as those ruling the seas.

Some saw time and death as equals, a pairing with special meaning for castaways. One day in 1654, the philosopher Pascal had an epiphany on the theme. As his horse-drawn carriage crossed a bridge over the Seine, two horses broke away and fell into the water, while Pascal and his carriage teetered on the edge. As he stared into the abyss, a theme of precarious balance lodged in his mind that would haunt him forever. Humanity perched on the edge of the abyss, sleeping on the soft pillow of ignorance (to para-

phrase Montaigne). Unfortunately for those in the longboat, the soft pillow had been plucked away long ago.

Space-Time. Urgency-Pain. Those who've nearly died in survival situations, or studied their psychology, agree on the importance of these four
horsemen of trauma. They disagree, however, on how to survive their
arrival. To psychologist John Leach, the key to surviving a long-term
ordeal is to adopt an "active-passive" approach and face calamity in a Zen
frame of mind. "Passivity is itself a deliberate and 'active' act," Leach wrote
in *Survival Psychology*: "There is strength in passivity." No less a survivor
than William Bligh would agree. When a crewman in the *Bounty*'s launch
asked about rescue, Bligh reportedly said that the only way to stay sane
was to forswear thoughts of the future. "Think if you like of the distance
we have come," he said, "but never in your mind run forward faster than
your vessel."

Dougal Robertson, who survived a shipwreck, would disagree. The
similarities between Robertson's 38-day ordeal and that of the *Hornet*'s
men are remarkable: their boats were wrecked in nearly the same place and
they drifted through the same stretch of doldrums; the length of their voyages differed by a mere five days. Even the initial choice to forgo the Galapagos on ten days' rations was the same: "Since no estimate I have heard of
puts a man's survival beyond 10 days even with very limited quantities of
water," Robertson wrote, "any attempt to reach the Galapagos was almost
certain to fail." To Robertson, a passive approach was an acceptance of suicide. Only an active attempt to thwart death promoted survival. "The
enormous difference between actively fighting for survival and passively
awaiting rescue or death effects a complete change in the castaway's out-
look," he wrote: "He becomes master of his fate and will devise means to
survive which no textbook can prescribe for him."

Robertson's approach seems more appealing to Western readers, but
danger arises when human ingenuity cannot halt the march of thirst and
hunger. Day 30, the point at which the *Hornet*'s men now found themselves, was near the breakpoint for the Robertsons, too. On Day 30, they
dined on shark and turtle, but a mishap the next day while bagging a turtle turned them against the maligned Robin Williams. They'd lost prey
before, but on this day the anger spilled over until Robertson and his wife
dredged up past sins. "The barrier of bitterness which had gone from

between us with the nearness of death rose once again to divide us, and Lyn wept as I flung savage recriminations," he said. The rancor among all of the adults grew more poisonous, culminating finally in threats of physical violence on Day 35. Their rescue came three days later, but one wonders what would have happened if they'd stayed on the boat any longer.

Crowding contributed to the rage. Samuel commented earlier that "cramped space" was one of their worst torments; this had special meaning now. Every inch of space taken up by a castaway meant that much less space for his neighbor. There was always some irritation, be it working out a cramp or shifting weight off a salt water boil. The "social density" of the boat was too high, the buffer zone between crewmen minimal. Social psychologists have observed the existence of a self-regulating "personal space" among animals: birds, for example, spread themselves evenly over telephone wires with calculated precision, alighting and leaving when newcomers land too close. Although humans tolerate invasion of that space throughout the day—in bus lines, movie theaters, and restaurants, for example—such invasion is temporary, and researchers calculate the ideal distance between people as 1.2 to 1.5 meters. This shrinks when tasks demand closeness—but the two spheres where space is most often violated for long periods with the greatest violence are oceangoing vessels and prisons.

Rats, the most social of mammals, thrive in such environments, and, not surprisingly, they are used to study why life there turns dicey. As W. Brad Johnson, head of the U.S. Naval Academy's Department of Leadership, Ethics and Law observed, rats break down and kill each other in overcrowded conditions. Although murder isn't a regular occurrence on Navy ships, "you worry about aggressiveness and changes in mood." He referred to a 1962 study by John B. Calhoun in which a large population of docile lab rats were turned into a ratcity of killers as their numbers increased in a confined, inescapable area. In time, almost every one of the community's 81 rats developed some form of abnormal, violent, or antisocial behavior: murder, rape, infanticide, and cannibalism increased in what Calhoun called a "behavioral sink . . . the outcome of any behavioral process that collects animals together in unusually great numbers."

One finding concerned the division of resources and space according to dominance, called "leadership" in humans. Dominant male rats chose pens with one opening, at either end of the enclosure, making them easy to defend. Peace prevailed here, compared to the center spaces, open to all sides, where chaos reigned. In this great muddled middle, two types of "citizen" patrolled the mean streets. "The first . . . moved through the community like somnambulists," Calhoun noted, a dazed state that appeared in varying degrees. While some rats acted like automatons, others maintained basic rituals of survival. Extreme cases lay down and died.

However, it was the second group, called "probers," that became the most serious threat. Probers lurked at the edge of a dominant male's territory, searching for weakness. In the middle pens, they raped estrous females, stole food, raided nurseries and ate the young, and attacked and ate the weak or dying. The pressure was so intense on females that they abandoned their cubs at birth or stopped bearing litters. Like a hive without a queen, the ratcity began to die.

Something like Calhoun's behavioral sink developed on the longboat, pushed to the edge by starvation and overcrowding. At both ends of the boat a leader had emerged: the bow and stern were their respective "territories," with midships serving as a buffer zone. Mitchell had taken station at the stern since the beginning, but now Harry Morris emerged as leader of the bow. If nothing else, he was a spokesman for the darkest thoughts of the crew. One night between Friday, June 1, and Sunday, June 3, he said to the others up front that he'd kill the captain if the American Group did not appear. "He's headed us from one island to another, and for what? With another captain, we'd've reached Clipperton long ago." While some men mumbled agreement, others defended Mitchell, saying he'd done his best. To such dissenters, Morris asked: Was Mitchell's best good enough if it only succeeded in getting them killed?

Why did Morris emerge as Mitchell's rival? He did not have a "community" on the boat like the Portuguese or Americans; in many ways, like Mitchell, he was a man alone. Hints dropped by the Fergusons, Jimmy Cox, and John Thomas reveal a spirited man, quick and witty, probably a leader in the forecastle before the *Hornet* burned. His rescue of Richard the Lionheart did as much for crew morale as Mitchell's assurances that they'd be rescued. Samuel disliked him because he was "impertinent," but Henry was fascinated by his worldliness and ability to laugh away cares.

Like rats in the middle pens, the men amidships kept their heads low. Poised between the poles of Mitchell and Morris, they mulled the mutinous words from the front and considered their options. Fred Clough was among them. Until now he'd kept his counsel and stayed faithful to the captain, but he knew something had to change or they'd begin to die. As the food dwindled, the men were "getting disheartened terribly," Henry observed. "Our chances of life are terribly small and are reducing from day to day." As Fred watched the level in the water cask sink lower, he knew that once they suffered thirst, sides would form up and someone would die.

Fred's thoughts frightened him. There was a growing coldness that started deep and spread to the extremities. It was as if he gazed at the world through a sheet of ice. He saw things he loved through the ice—a finely turned ship, his family and home—but cracks ran through it that only deepened with his urge to live. Every thought was filtered by the ice, including the threats against Mitchell and whisper of cannibalism. All was depersonalized.

One thing was clear: the time for decision grew short. "Short it must be," wrote Henry, "for one end or the other must come soon." Over the next three days—Friday, June 1, to Sunday, June 3—the fifteen men in the boat trembled with expectancy while awaiting the "uncertain isles." Each day merged into the others. The trades blew so briskly that they averaged 120 miles a day: too fast to troll for fish, yet mercifully cooling the air. Samuel reported his deterioration with a lack of passion that seemed surreal: "Managed this A.M. to crawl more than [a] step forward and was surprised to find I was so weak, legs and knees particularly." Though Henry dreamed of death, it was in ways made bearable by imagination: "What would I not give to be with [the family] were it but to die with them around."

Mitchell teetered on the edge of the panic against which he'd struggled for so long. On Friday he refused to take a noon sighting: Henry said it was to preserve the instruments, but Mitchell's tone suggests despair. "Have spent most of the day in prayer," he wrote on June 3. "Oh my Father, spare me if it's Thy will, otherwise, prepare me for death."

This echo of Christ at Gethsemane hints of strange thoughts in Mitchell. His thoughts *did* trouble him, but he never dared say what they were. He apparently feared insanity, and the best way to fight that was to work, plan, and *do*. In addition to handling the boat, he looked for clouds, an old mariner's trick borrowed from South Sea islanders during their epic voyages. He searched for rising cumulus clouds piling up on the thermal

Frank Vining Brown painting of the *Hornet* racing *Flying Cloud.*

Courtesy of The Mariners' Museum, Newport News, Virginia

The *Hornet's* "sailing card," an advertisement for the journey.

Courtesy of The Mariners' Museum, Newport News, Virginia

Captain Josiah Mitchell.

Courtesy of The Mariners' Museum, Newport News, Virginia

Josiah Mitchell's house.

Courtesy of The Mariners' Museum, Newport News, Virginia

Charles Rosner painting of the *Hornet* on fire.

Courtesy of The Mariners' Museum, Newport News, Virginia

A *Harper's Weekly* illustration of the fire to go with Twain's article.

Courtesy of The Mariners' Museum, Newport News, Virginia

The title page of Henry Ferguson's journal.

Courtesy of The Mariners' Museum, Newport News, Virginia

A page from Samuel Ferguson's journal on the day the *Hornet* burned.

Courtesy of The Mariners' Museum, Newport News, Virginia

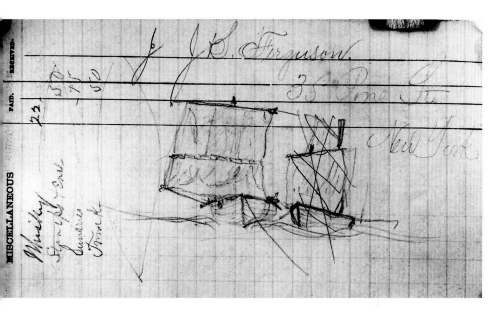

Henry's sketch of the quarterboats under sail.

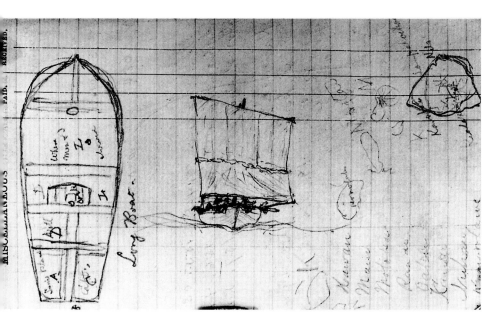

Henry's sketch of the layout of the longboat

Josiah Mitchell and the two Fergusons, after the ordeal.

Courtesy of The Mariners' Museum, Newport News, Virginia

Fred Clough as a young man.

Courtesy of Alderman Library, University of Virginia

Laupahoehoe: photo from 1875, showing the little village where the survivors eventually landed.

Courtesy of The Mariners' Museum, Newport News, Virginia

Mark Twain in the mid-1860s, about the time he wrote the *Harper's* article that he hoped would make him famous.

Courtesy of The Mariners' Museum, Newport News, Virginia

Fred Clough as an old man.

Courtesy of Alderman Library,
University of Virginia

An oil painting of Henry
Ferguson as an old man.

Courtesy of The Mariners'
Museum, Newport News,
Virginia

currents over islands; at night he looked for phosphorescent lines in the water—hints of waves that struck a shore and bounced back to sea. There were traps to guard against, too. Near the horizon, clouds seemed to move slower and attain a darker mass, due to the oblique angle of view. Some remained motionless long enough that it was easy to mistake them for low flat islands or high volcanic rims.

Such illusions frightened Mitchell. At first his emotions were held in check by years of training, while his body was used to hard work and responded easily. But the rift between mind and body had grown deeper and there were times when the two no longer worked together but more like self-canceling machines. He could endure physical pain, but enduring his emotions was terrifying. The smallest things sent him into a dark depression; at other times, tiny mercies nearly made him cry. "The sun shines and God is merciful," he said on June 2. His body felt so beaten that sometimes he had trouble hanging on to the tiller. The sun's warmth relaxed his muscles, a momentary ease that reminded him of long-forgotten rest and the promise of relief from pain.

More than anything else, Mitchell feared losing his ability to command. He feared the day he'd wake and be physically unable to take the helm, his arms and hands acting in mutiny against his will. As rebellion percolated around him, he watched for signs of rebellion within himself. Surely he could fight that, he hoped, but that might have asked too much of biology.

By now, starvation had taken firm hold of them all. Their faces and frames were emaciated; the wasting of their muscle and subcutaneous fatty tissues was well advanced; they shrank in weight and stature so dramatically that their shoes were too large and their clothes flapped like rags. Swelling set into their knees and ankles; their nails grew slowly; some noticed that their hair fell out in clumps. Their skin, especially on the face and hands, had blackened from the sun and salt. They were assailed by muscle cramps and soreness; cuts and scrapes bled less freely but took longer to heal. Their pulse rates and general metabolism slowed.

They looked and acted like old men. Their eyes had developed cloudy lenses and the whites looked unnaturally blue. They talked slowly, a development so disturbing that some shut up tight as clams. With the loss of internal heat, their tolerance to cold dropped until they lay shivering in a fetal position on all but the sunniest days. They always felt sleepy; if they moved too fast, they suffered momentary blackouts in which it was far too easy to fall overboard.

But the most insidious changes were mental. The rules were changing in the basic way they perceived reality. It was hard to focus on the horizon, and many were plagued by a ringing in the ears. Their hearing had grown more sensitive, which made the conspiratorial whispers up front audible to those in the middle and back. The ordinary sounds of the boat grew unbearable: the creaks as boards expanded, water lapping against the side, sail luffing in the wind. They swung between black depression and anger, most often during meals. The old class suspicions of ill treatment turned into articles of faith, the men up front certain that Mitchell favored himself, the Fergusons, and Mr. Thomas when doling out meals.

Hunger was the scourge of the poor. Since they rarely had reserves of food or money, they suffered most from any shortage: one of the bitterest complaints during the Great Famine of 1848 was the fact that the English and great landowners profited from higher food prices while thousands of poor Irish died in the streets and fields. Some men on the boat were old enough to remember those days. The hard economy of supply and demand prevailed in Western thought, and although the men of the forecastle were neither economists nor political philosophers, they knew the tenor of the times. Economists swore by the name of English clergyman Thomas Malthus, who early in the 19th century concluded that population increased geometrically unless checked by famine, disease, or war. Malthus was as influential as Darwin, their theories bastardized into a Social Darwinism that claimed the poor were unfit for survival, a "fact" proven by their poverty. If allowed to increase, they'd drag society with them.

On the night of June 3–4, whispers up front were born of old angers and fears. Resentment against society mutated into accusations against Mitchell himself. The irony was that Mitchell was one of the fairer captains. The accusations were unfounded, but as society's agent he was close. Such accessibility made him ripe for revenge.

The men blamed Mitchell for their torment, not Sam Hardy for his carelessness, or the sea. They said Mitchell did not try to save the ship or extra provisions, as seen by the way he'd given their share of stores to the quarter-boats. "Look how he hands out the choicest bits to the two high-hats," Harry Morris said. "There's money in this, I bet." There was always money in a rich man's dealing. Almost as suddenly as Parr's boat had exploded, Mitchell was turned into a focus of hatred.

All this was said at night in earshot of Jimmy Cox, who pretended to sleep so they wouldn't know he overheard. Jimmy was terrified. If he argued in Mitchell's defense, they'd say he was the captain's pet, thus sealing his fate with those in the stern. He could warn the captain, but the stern was always watched and he might be caught and killed. But if he didn't warn the captain . . . well, he couldn't stand that thought at all.

Jimmy was devoted to the man. Captain Mitchell had saved his life, rescuing him from Mr. Parr, and in so doing adding one more mouth to the sad economy of their stores. If not for that act, Jimmy knew he'd be dead. Cabin boys rarely fared well as castaways: their straws were always shortest in the cannibal lottery. Either that, or Parr's boat had foundered in a storm. Jimmy had said he'd repay the captain, but now that promise was put to the test and he held Mitchell's life in his hand. He couldn't live with himself if he didn't warn the captain and something happened . . . but if the men up front saw him do so, his life wasn't worth much, either.

Sometime after midnight, when sounds in the boat died to the shifting of men asleep, Jimmy crawled past John Thomas and Fred Clough, past the skeleton that was Samuel Ferguson; he glanced at the shadow by the tiller and turned to Henry. They'd become friends on the *Hornet*; if seen by the others, he had a better chance of lying than if he went to Mitchell. He plucked at Henry's trousers; when the younger Ferguson jumped, he whispered to be still. "You gotta know, Harry Morris and the others say they'll kill the captain if we miss the islands."

Henry recognized the messenger's voice but was stunned by the message. The suspicions he'd cobbled together himself were now being confirmed. "What do they plan?"

"I'm not sure," Jimmy said. "I can't say more. If anybody sees me, they'll suspect what I'm doing and kill me as a lesson to others. Be prepared, Mr. Ferguson, and please tell the captain. I'll come back tomorrow night if I can." The dim shape was swallowed by the gloom.

An elaborate game of denial was played in the stern on the morning of June 4, the same day the bread crumbs and raisins ran dry. The dawn was rough and cold, but by noon the sea had calmed to regular swells and the day turned to one of "pleasant sunshine and warm." The reading was Lat. 17°06' N, Long. 130°30' W, a position putting them in line with the American Group "if they're where the book places them," Mitchell said. Samuel spent an hour getting into dry clothes and contemplating his bones. "Have been trying for the last ten or twelve days to get a pair of drawers dry enough to put on and today at last succeeded," he wrote. "Was much surprised to see how much my legs had wasted away, above my knee barely thicker than my upper arm used to be." His skin had a bluish, chalky cast, like that of a corpse. "Still, I trust in God's infinite mercy and feel sure He will do what is best for us," he dutifully said.

Only Henry seemed terrified that day: there is a good chance he did not tell Samuel or Mitchell about Jimmy's nighttime visit, a lapse attesting to the depth of his fear. All that was left to eat was the ham, a few oysters, and the bouillon. They hadn't caught a fish or bird in days; the water dropped steadily. "Men growing dreadfully discontented and awful grumbling and unpleasant talking is arising," he wrote. "God save us from all strife of men and if we must die now, take us Himself and not embitter our bitter death still more."

Henry's curse was imagination. He was the most imaginative of the diarists and now he suffered for it, dying in grisly fashion a hundred times. Every sudden lurch by a man up front, every shift to ease the pressure on tired joints became in his mind the vanguard of the attack. Terror sharpened his mind. He did not slip into a near-comatose state like the others; his observations were sharp, conspiring to keep them alive. If it were his fate to be murdered, he would at least know the reason and take it down for others to read.

As one later observer said of some literate Holocaust survivors, Henry stayed alert through "the relieving gift of self-expression." The act of writing diminished the fear. Leon Szalet, a Polish-Jewish businessman, said that when he decided to record his experiences in the Sachsenhausen extermination camp, "a strange mood took possession of me, a mixture of despair, fear, and boundless curiosity. So must an explorer feel who has fallen in the power of a cannibal tribe." Child psychologist Bruno Bettelheim felt split in two—one half observed the horror around him, while the other suffered with his fellows. Henry felt a similar split. He wondered, like Bettelheim, whether he'd transform into something feral, or simply go insane.

But if things looked bad to Henry during the daylight hours of June 4, they got worse that night when Jimmy returned. Henry had dreaded another visit, but also expected it from the glances he'd received all day. *God, please let it be better than last night's news,* he thought, but another day of empty sky and sea had passed and rage expanded to fill the emptiness. When Jimmy crawled forward until he could touch his friend's shoulder, his whispers were chilling.

June 5 dawned to robin's-egg skies and high rolling seas, with a steady wind from the east smelling like a fresh new world. To Henry, it was illusion. The dawn saw him scribble a note in his journal, then pass it to his brother. "Cox told me last night that there is getting to be a good deal of ugly talk among the men against the Captain and us aft," it began. He named Harry Morris, Jack Campbell, and, surprisingly, Fred Clough, whose anger had finally won out, as the leaders of the plot against them.

> They say that the Captain is the cause of all, that he did not try to save the ship at all, nor to get provisions, and even would not let the men put in some they had, and that our allowance aft we are favored. Jack asked Cox the other day if he would starve first or eat flesh. Cox answered he would starve. Jack then told him it would only be killing himself. If we do not find these Islands we would do well to prepare for everything. Harry is the loudest of all.

The note got Samuel's attention. As Henry watched, he turned white under the scabrous layers of sun and salt. He grabbed Henry's nub of pencil and scrawled beneath the initial note, "We can depend on Charlie Iron, I think, and Mr. Thomas and Cox, can we not?"

"I guess so," Henry wrote back, "and very likely on Peter [Smith], but there is no telling. Charlie and Cox are certain. There is nothing definite said or hinted as yet, as I understand him, but starving men are the same as maniacs. It would be well to keep a watch on your pistol so as to have it and the cartridges safe from theft."

Samuel's hand leaped to his coat pocket for reassurance and felt the small pistol and cartridges. The men up front were watching his movements, hate undisguised, on guard for suspicious signs. The least hint of knowledge could prove disastrous. Mr. Thomas said something to Mitchell about the fractured mast and ragged sail needing repair, a job they felt too weak to handle. "Sail and block show signs of failing and need taking down, which is something of a job as it requires the shinnying up the mast," Samuel wrote. What if Mitchell ordered a crewman up the mast and he refused to go? Would the mutiny begin?

Mitchell had to be told. Perhaps he already suspected, but Samuel wasn't sure. "Bad news from forward," he wrote in his journal, "discontented and threatening complaints of unfair allowances, etc., all as unreasonable as foolish." Once again he dismissed the cause as something beneath him, but he could no longer dismiss the threat itself if he hoped to survive. He felt "miserably" weak, as if Henry's news added weight to his limbs. "But try to keep up the best I can. God will help us, I am sure, although we may not all live to be delivered." He put his hand on his pistol, but it brought him little comfort. "God have mercy on us," he said.

It is uncertain when, exactly, Mitchell learned of Cox's warning. He calmly issued orders in the morning, talked with Mr. Thomas about the sail and block, mentioned that if the islands were not where the charts put them, they'd be forced to swing northwest into the shipping lanes and head for the Sandwich Islands. "We'll live as best we can," he said, neglecting to add that Hawaii was nearly 1,500 miles away. At noon he took a sighting that placed the boat at Lat. 16°46' N, Long. 132°10' W. He lowered the rations to a single noontime meal of a little ham and an ounce of water, with extra sips at 8 to 9 o'clock each morning and 5 to 6 o'clock each night.

By 2:00 or 3:00 P.M., however, he knew. "A conspiracy formed to murder me," he wrote. "Minds unquiet." As always, the surface was calm, but his mind was not. Jimmy's warning certified what he'd come to suspect. There was an edginess to the men: guilty eyes and averted gazes among the youngsters, sullen stares from Harry Morris and the older hands. He suspected the Frenchman of being some sort of leader before Cox's news. The boy had pleaded for his life to get off Parr's boat—now he was trying to save his savior, even if he put himself in jeopardy.

Mutiny was the abrogation of everything that mattered on a ship, the equivalent of civil war. Thought to originate from the French in the 1500s, the word itself implied violent revolt on the high seas. Unlike revolution, defined as an "impersonal attack," shipboard mutiny was always personal due to the close working relationship between officers and men. Historians have noted an intimate, familial quality to the violence, almost like fratricide. The most famous mutineer in history, Fletcher Christian, was sponsored and vouchsafed by William Bligh, and to his dying day Bligh would never grasp why his friend turned on him. Revolutions tore nations apart, but mutiny destroyed something more immediate—the bond between friends.

Thus, we see the double-edged nature of Henry's entry for June 5: "No signs as yet of the Islands. God deliver us, our stores are almost spent and will be entirely if we do not find them soon. Dreadful forebodings. God save us from all such horrors. Some of the men getting to talk a good deal." Then, "Heart very sad."

Heart very sad. Henry saw in an instant what chroniclers of mutiny rarely capture: the sadness of insurrection, the rupture of bonds forged in hardship or pain. Though he barely knew Jack Campbell, he'd come to enjoy Harry Morris's wit and spirit. More than anything else, he regarded Fred Clough as a friend. Fred had been the one to catch him in the shrouds, and after he'd paid his fine had taught him more marlinspike seamanship than any other sailor aboard. Fred was a Yankee farmboy raised not far from Stamford, so they'd had much to talk about. They'd bailed together all night when it seemed that any second they would drown. Henry couldn't understand the betrayal, and felt stabbed in the heart.

Perhaps this familial quality is what intrigues landlubbers about mutiny. While Marxist theorists see mutiny as a class struggle, others believe that resistance to authority is basic to man's nature. The biblical story of man's fall is mutinous, since Adam and Eve rebelled against God's most basic command. Maritime historians like Edmund Fuller and Leonard Guttridge have defined specific *kinds* of mutiny based upon a mutineer's legal status, and this informs his moral right to rebel. Mutineers held in slavery are deemed most justified, while those who have submitted voluntarily to legitimate authority, like soldiers and sailors, receive less sympathy from society and history. Sailors almost always rebelled without legal protection. Before the 1915 Seaman's Act, most U.S. sailors were prisoners of their contracts, and such custom of centuries was cast in stone when the U.S. Supreme Court barred sailors from Thirteenth Amendment protections forbidding slavery and involuntary servitude. "The contract of a sailor has always been treated as an exceptional one," the justices ruled in the 1897 *Robertson* v. *Baldwin* case "involving to a certain extent the surrender of his personal liberty."

A ship on the ocean is a world of its own, so unique in its remoteness that emotions soon dissipated by larger society can instead bubble and boil within its cramped confines. Charles Vidil, a French scholar of naval mutiny, believes shipboard life the ideal environment for breeding "the disturbance of minds, the spreading of false rumors, the growth of group suggestion" that leads to insurrection. The secret nooks and dark crannies, the harsh division by class, the constant threat of the sea—all made ships as well-designed for breeding mutiny as Cape Horn was for killing sailors.

Sea captains like Mitchell believed that mutiny reflected their failure of leadership: "Mutiny in my ship!" stormed 18th-century British admiral Cuthbert Collingwood. "If it can have arrived at that, it must be my fault, and the fault of every one of my officers." Yet the act was punished with little of the mercy that such statements imply. In the 19th-century merchant service, the mere attempt to mutiny was punished by five years in prison and fines of $1,000, while actual success carried double the penalty: 10 years' imprisonment and $2,000 in fines. The military, of course, was harsher. Aboard the U.S. Navy brig *Somers* in 1842, three suspected mutineers—including Midshipman Philip Spencer, son of John Canfield Spencer, secretary of war under President John Tyler—were hung from the yardarm. The gruesome ceremony was designed to scare other mutineers from their intentions while putting blood on everyone's hands. Nooses were placed around the condemned mens' necks; the hanging ropes were tossed over booms so that the trailing ends hung down; groups of sailors were ordered to grab these ends. At the command of "Whip!", they ran across the deck, hoisting the three kicking bodies high into the air. The captain ordered his men to give three cheers.

Such ceremony rarely washes clean the taint of mutiny. It clings to a ship after the last officer is dumped overboard and the last mutineer hung. Mutinous ships acquire a curse, while officers seem brushed with a mark of Cain. After the *Bounty* mutiny, Bligh's life was filled with conflict, acrimony, and more mutiny. His voyages aboard the *Resource* and *Providence* were disasters. He was thrown off the 64-gun *Director* during the 1797 Mutiny of the Nore, court-martialed while commanding the *Warrior,* and in 1806 arrested by his own militia while governor of New South Wales. Aboard the *Somers*, the ship's surgeon committed suicide a few days after the mutiny, while a lieutenant told Herman Melville about the kangaroo court in which the jurors could not reach a verdict, so the captain stepped in and the mutineers were executed. The man was so consumed by guilt that he turned to drink and eventually died of alcoholism.

Even more than shipwreck or storm, captains feared mutiny. The act of rebellion did more than strip them of their ship—it judged their authority and destroyed their good name. One reason for the constant activity on a ship was this fear. When the British Admiralty's Articles of War were drafted in 1749, four of the thirty-six articles, or 11 percent, dealt with the act of mutiny. Such rebellion was a stake through the heart of the system's existence, so the death penalty for mutiny was mandatory. Anyone who heard mutinous talk and failed to report it was subject to court-martial. Anyone with grievances, such as "the unwholesomeness of the victual," must complain privately or be court-martialed, since making public complaints could "stir up a disturbance" and lead to mutiny.

Then-current wisdom dictated that the best way to keep sailors quiet was by keeping them occupied. "The adage that idleness is the root of evil is with no people more strongly verified than with sailors and soldiers," said Rear Admiral Richard Kempenfelt of the British Navy. "The only way to keep large bodies of men in order is by dividing and subdividing them, with officers over each, to inspect into and regulate their conduct." Controlled and busy men had few chances to mass together in an uncontrolled, idle fashion. "The people, left to themselves, become sottish, slovenly and lazy, form cabals, and spirit each other up to insolence and mutiny."

Such language itself smacked of the lofty prejudice found in Samuel's diaries; in close quarters, this led to trouble. Mutineers like Fletcher Christian and the *Somers'* Philip Spencer were portrayed as madmen, and in truth there was something mad about facing the force arrayed against them. Mutiny was a desperate act, an "incoherent protest" against faulty leadership or intolerable conditions, and the *Hornet's* mutineers had convinced themselves that Mitchell's seamanship was dangerously flawed. He'd set course for three islands and missed every one, always blaming the wind. His decisions had taken them thousands of miles from land or other sail. Their food was running out and their water would be next. He'd said they'd make the American Group by Wednesday, June 6, but even as he steered that course he was heard telling Mr. Thomas that the islands might not even be there. If so, why in hell were they heading to them?

What other explanation was there but that the Old Man had gone mad? They might not have an alternative plan, but in their eyes they were doomed if Mitchell stayed at the helm.

For his part, Mitchell was subject to the beliefs and the prejudices of his era. Arthur Clark, who captained several clippers, said that crews filled with "Liverpool Irishmen" were wild, depraved, and obscene. Such men could only be ruled by an iron fist; their code of ethics condoned clubbing or stabbing an officer, he claimed. Though Clark did admit that much of the violence stemmed from class and the inability of non-native crewmen to advance, he saw nothing wrong with the system. A captain must be severe: it was ultimately his character that got a ship to port. A clipper captain was a benevolent employer in charge of a pack of rogues who rarely appreciated their good fortune. Without him, they'd be destitute, behind bars, or dead.

Such was the chasm made evident by mutiny. Captains were "scoundrels" while crews were "bloodthirsty" swine. A common belief among sailors was that all captains profited from cheating men out of their rations, so why should Mitchell be different? He hadn't let them bring extra food, they said, forgetting after 30 days the panic and urgency as the *Hornet* burned. They lived in a different kind of furnace, where violence seemed the only way to survive.

"Don't worry, boys, we'll make it," Mitchell tried to assure them during the afternoon of June 5. "You'll see those islands with tomorrow's light." Even Harry Morris wanted Mitchell's words to come true. They sped west through a dry evening with steady winds, praying that this would be their last night at sea. Mitchell prayed, too, but that night, he also grabbed the hatchet with which he'd cut the towlines to the quarter-boats and tucked it under his thigh. That night, the crewmen kept their hands on their knives and took stock of the other weapons: the captain's hatchet, Samuel's pistol, the two oars. There was nowhere to hide on the longboat, nowhere to run. Once violence started, it would consume them all.

That evening, as the light faded, Henry wrote this prayer:

Oh eternal God who causest both the storm and calm, in whose hand is the power of life and death: we beseech thee to look upon us Thy creatures in our extremity. Spare us. Good Lord, spare Thy people who cry unto Thee for help. Thou who didst feed Thy people in the desert, suffer us not to die with this famine that threatens us, Oh save us Lord or we perish. Spare us for Thy mercy is great. Lord Jesus, who didst command the storm to cease and didst preserve Thy disciples from drowning, help us we beseech Thee, that we being saved by Thy defense may evermore serve Thee and praise Thee as we have never done before. We thank Thee, Oh Lord, for Thy great mercy in keeping us safe for so long, and for blessing our food to us. Grant us still Thy protection and preserve us for Thy great mercy's sake.

Or if it be Thy Holy Will to summon us from this world, give us grace to use the remaining time in preparation for the final judgment. Give us true repentance for our sins, and grant that through the merits of Christ Jesus who died on the cross to save us, they may be forgiven us. Give us patience and resignation to Thy will and keep us in thy spirit of peace and charity. All which we ask for the sake of Him who suffered hunger, thirst and death for us, who with Thee and the Holy Ghost we worship and glorify, one God, world without end—Amen.

He said it through the night, muttering with renewed strength with the approach of dawn. Yet with the light, they saw only the sea. Their position put them in the midst of the American Group, yet all they saw around them was seaweed and a floating piece of wood that looked to Henry like "an old tree." They stood silently in the boat, gazing to all compass points for the lowest silhouette—for any shadow that could be an island or atoll. But there was nothing—nothing but water and the sobs of Thomas Tate, which seemed to speak for them all.

Like Henderson's Island, the American Group had existed only in the imagination of another captain, long ago.

DELIRIUM

A S THEY GAZED AROUND THEM for land that never existed, shock turned to anger, anger to despair. Land avoided them somehow. They waited for Mitchell to say something, anything—it was his place to devise one more scheme for salvation, though everything else had failed.

A crew of scarecrows watched him, and Mitchell resented them all. What did they expect, that he could win against the ocean? Man was barely tolerated in this place, allowed by the inattention of the bitch goddess to roll the dice another day. For a moment his anger flared so bright that he clutched the hatchet, welcoming an attack. *Come and get it over with,* and perhaps for a brief moment a madness like Harry Morris's gleamed in his eyes. He'd take some with him before he died. Rage threatened to sweep all of them as Mitchell struggled for some miracle.

He had two options. Although no mention was made, he would have seen on the Imray chart a reference to yet another tiny island, an unnamed speck lying five degrees west and not far north if they continued toward Hawaii. At approximately 19° N, 141° W, Imray promised an "island, 40 ft. High. 4 miles long. Very barren. Seen Dec. 28, 1848," and like the Siren calls of Henderson and the American Group, it promised too much. For it was not there.

Maybe the reference to barrenness warned him off; maybe he'd developed a sixth sense for nonentity. Instead, he chose a known quantity 1,200 miles west. "Bowditch was wrong," he sighed. "All we can do is run for the Sandwich Islands and trust in God's goodness for food."

"*God's goodness?*" Fred cried, and laughed bitterly. Such laughter from Fred had a crazy quality, since like Henry and Jimmy Cox the men depended on his cheer. No longer. "You call it goodness that one or both quarter-boats are sunk? Can we *eat* God's goodness? If you can, Cap'n, welcome to it, but I'd like something more filling. I place my faith in meat and bread."

On the *Hornet*, such talk was mutinous and Clough would be clapped in irons. But everything had changed. All the tired assumptions about man's place and trust in higher authority—all gone. Mitchell laughed softly and opened his hands. "What would you have of me, Fred?" he asked. "Do you know a better heading? If so, let us hear it. I've done the best I can."

It was a vulnerable moment, for he admitted weakness, something a captain never did. But in so doing, he made himself human again. *Of course* they had no better solutions—just anger and frustration. "At least we know the Sandwich Islands exist," Fred conceded. "Though it's probably our bones that'll wash ashore."

They bobbed up and down like a cork; Fred's words hung like a curse in the air. In the lull, Charles Kaartman, one of the Danes whom Samuel trusted, cleared his throat and asked what they would do if one of them died. "That won't happen," Mitchell replied stubbornly.

"Beggin' pardon, Captain, but I'm not sure of that," Kaartman said. The men in the bow bent forward, tense and attentive. Mitchell could guess where this was headed, but hoped to avoid it if possible. He stared west at another squall-line forming and answered that they'd read a service over the poor devil and bury him at sea.

"That's not what he means," Harry Morris interrupted. "That would be a waste of meat."

Mitchell stared at Morris, surprised by his bluntness. "You'd sink to that?"

Morris gazed back evenly. "What would you suggest, considerin' the state we're in?"

Neither man blinked or looked away. Despite Mitchell's caution, Morris had drawn him into a confrontation. Backing down now meant the end of his authority. But having reached this line, no one wanted to cross it, not even the conspirators. "What would you have of us, Captain?" cried Joe Campbell, breaking the tension. "Look around. Do you see a single thing to eat? Soon there won't be drink neither, and when that happens, we'll go mad."

"Which is worse?" asked Kaartman, the calmest voice despite his choice of subject matter. "A custom we know but do not mention, or a boat filled with corpses and madmen? You know the answer as well as the rest of us, Cap'n. It's the natural order of things to stay alive."

"I'll not draw lots to kill a man for food, not on my boat," Mitchell said. "Not while I've got strength to prevent it."

"We're not suggesting lots," Campbell said, though the sidelong glance at Harry Morris suggested that not all agreed. "Not yet, at least. But we won't shrink from using the flesh of one who dies. That won't be long for some . . . and it'll keep the living going another few days."

"It will not come to that," Mitchell answered, but in his mind he knew a subtle power shift had occurred. The sailors had not asked his permission: they'd informed him that, once the pain of starvation grew unbearable, they'd eat the dead. Mitchell had no choice in the matter but whether to partake, too. In a sense, Kaartman asked his blessing and Mitchell refused to give it, but neither had he forbidden their decision. Doing so would force a confrontation, and on the day when his navigation again came to nothing, his command would crumble as well.

Wisely, he objected to a greater evil than had been suggested—the sacrifice of the living. By setting limits, he kept the pretense of command while never actually issuing orders. He played for time, the only sure resource left to him.

Samuel faced a similar problem. Although his name was not mentioned, he knew the crew envisioned dining on him. He was damned if he'd be someone's lunch, and he had the firepower to back his feelings. Yet there were as many dangers in using his pistol as in never using it. In Samuel's Starr .44, the roll-your-own paper cartridges of ball, powder, and percussion cap tended to misfire when damp. Samuel had done his best to shield the rounds in his coat, but everything was wet after a month at sea. If he was forced to pull the trigger, the charge might not go off and the men would tear him apart. Or the gun could misfire, detonating rounds in adjoining chambers and injuring himself, Mitchell, or Henry.

Henry was most horrified by Kaartman's suggestion: the idea of watching others tear into his brother's body seemed more than he could bear. "Horrible!" he wrote: "God give us all full use of our reason and spare us from such awful things." Even as he watched, Samuel approached that point where the starving men would claim him. At times he could barely lift his head. "Sam holds out well," he wrote, "but is growing weaker and weaker, I fear, as indeed we all are."

The idea of being consumed began to haunt Henry Ferguson. His brother Samuel was dying of consumption, the ship was consumed by fire, his friends in the quarter-boats were consumed by the sea. Their little group in the longboat was falling into savagery. Swordfish, sharks, and waterspouts all waited their chance, each an expression of a Nature determined to rub out his memory. Of even greater danger were his comrades. Man might be on the eve of an age of science, but a very unscientific beast lurked within.

Cannibalism was the shorthand of that fear. As ethnologist Konrad Lorenz noted, cannibalism is rare among warm-blooded vertebrates and almost unknown in mammals, probably for the simple reason that conspecifics "do not taste good." Yet man seems the exception, a practice concurrent with his development of tools. *Australopithecus*, the inventor of pebble tools, used his invention to kill members of his species; the Promethean discoverer of fire, Peking Man, used the discovery to roast his kin. In Britain's Iron Age, warrior Celts consumed large quantities of human flesh; in one four-night feast in 1487, Aztecs were said to sacrifice 80,000 prisoners to the gods, their flesh in all probability fed to a protein-starved citizenry.

Henry could not think of what might happen on this boat without revulsion, yet he could not force his mind from the taboo. The obscenity drew him as strongly as it repelled, and most repellent of all was the fear that hunger would make him a cannibal, too. "As I feel now I don't think anything could persuade me," he wrote, "but can't tell what you will do when reduced by hunger and crazy." He recognized now the fragility of norms. "Darius, after he got the kingdoms of [Persia], called into his presence certain Greeks who were at hand, and asked what he should pay them to eat the bodies of their fathers when they died," began Herodotus in his famous passage in which cannibalism illustrated the relativity of culture and law:

To which they answered that there was no sum that would tempt them to do such a thing. He then sent for certain Indians of the race called

Callatians, men who eat their fathers, and asked them . . . what he should give them to burn their fathers when they died [as did the Greeks]. The Indians exclaimed in horror and asked him not to use such language. Such are the rules of custom, and Pindar was right in my judgment when he said: "Custom is King over all."

There were several variants of the cannibal custom, each tied to a purpose or goal. All were known by 1866, though most were news to Henry. "Gastronomic" cannibalism provided needed supplements to the diet, "medicinal" cannibalism was thought to ward off sickness, "mortuary" cannibalism (eating one's relations) maintained an after-death connection to family members. "Sacrificial" cannibalism was probably the most widely documented by explorers: it helped one gain a victim's strength or wisdom, satisfied the gods, or exacted vengeance on an enemy. "Political" cannibalism—publicly polishing off a captive to terrify opponents—ventured closest to pure evil, but was also the rarest. The more common variant contemplated now by Henry dominated headlines and, more than any other, spoke to fears of society's breakdown.

"Survival" cannibalism had a long pedigree. It occurred when conditions grew so harsh that the rules regulating day-to-day life were no longer effective; it inhabited the landscape where civilization was stripped away—famine, drought, or disaster, events that humbled man. While other "brands" of cannibalism contained some intellectual or ritual component and were freely "chosen" to fulfill a purpose, survival cannibalism was the individual's last gasp; there was a choice, but at the most basic level of choosing to live or die. Evolutionary biologists claim that at that level there is no choice, while the world's religions typically refuse to condemn survival cannibalism, siding for once with scientists. When every cell cries for nourishment, normal morality checks out. When it returns, it never seems the same.

Records of survival cannibalism burrow like moles through every age, rarely seen, always there. Herodotus wrote of *anthropophagi* barely subsisting in the harsh climes beyond the Caspian Sea. The Egyptian physician Abd al-Latif wrote of a cannibalism so widespread during the great famine of A.D. 1201 that "this mania for eating people . . . no longer caused surprise. The horror people felt at first entirely vanished; one spoke of it, and heard it spoken of, as a matter of everyday indifference." Medieval siege survivors told of eating their way through family pets and rats before turning to the recently deceased; Napoleon's soldiers resorted to cannibalism during the retreat from Moscow. Early Arctic explorers seemed to have a knack for discovering, or becoming, gruesome leftovers. A Gulf of St. Lawrence expedition in 1829 found a rude hut containing "the carcasses of four human beings with their hands, legs and arms cut off and their bowels extracted." A kettle held more remains. Artifacts around the bodies identified them as the crew of the British ship *Granicus*, wrecked near the Arctic Circle the previous year.

The American incident even more famous than the *Essex* was that of the Donner Party in 1849. Henry was still an infant, but Samuel and Mitchell remembered the headlines. Equal in horror to accounts of Indian attacks, the tale of the midwestern farmers and businessmen trapped in a lonely snow-filled mountain pass on the California Trail was *the* nightmare story of the Great Western Migration. Of the party's original 87 members, five died before reaching the mountains, 34 died in the winter camp or while trying to seek help, and an infant succumbed to sickness after rescue. Two Indian guides sent to save the party were killed and eaten, too. When it was over, there were 42 dead and 47 survivors. Of those who lived, friends ate friends, and kin ate kin.

The Donner Party tragedy was so well-known that two lessons impressed themselves on the 19th-century American mind. First and foremost was that when one person broke the cannibal taboo, it was easier for all to engage. With each death, the harvesting of flesh became more efficient. Some meat was stripped from bodies and roasted immediately, while some was dried for later use—just like the fish on the longboat. That acceptance of cannibalism, after early resistance, was the change Henry most feared in himself.

The second lesson of the Donner Party was that individuality was a bad idea, echoing de Tocqueville's "tyranny of the majority" to the *nth* degree. Although males died at twice the rate of females in the Donner Party—possibly because of women's smaller size, greater proportion of subcutaneous fat, and lower basal metabolism—more females were actually proposed for sacrifice. During a trek across the mountains by a group called the "Forlorn Hope," one man argued that a woman who fell behind should be killed and eaten. When this was opposed on the grounds that she was a wife and mother, the same opinion-maker pointed to two other women who were not mothers and whose husbands had died. Luckily for these women, the group crossed the trail of the Indians who'd brought relief and who were now collapsed in the snow. They killed and ate their former saviors; in a grisly sense, the Indians saved them again. The lesson was simple: differences could be deadly. It was best to blend into the crowd.

The underlying horror of cannibalism for Victorians was the fear that one became less civilized, forever. There was a reverse cannibal agenda in this that arose in the Age of Discovery even as *cannibal* appeared as a term. Simply put, those peoples who engaged in cannibalism were seen as less than human and so could be exterminated, exploited, or enslaved.

From the beginning, the cannibal agenda proved useful for rationalizing conquest or control. The New World, ripe for exploitation, was filled with cannibals in need of conversion; the poor, ripe for exploitation, turned to cannibalism during famine—and also required control. Christopher Columbus was credited with introducing *cannibal* to the lexicon: Frank Lestringant, a French professor of Renaissance literature who surveyed the writings of European explorers and missionaries, traced the term to the Arawak *caniba*, believed to be a corruption of *cariba*, or "bold." Aztecs, Aborigines, Fijians, New Zealand Maoris, American Indians, Congolese headhunters—in every locale where a colonizing frenzy took shape, the native peoples were characterized as eating others, lacking law and religion, eschewing private property, and violating the incest taboo. The finished landscape was that of an anti-Eden badly in need of repair, a Garden that had shifted "away from the tranquility of Paradise" toward savagery, where the "ferocious appetites and unrestrained sexuality" of the natives represented "the precise opposite of Christian society, as conceived by the Renaissance," Lestringant said.

Yet savage freedom was also implied. When a man ate human flesh, his moral character was permanently savaged, too. One popular anthology of the 19th century used such visceral frisson as a marketing tool, boasting on the title page of tales of "poor wretches forced to abandon their floating homes without food or water, thus compelling them to resort to CANNIBALISM, WITH ITS ATTENDANT HORRORS." One frequently reprinted account mixed the loss of love with the loss of humanity: the fiancée of a young ship's cook said she was "driven to the horrid alternative to preserve my own life to plead my claim to the greater portion of precious blood as it oozed, half congealed, from the wound" of her

loved one's "lifeless body." A captain in a 1710 incident in the Pacific noticed his crew's transformation as they ate the ship's carpenter: "That affectionate, peaceable temper they had all along hitherto, [I] discovered
totally lost; their eyes staring and looking wild, their countenances fierce
and barbarous." Among the Donner Party, survivors "dreamed maniacal
dreams of hunger, and awoke trying to sink their teeth into the hands and
arms of their companions." The guilt never really left them: as they ate,
they wept in shame and at night "wailed and shrieked" in their dreams.
Savagery seemed permanently etched in some. Lewis Keseberg, the last
man rescued, reportedly said the flesh of Mrs. Tamsen Donner was the
best he'd ever tasted. Years later, still professing a preference for human
brains and liver, he opened a restaurant in Sacramento.

It was at sea, however, that survival cannibalism achieved its greatest
level of ritual, one so accepted as to be called "the custom of the sea." *Custom*, like "habit" or "fashion," a duty paid by one so many could survive. Just
as sailors knew that drinking seawater drove men to madness, they
accepted the necessity of eating one of their own for others to live. The
procedure was simple: a victim was selected by drawing lots, then killed
and bled so the blood could be drunk (since thirst was greater than
hunger). The heart and liver were eaten next, since these were most per-
ishable, then the rest of the body was butchered.

Unfortunately, a customary hypocrisy existed in the way the lots fell.
There was a strange consistency in most accounts: though it was supposed
to be random, the order of sacrifice followed a pattern. First to be eaten
were those who died of natural causes, an understandable choice since
guilt and murder were not involved. But after that, the burden fell regularly on the most isolated and vulnerable. Slaves were eaten first, then
blacks before whites, women before men, passengers before crew, unpopu-
lar crew members, boys, then crew. The ship's hierarchy was rigidly maintained: cabin boys and apprentices died first, followed by "idlers"
(carpenters, cooks, stewards, sailmakers, and boatswains), then seamen and
officers. It's beyond belief that random drawings accounted for this order.
What becomes evident is that little fairness existed in the drawing of the
lots. Fairness was an afterthought, added to the accounts by survivors.

The granddaddy of all seagoing cannibal accounts was the wreck of the
French frigate *Medusa* in June 1816. Two survivors wrote accounts, which
inspired Théodore Géricault's monumental painting *Radeau de la Meduse*.

The English translations became bestsellers. Of the 150 soldiers and sailors stranded on a flimsy raft 40 miles off the coast of Senegal, only a tenth survived the two-and-a-half-week ordeal. The *Medusa's* fame arose not only from cannibalism, as corpses were eaten, but also from the apocalyptic madness that gripped the raft, largely explained by the fact that there was only food enough for one meal, but barrels and barrels of wine. As the castaways drank to excess, mutiny broke out and officers counterattacked to quell the rebellion. Strange derangements arose: erstwhile saviors told their friends that "they were going to fetch succor, plunged headlong into the sea, and perished," while others believed their raft-mates mocked them "by holding out temptingly the wings of chickens and other delicacies, and for this they rushed on them with drawn swords." By Day 4 on the raft, "those whom death had spared . . . fell upon the dead bodies with which the raft was covered, and cut off pieces which some instantly devoured." They also ate sword belts, linen, hats, and excrement. Thirteen sick and wounded were thrown overboard to save rations. When rescue came on Day 17, there were 15 survivors, and of these, six died soon after rescue.

Above all else, the *Medusa* illustrated a simple rule of violence: once begun, it assumed a life of its own. There comes a point when adopting group madness seems the wisest choice, and only an extraordinary act of will, or an extremely lucky accident, can break the chain. The crew's cannibal embrace, the captain's acquiescence . . . both created the moment when the tiny world of the longboat shifted to delirium.

Perhaps there is a point at which acceptance of one madness opens a door to all others. Although eating others would seem to make sense as starving individuals grasp for the last available nutrients, studies have shown that when the cannibal act shifts from eating the dead to eating the living, it becomes group suicide. The "cruel mathematics" of cannibalism, as Nathaniel Philbrick called it in his study of the *Essex,* seem logical, since each sacrifice provides survivors with meat while reducing by one the number of people with whom it will be shared. But anthropologists have determined that this is an illusion. Although the average healthy adult provides about 66 pounds of edible meat, starvation victims are another matter. Autopsies reveal a dramatic loss of muscle tissue and a complete absence of fat, both consumed in the body's need for nutrients and turned into an indigestible glutinous material. The internal organs have shrunk as well. Given these changes, the body of a starvation victim yields barely half the edible mass of a healthy adult, and usually less. Eating the number of unhealthy adults needed to regain a modicum of strength would quickly deplete the manpower of the boat: worse, it was also a futile gesture. The flesh of a starvation victim lacks the fat required by the human body to digest meat. A fat-rich turtle might save them, but all the meat from all the men on the boat would be nearly useless without a corresponding source of fat to aid digestion.

At this point, a lucky accident occurred, possibly saving those in the longboat from leaping at each other's throats like the madmen of the *Medusa*. The block—the wooden pulley attached to the top of the mast through which passed the halyard to raise and lower the sail—was failing. For the past few days its sheave—the wooden wheel over which the rope passed—had stuck, the first sign when a block starts to deform. Although one of the most ancient mechanical devices on any boat, the block is quite essential, for without it they'd lose all sail control.

That morning, as the crew agreed on their final destination, the inevitable occurred. Mitchell pulled on the "falls," the trailing end of the halyard, to adjust the sail for their more northerly course, but the sail refused to budge. He pulled again—but no good. The sail was stuck fast. The men looked at each other, sick at heart. Despite their weakness, someone would have to shinny up the mast and bring down the block for repair.

Mr. Thomas tried first. The mere act of standing nearly ended the attempt; his vision turned white and his heartbeat pounded in his ears. He clung weakly to the mast and heard voices ask if he was all right, but these came as if from a tunnel. When the sickness passed, the real ordeal began. A month ago, the act of going up the mast would have been as natural for Thomas as breathing or walking, but now he clung to the pole like a green hand on his maiden cruise. In a seaway, a masthead's movement is grotesquely amplified and swings at the top like a pendulum. Thomas clung to the mast like an insect on a stick; his face went white and he shut his eyes. No crewmate laughed, for each could feel his nausea. He got to the top and found the problem: the wooden pin on which the sheave turned had bent, jamming the flanges sideways in the groove.

He'd have to take the block apart and carve a new pin, but first they must fashion a temporary block through which to reeve the halyard. A clew-iron, the round shackle securing a sail's lower corner, could serve as a wheelless "bull's-eye" block, but the metal would sever the rope if left too long. Thomas had begun lashing one to the top of the mast when his vertigo caught up with him. He slid down the pole, ashamed of himself—but it was quit or fall into the sea.

Joe Campbell, a conspirator, volunteered. For now the conspiracy was forgotten—every sailor understood that they'd turn beam-end to the waves and founder if they lost all power from the sail. "I'll take over, Mr. Thomas," Campbell said, while others helped the third mate down. "Take it slow, in steps," Thomas gasped. He sank against the thwart and seemed to faint away.

It took Campbell two tries to finish the job. On the first trip, he completed the lashing of the clew-iron, then rove the halyard from the broken block and into the bull's-eye. He slid down the mast, shuddering. "You want me to take over?" asked Morris, but Campbell said he needed a breather, was all. He shinnied back up, cut loose the lashings of the damaged block, and passed it down. With that, exhaustion washed over him: every muscle quivered like aspic and he dropped down to waiting hands. Both Thomas and Campbell were out for the rest of the day: their exertions were a success, though only temporary, for the sail raised and lowered indifferently. As soon as they fixed the pin on the block, someone would have to go up again.

The night of June 6–7 was filled with dreams of food. Thomas Tate gnawed on his fist and whimpered in his sleep that no meat remained on the bone. Henry remembered every morsel of food he'd discarded and said, "We think with remorse of how much we have wasted when we had plenty." He thought of his dog Toby at home and the scraps they fed him from the table: "If I only had what Toby lives on, I would do well." He remembered the pigs' swill at a neighbor's farm in Stamford and imagined how the mess "would supply us all."

That night his dreams were forbidding. He saw himself covered in blood as when they'd slaughtered the turtle, lips red, hands dripping with gore. He smiled as he ate, his entire body recalling the creamy globs of turtle fat, the yolk sacs bursting on his tongue, the rush of nutrients like a healing river. It was the most sensual dream he'd ever experienced, more sensual than any concerning the luscious Josie Taylor or the delicious sisters Elie and Maggie Wendell. He stripped them of their doilies and dove in with a knife and sharp teeth. What delights there were to sample among the well-fed girls of Stamford town.

"May He preserve our reason," Henry wrote the next day.

Fred Clough's dreams were more peaceful. He was watching a rosy sunset to the west, the herald of a storm, when suddenly, in a blink, he was home in Thomaston with a feast on the table. He saw and smelled the foods he loved: turkey and oyster dressing, hashed fowl, potato puffs, tomato sweetbreads, onion ormoloo, molasses gingerbread, and a chocolate pudding quivering in its bowl. He felt like royalty, but no king ever loved the riches spread before him as much as Fred loved his dream-meal.

No such blessing came to Mitchell. He no longer slept after Cox's warning. Thursday, June 7—Day 36 in the boat—was a "beautiful June day," Mitchell recorded. They ran all day to the west and made a reading of Lat. 16°36' N, Long. 136° W, averaging 200 to 250 miles from noon to noon. It seemed like cause for hope, but for him no hope remained. "Failing fast . . . a day or two more and all will be over. Oh God, have mercy on us and forgive us our sins." Forgive us the boats left somewhere behind, he thought, and some of the men noticed his glances over his shoulder. If only he'd see a speck, the faintest dot, then his sins would be expunged. Forgive us the sacrifice of others in the name of duty. But the sea behind was like the sea in front, and that sea was no longer a comfort for him.

All that day and into the next they rode before the northeast trades. Mr. Thomas worked on the damaged block, shaving a new pin down to size, repairing the sheaves. "Men quiet and all seem resigned," wrote Mitchell. "A better feeling prevails." But he knew it was only because they were all too weak even to feel mad. They'd become automatons instead.

Clough watched Thomas in his endless whittling and slipped into a fugue. He looked at what remained of himself and realized he was being whittled like that slip of wood. He lay and slept in every strange contortion, muscles numbed and cramped, pain centered in his hands, arms, back, and legs. The pain throbbed like a heartbeat; the skin on the back of his hands was burned, peeling, and always seemed to bleed. His nose felt huge and chapped, too sore to touch; the skin beneath his clothes looked pasty white and wrinkled, like that of a waterlogged corpse. He was the Flying Dutchman, doomed to sail the seas and never rest, perched at the lip of death but never dragged in.

That day, Henry imagined showing up for Class Day at Trinity. "How different it is at College today," he said. "All enjoying themselves." The class of 1866 was clad in gowns and mortarboard, "bidding their farewells." He envisioned himself appearing at the podium, skeletal and ragged, leering at the crowd. "Little did I think last year that I would pass the next Class Day in this manner," he told them, smiling with the irony. The seniors, so full of hope and promise, gaped at the skeleton above them, skin burned black as the gowns of graduation, eyes sunk in its skull. This is what awaits you, Henry told his friends. I have seen the future. It is in the sea.

That afternoon of June 8, Mr. Thomas fixed the block; after some difficulty, he and Mitchell lowered the sail. Now it was Harry Morris's turn to do the impossible. He wriggled to the top of the mast, cut loose the clew-iron, then lashed tight the repaired block in its stead. He rove the halyard through the hole and over the greased sheave. "Get down, Harry, good work," said Mitchell. Morris dropped back to the boat as if slain. The rope ran through the block like silk, raising the sail as smoothly as ever. Harry crawled back to his place and hung over the side, wracked by heaves. They gave him an extra ration of water that night, the best they could spare.

The next day, June 9, a Saturday, Mitchell divided the last tin of soup and broth, then dropped the tin overboard. Like the message in the bottle, it floated off and disappeared. "That's it, boys," he said. "The last of the stores." It was the 38th day in the boat and Mitchell grimly wrote, "We still live. High seas and fresh Trades, running for Sandwich Islands. Some of the men will be able to reach there, they are young and strong." He looked at his men. Youth passed like life, but nothing in his life prepared him for what they'd endured. Would he live? "I never shall," he added, "except for the great mercy of my Heavenly Father."

But mercy was like an island: out of sight, out of reach—always over the horizon.

THE LOTTERY

W HO WOULD LIVE, WHO DIE? All neared death, signaled by the swelling of their hands and feet, the paper-thinness of their skin, the bruised pigment around their pus-filled eyes. These were the vestments for the gamble they'd soon take, the dress-code for the lottery, though in theory, they could actually starve much longer. Antonio Viterbi, a Corsican lawyer sentenced to death in 1821, lasted 17 days without water or food, but with water the time expanded geometrically. An Italian researcher in 1890 fasted repeatedly in a friend's laboratory, each time for 30 days. In 1931, an inmate in the French penitentiary at Toulouse existed for 63 days on water alone. The master starver was a collie named Oscar: near death on Day 45, he recovered after feeding, then survived another 72 days without food.

On June 10, Day 39 in the boat, the men were obsessed with food. "We are fast starving to death," said Mitchell, driven to take "what nourishment we can get from boot legs and such chewable matter." Over the next days they mimicked termites in a lumber yard. On June 9, they cut their boots into small pieces and chewed the leather; on June 10, the one-pound ham bone was scraped with knives and devoured. "Our ham bone has given us a taste of good today," wrote Henry. "Certainly never was there such a sweet knuckle bone or one which was so thoroughly appreciated." Mitchell cut its canvas cover into equal pieces, the last division of food he ever made.

On June 9 or 10, they cut through a shoal of flying fish and four fell in the boat, which were cut into fifteen pieces and instantly devoured. Instead of relieving hunger, the small portion of protein and fat turned them ravenous. They attacked the small oaken butter tub, breaking it apart and dividing the staves. They gnawed the wood for tastes of rancid butter and saline. The forgotten shell of the green turtle was scraped and eaten. They chewed up the last tobacco.

By June 10, they sipped a porridge of scraped boot leather, water, and wood shavings from the butter tub. They ate pieces of leather tacked to the thwarts or wrapped around the oars, and for dessert downed thin strips of shirts and handkerchiefs, developing a taste for fine clothing. Cotton held its flavor best, but bits of silk handkerchief slid so delightfully over the tongue and down the gullet that one imagined a cream pudding or fine Madeira wine.

Jimmy Cox became convinced one could go mad from dreams of food. Every cell in his body felt besieged by hunger, every thought occupied by visions of past meals. He'd drop off and see bread, fowl, and *meat!!*, steaming from the oven, the smells like opium. He'd seize the closest dish and bring it to his lips, but then would wake and see the same empty sea.

The real danger now was thirst, and dehydration quietly ensnared every castaway. The trades that kept them scudding west pushed storm clouds from their path; they'd had no hard rain to refill the cask in weeks, and were down to a sip of water in the morning and another before dark. The salt that encrusted the leather boots, leather strips, pieces of cloth, and ham they devoured poured fuel on their thirst, forcing their kidneys to extract extra fluid from their bodies to excrete the additional salt. Excessive amounts of sodium in the body can bring on convulsions, a condition called *hypernatremia*, which Possene and Neil Turner may have had.

The tortures of thirst were certain unless rain replenished their stores. The adult human is about 70 to 73 percent water, a level maintained within narrow limits. In a normal day, the process of replenishing water accounts for a .25 percent fluctuation in body weight: when a person loses more than .50 percent, he feels thirsty. Water loss is continuous, through the lungs, skin, and urine, and although some fluid is replaced by a spongelike effect of the skin, it is primarily by drinking that water is restored. When this is not possible, one suffers "dehydration exhaustion," a condition in which circulation slows from a decrease of blood volume. In a hot climate, the blood can lose two or three times its normal volume; soon, without circulation, cells begin to die.

Researchers speak of three "types" of thirst: Ordinary Thirst, found in humid lands, where the air is filled with water vapor and the body is little affected by salts outside the system; Desert Thirst, where water in both liquid and vapor form is absent and free salts are lacking; and the Thirst of the Sea, where vapor is plentiful, potable water is not, and free-floating salts abound. Desert Thirst kills fastest, but all proceed in the same manner. Humans can tolerate water loss of up to 3 to 4 percent of body weight with moderate impairment: the skin flushes, heat is more oppressive than usual, and weariness, impatience, and vertigo are noticeable. At 5–8 percent, it is hard to stand, and at more than 10 percent, general deterioration sets in. It has been said that the limits of dehydration occur between 15 to 25 percent, when victims go mad and die.

On the ocean this final phase lasts as long as 10 to 15 days, while in the desert it is much shorter—a few hours to an entire day. In either place, the process is not a pretty one. The victim experiences restlessness, delirium, and hysteria; the tongue swells, swallowing becomes impossible, the mouth goes numb. One survivor recalled that his tongue, "cleaving to the roof of my mouth, was as useless as a dry stick until I was able to loosen it by a few drops of my . . . urine." The face shrivels; the eyes sink, molding to the skull. Vision dims, partial deafness sets in, and bloody cracks crease the skin. After a 12 percent loss, a person can no longer swallow water even if offered: he is helpless and must take fluid intravenously or by a stomach tube.

Although the men in the boat had not reached this point, they had entered the "cotton-mouth" phase. At this point, the saliva is thick and foul-tasting; the tongue begins clinging to the teeth; the voice grows cracked and the throat sore. Fred felt a lump grow in his throat that a day's worth of swallowing could not dislodge; Samuel felt sharp pains in his forehead and neck; Mitchell felt as if his skin stretched thinner and thinner. Some hallucinated.

This is a dangerous time. Although rational thought is still possible, increasingly illogical choices determine the path of the body and mind. A mind is pushed by thirst as a boat is pushed by wind: thirst becomes a deterministic force, and the imagination takes new and frightening directions. Although the first physical symptoms of thirst are similar to hunger, its mental effects are an evil twin. Where a starvation victim imagines sumptuous meals, those suffering thirst imagine themselves as insects in "the focus of a burning-glass," one desert traveler said. "The throat parches and seems to be closing. The eye-balls burn as though from a scorching fire."Relief is still possible at this stage, although extreme. The most common salvation was drinking one's urine, but urination could be so painful that people cried aloud in agony. By June 10–11, the ravages of thirst were well-advanced and the men's throats felt afire. Samuel doubted he'd last much longer on two daily sips of water: "I don't feel the stint of food so much as I do water," he wrote, marveling that "Henry, who is naturally a large water-drinker, can save his one-half allowance from time to time." Such self-control was beyond his power.

What Samuel saw as self-discipline, Henry knew as despair. His brother was dying before his eyes. Samuel was weak as an infant, barely moving in the bottom of the boat for hours at a time. He only came to life when water passed his lips, so Henry saved his morning ration and shared it through the midday heat with Samuel. It was endure the thirst or watch his brother turn to dust, but in the evening, the day's last sip never tasted so good.

By June 10–11, most sailors bridged the morning and evening rations by drinking their urine. Henry does not mention it, but the omission was probably out of delicacy. The men up front talked quietly at night about who should be the first to die. Some favored Thomas Tate, whose sobs grew weaker; others thought Neil Turner would be the first as the abscess in his hip bored deep and he moaned he was ready to die. All would be happy if Possene died first, but his will to live was as prodigious as his appetite. After the food ran out, he ate two handkerchiefs, two cotton shirts, and his division of boots, bones, and lumber. Possene wouldn't die quickly, unless someone helped him.

The great favorite was Samuel. Henry watched as others stole glances at him with what resembled greed. He wondered whether Samuel knew how patiently they waited. "He will die Saturday," Joe Campbell hoped, but Saturday passed and Samuel endured. Sunday and Monday, too. Henry wanted to laugh at their disappointment, but mockery would be a dangerous gesture.

At least most were quiet about their hopes, but not Harry Morris. The Frenchman kept his eyes on Samuel's face, noting his failing strength with care and cheer. "I think he will go off pretty soon, don't you, Mr. Thomas?" he said one night.

"Leave the poor devil to his rest. What does it matter?"

"It matters because we'll eat him."

It was truly a race for life now that dehydration was a factor. The 200-mile clip each day was in their favor, and most believed they could endure the hunger until Hawaii. Thirst, however, was another matter. Death by blazing thirst seems so excessive that its very existence challenges the notion of a just and kind God. The body's integrity becomes a myth and what remains is a travesty of all that was thought human. For life to continue in such a state seems impossible, yet in 1906 a 43-year-old sailor-turned-prospector named Pablo Valencia showed that it could be done. Valencia survived seven days without water in the Arizona desert, subsisting entirely on his own urine and a few drops of moisture from a crushed scorpion. When finally discovered, he'd degenerated to a "living death," wrote his rescuer, W. J. McGee:

> his ribs edged out like those of a starveling horse; his . . . abdomen was drawn in almost against his vertebral column; his lips had disappeared as if amputated, leaving low edges of blackened tissue; his teeth and gums projected like those of a skinned animal . . . his nose was withered and shrunken.

McGee could have been describing a creature from the Grand Guignol. The skin around Valencia's eyes was pulled back into a "winkless stare"; his skin was a "ghastly purplish, yet ashen gray"; his extremities were laced with so many bloodless cuts that the effect was one of "dry leather." Yet just as amazing was his recuperation. When McGee rubbed water onto his leg, the skin shed off, then absorbed liquid as "greedily as a dry sponge." In thirty minutes, Valencia could swallow water in feeble gulps; within an hour he could drink, and in two hours, ate "bird fricassee." He walked within a day. By then, his skin had softened and his numerous wounds were leaking blood—he begged constantly for "agua, agua," as his cells soaked up fluid. Within a week, he was again a picture of health, the only sign his hair, which "turned iron-gray."

One temptation in such distress was to drink seawater, but the results were just as grim, if not worse, a last-ditch expedient sailors associated with delirium, madness, and death. Fiery thirst results when water from the rest of the body is sucked through the stomach lining to dilute the higher concentration of salt in seawater; when more seawater is drunk to quench that thirst, a fatal spiral begins. Cells contract when dehydrated, and in the brain, neural shrinkage causes delusions and insanity. A 1943 British survey of shipwreck deaths concluded that "seawater poisoning must be accounted, after cold, the commonest cause of death . . . there comes a breaking point in the dehydrated person's resistance, when . . . he succumbs to the temptation of drinking the fluid which is all around him." This is done furtively, "after nightfall or during the process of bathing the head and face." As in accounts of cannibalism, a moral tone ensued regarding class and nationality: "This giving way . . . varies in time, occurring very early in Lascar [Indian or Southeast Asian] seamen and late in the men of stouter morale, more especially if they are in a position of authority."

But in the end, the temptation to drink overwhelmed all castaways. An immediate slaking of thirst was followed by an unmerciful need for water, requiring more copious drinks. Soon the victim grew silent and listless "with a peculiar fixed and glassy expression in the eyes." Within two hours, delirium set in, starting quietly, then "violent and unrestrained." Death was almost certain: "the most common ending was for a victim to jump over the side of the raft into the sea."

By the night of Monday, June 11, it is likely that some in the longboat were drinking seawater. Their behavior grew erratic; they raised their voices, then shushed for quiet, making it plain to Mitchell that all did not bode well. As if starvation and dehydration weren't enough, they may have also suffered from extreme magnesium deficiency, known to cause violent or bizarre behavior. Sometime after midnight, Jimmy Cox crawled aft again and whispered a bizarre story into Henry's ear. Harry Morris had convinced the men that Mitchell saved the ship's treasury during the fire, smuggling it aboard the longboat when no one noticed. He stowed it under his seat by the tiller, the reason he never left that spot, Harry said. Clipper captains were given huge sums to transport between coasts, and Mitchell was guarding a million in gold coin.

A million, Harry emphasized. More gold than *all* of them would see in their lives, and by rights, it should be theirs. They'd rush Mitchell while he slept, then dump him over the side. The Fergusons, too. They'd split the gold and no one would be wiser. If Jimmy helped, he'd get an equal share. If not, they'd kill him, too.

"That's insane!" Henry said, and Jimmy warned him to keep it down. "A million in coin would break through the bottom. No man could carry it all."

"They say you two helped. Your brother's a banker, right? They say he arranged it all."

Henry was stunned. It came down to this, a floating dream of El Dorado, sacks filled with pieces of eight. A redistribution of the wealth in the age-old tongue of piracy. Maybe some would die in the attack, but they were dying anyway. They'd rise to the top of the heap, if only briefly, before they fell mad and died. They'd dine off the corpses of the rich, just as the rich for ages had feasted off the poor. They'd sail to some unknown paradise and start over again.

It sounded lovely, as only desperate visions can. A dream of apocalypse and paradise that swept them all away. Henry felt his heart flutter in his chest; he was truly frightened. How could one person turn aside such hatred? Despite one's efforts, events spiraled out of control.

"What will they do when they kill us and find there's no gold?" he asked.

"Kill each other," Jimmy said. There was silence, then from the darkness his voice sounded as old as the captain's, maybe older. "I tried to argue, Mr. Ferguson, but they're past listening. I'm just a boy, they say. I'm too young to know the way things are."

THE MORNING OF Tuesday, June 12, was spent waiting for a sign. A moment of inattention or weakness: any signal would do. The two groups faced each other across the no-man's land of the water cask, but no one took the initiative. The pain of thirst and hunger were still dominant. It was easier to wait, lulled by constant wind and waves.

The stares . . . these too were constant, unblinking and unwavering. It was obvious to Fred that someone had told the stern about the forecastle's plans. He thought he knew the culprit. A day ago this suspicion would have enraged him beyond reason: there's a traitor among us, he would have cried, and such bilge is best dumped overboard. Late last night as the others slept, he felt someone brush past him in the darkness; a few seconds later, he heard whispers in the stern. When he recognized the voices of Cox and Henry Ferguson, he knew the truth.

Surprisingly, he did not care. He knew that if he reported his discovery, the men up front would kill the cabin boy and maybe even eat him, just to show Mitchell who was in charge. He could decide the boy's fate like a Roman emperor. Thumbs up, or thumbs down.

Fred thought about such power, and did a mental shrug. Why shouldn't Jimmy remain loyal to Mitchell? It was the right thing to do. The Old Man had pulled him off Parr's boat; there was an equal chance it was the spar from that boat they'd seen floating after the storm. Fred could hate the captain and two brothers for what they represented, but he couldn't blame Jimmy Cox for risking all for the man who'd saved his skin.

So he held his tongue, sparing the life of a cabin boy.

He watched Mitchell get the noon fix, as religious about his daily reading as Samuel Ferguson with his little red Book of Common Prayer. Mitchell made the calculations, wrapped his chronometer in faded red silk before thrusting it in his pocket, and returned the sextant to its watertight compartment in the stern. They were 600 to 700 miles from Hawaii and making good time, he said. He opened his journal to record the position when he said in surprise, "I'll be damned. I'd forgotten today is my birthday. I'm 56 years old."

"Happy birthday, Captain," Fred and some other crewmen said.

As had the incident of the broken block, the announcement of Mitchell's birthday delayed the mutiny by at least a day. It wasn't right to kill a man on his birthday, not after all they'd been through together. Mitchell sensed the break in tension and knew it as a reprieve. "Still permitted to live and write," he scrawled with relief. "God grant it may be to me a new birth day for the soul." The day was pleasant, their clip was brisk, and if he dared entertain hope, was that a sin? "We have been spared so long, 40 days today, that we dare think we may arrive," he said, and dreamed of the islands ahead. The women there had a fancy for yellow wreaths, not the grays and blacks of his New England home. Small communities of captain's wives had formed in ports like Hilo, Lahaina, and Honolulu, and he wondered if Susan would like it there. They were said to flourish in Hawaii, and in the middle of a lonely ocean had found friends.

Mitchell wondered if Susan remembered his birthday or had forgotten it, like him. His head had troubled him yesterday, but recalling Susan's depression troubled him more. He felt at a loss for what to do. She felt abandoned by everything: him, their grown children, young Flora who grew more independent daily. He'd asked Susan several times to accompany him on trips, but she could never stand the sea. Such requests produced recriminations, so he no longer tried. By now she was visiting Mary in Detroit; perhaps her absence from Freeport kept her ignorant of the *Hornet's* disappearance. She always stayed on a farm outside the city during these visits: such returns to the country were the only time when she was her old happy self, "carried away and beyond this animal life into the more real and ideal."

He wrote a birthday letter to his family in the back pages of his journal, one that might make it to them even if he did not live. "Again I am still spared," he began:

It's the 12th of June, a lovely day as my birthdays have ever been. I pray God it may be a birthday of the soul born into Christ. Oh darling wife and children, I think if I am ever permitted to see you again, I shall try to be more of a dutiful father than I have ever been. No parent could love his children more, but I feel that I have neglected my duty in not leading you to Christ. Should this ever reach you girls and Harry, *do not fail* of making Jesus your friend, *now* early in life. You can always rely upon Him steadfast and sure. I trust and pray that my sins are pardoned and that we shall all meet in heaven at last. You never can realize what a trial this has been. And still by God's great mercy preserved forty days today on the ocean with not stores enough to last a week, and sailed over 3,000 miles in an open boat with 15 men crowded into her. The ship was burned very carelessly by the Mate. Oh how much suffering it has caused. We are very nearly starved. It's with great difficulty I can stand. Growing weak fast, sands will soon be run. God bless you all now and forever and may you all be happy in this world and the world to come.

Samuel also considered the world to come. While others neared the Sandwich Islands, he approached a different kind of Paradise. He'd lived with Death a long time, almost like a cordial neighbor whose presence was felt but whose face was never seen. Now Death had come to visit and Samuel couldn't hide forever. But maybe he could use the little time left for one meaningful deed. He took the pistol from his pocket and inspected it— he thought the cap was wet but didn't dare test it, since doing so risked misfire. He slipped it back into his pocket and must have slipped into a frequent faint, for the next thing he knew, it was evening and Henry pressed water to his lips. He could make out light and shadow, but little form. His sight improved and he could make out his brother's face. "Henry," he croaked, "take the gun tonight and put it in your pocket. I'm useless if something starts." He took a deep breath. "I may be going blind."

There was silence, and Samuel wondered if he'd blacked out again. There was no longer any way of knowing: his conscious life turned on and off like a lamp, minus the tell-tale sputter. "If I die, I want you to do something for me," he added.

Out of the darkness, Henry answered, "Anything."

"I want you to throw my body overboard before the others get me. It's better that you do this than watch me be eaten." The effort to talk was so exhausting that he could feel himself slip back toward unconsciousness. "Promise me, Henry," he insisted. "Do it at night, when the others can't see you." Before Henry could protest, Samuel had fainted away.

Henry lowered his brother to the floor. *Throw my body overboard.* A line from Aristophanes entered his head: "Whirl is king, having driven out Zeus." When sanity was abandoned, chaos took over. Out here, Whirl was king.

Henry laughed, a little insane himself. They drifted aimlessly in this boat, acting out their comedies. Some men were heroes in death, but they played the fools.

That night, he had the strangest dream. He dreamed in the island sense, for the Hawaiian for *dream* was "spirit sleep" in which a wandering consciousness receives messages from the spirit world. The *Kanakas*— "the people," as Hawaiians called themselves—accepted the "wandering spirit of sleep." Waking and sleeping were two sides of the same mind.

All was dark in Henry's dream, but in the distance he saw a tiny red flare and seemed to fly toward it from a very great height. The flare turned into a burning ship, its flames rising up to heaven in an incandescent pillar. Waves danced around the ship, reflecting the blaze. It was the *Hornet,* but a ship more huge than any clipper in imagination, masts towering thousands of feet, wreathed by a corona of smoke that was carried downwind. So much smoke could choke the whole world. Small figures danced in the firelight like puppets, some on fire themselves. Others danced with hands upraised, the gesticulations similar for reverence and horror. Sparks fell like a curtain. The dancers screamed and leaped into the sea.

Henry awoke on June 13 to calm water and light wind. His eyes were glued shut with dried pus; he rubbed gently and the lids separated in sticky threads. His tongue felt like a black root stuck to the roof of his mouth; he could not speak until Fred rationed the water and a few drops loosened his tongue. Fred said something to Mr. Thomas, who glanced into the cask and told the captain he'd better take a peek, too. Mitchell staggered over: the water barely covered the wooden bottom. He cut rations back to two ounces a day, but even that could not delay the inevitable. By late tomorrow evening or early the following morning, they'd run out of water.

A man up front discovered a small flying fish had landed in the boat overnight. They tore it into silvery ribbons and divided it 15 ways. The tiny shred of meat lifted their spirits, and at noon Mitchell took his reading—Lat. 20°10' N, 149°50' W—which put them north of the Sandwich Islands by a fraction of a degree. He adjusted the course. They were just a day or two from land, he said.

Such innocent words brought the long-delayed mutiny to a head. Mitchell knew even as he made the statement that he'd made a grave mistake—the men in the boat had heard such promises too often, and they had never once come true. Voices rose up front about the chronometer's accuracy: they were all experienced sailors and knew what damage the sea could do. The chronometer could be off by as much as 30 minutes, and there was no way they could test it. They were adrift in every possible sense. Without an accurate fix, they'd die.

"We can still depend on the chronometer," Mitchell said, his throat harsh and raw. "I kept it in my coat and wrapped it up for protection."

That wasn't good enough, they said. Even 15 minutes of error could put them off by 210 miles. Harry Morris rose in the bow and clung to the mast for support. "I don't think you've known where we are since Clipperton Rock," he said.

They'd all forgotten how big the Frenchman was in his prime. In full health he stood nearly six feet and was solid as a post; the muscles in his arms and calves were knotted like cord. Now he was a scarecrow, his gray-streaked beard covering his cheeks and throat, his forearms thin as sticks, the backs of his hands oozing with sores. "Not only are you lost, I think you're lying," he said. He reached into his pocket for his jackknife. "I think you've been hiding something from us, and it's time to share it evenly, like the food."

The 13 men and boys between Harry Morris and Josiah Mitchell froze in place, amazed. This was it . . . the mutiny they'd expected . . . a situation that entered every sailor's mind, but one in which few ever participate. It came upon them suddenly, called up by Mitchell's innocuous estimate of their distance from Hawaii and Mr. Thomas's observation of their water supply, and there was no convenient emergency like the broken block to divert their anger. Harry Morris had struggled to his feet to make his accusations. Given his weakness, the physical statement was as powerful as the words.

"Harry, for God's sake, give it up," hissed Thomas, voice trembling. "Sit down before someone gets killed."

But Mitchell answered sadly that it was just as well that the moment was here. He heard a movement to his left and, glancing over, saw Henry draw the butt of his brother's revolver from the folds of his coat. He'd been unaware that Henry had taken it, and felt grateful for such foresight. Even now, the older brother lay unconscious, curled in a ball on the bottom of the boat, the only sign of life a faint fluttering of his eyes. He looked at the boy and told him to put it away. Henry rearranged the folds of his coat, but kept his hand on the gun.

"Do you really think I have gold coins stowed back here?" he asked, facing Morris again. He rose painfully from his seat and steadied himself against his vertigo. The troubles in his head were growing worse: it was the first mutiny he'd ever faced in his life, and he was forced to do so after 40 days' starvation. Worse than unfair, it was unsporting—and that angered him, an anger that gave him an energy surprising everyone, himself most of all. "How could I possibly sneak a million dollars into this boat? Yes, I know what you've been saying. *Nothing* is secret on this boat, not even the fact that none of us have moved our bowels for twenty days." He threw open the hatch of the watertight compartment that had served as his seat for so long. "There are no secrets here!" He glared at the men and invited one to take a look, then beckoned to Fred Clough.

Why the farmer's son from Thomaston? Although Fred's sympathies lay with his brother sailors, he was trusted by all, as shown by his role of guarding the water cask and helping Mr. Thomas with rations. By all accounts, he did so impartially. Although he was young and hotheaded enough to side with his mates in their frustration over the captain's mistakes, he could also admit Mitchell wasn't entirely to blame. But now words had given way to action, and Mitchell must disprove the tales of hidden millions for any hope to live. He could only do so at the word of a sailor—and not one was more trusted than Fred.

An anticipatory silence fell over the little floating world. Mitchell moved away from his seat and Fred looked in the compartment. There was at least one other stern compartment, over by Henry, and Fred threw it open, too. "What'd you find?"shouted Harry Morris.

"Nothing," Fred replied.

The word hung before them, followed by voices. "There's got to be something! He's hidden it somewhere."

"Where?" Fred cried, laughing at the absurdity of it all. Maybe some of his friends *had* drunk seawater: how else to explain their obsession? He told them what he saw, while those amidships could bend forward and see for themselves. The compartments supposedly filled with gold contained small pools of water, scraps and shreds of canvas, a piece of rope stiffened by the salt and sun. Fred thrust in his hands and held up the items, one by one. That was it, he said—they'd run through everything else like locusts in their efforts to survive. They'd even eaten wood. "There's no money, nothing!" he stated, staring straight at the Frenchman. "The captain made mistakes, but he never lied to us. He played straight since the beginning!" Fred slammed the hatches shut and realized as he did so that Mitchell had placed his life in his hands.

He turned to the stern and saw that his captain was watching him. Fred smiled at Mitchell for his trust, then wheeled back to the front. "You were wrong, Harry," he sighed, lowering himself gently. "There's nothing's there, and never was."

With that, the mutiny ended, but death by hunger, thirst, or misdirection remained. Mitchell might have thwarted rebellion, but the threat of cannibalism still hung over them. He could not stop their decision to draw lots, and knew it. All he could do was delay.

He tried bucking up their spirits that evening, explaining that on a line to Hawaii, they should be about 300 miles away. He constantly searched for confirmation: the columns of cloud rearing up on thermal currents, the seaweed and flotsam that signaled land. Even the distant star of a ship's light would be welcome, if only to make it less lonely out here. He did see a sign, but behind them. The sun was sinking when Henry looked back. "Look at that, it's beautiful!"

They all glanced back and saw a double rainbow. The sharpest arc bled from fiery red to an inner, prismatic purple; both legs seemed to touch the sea. The sky beneath the curve seemed unnaturally clear, the blues and whites within its arc approaching a kind of perfection few had ever seen. Above the main rainbow curved its pale brother, its colors a reversal of the first, legs fading to mist above the sea. "Cheer up, boys!" cried Mitchell. "It's a prophecy. It's the Bow of Promise!" But no one responded. They didn't believe in omens anymore.

That night, Henry saw a new moon. Maybe, he thought . . . maybe Mitchell was right and they'd been preserved for a purpose. Maybe salvation was near. But the morning of Thursday, June 14, was unforgiving. The wind was strong and constant; the sun glowed white-hot from a cloudless sky. At noon, Mitchell took the daily reading—Lat. 20° N, Long. 152° W—and croaked that they were only 100 to 200 miles distant. "God has been very merciful," he wrote, yet added ominously that water remained for only one more day.

One more day. After tomorrow noon, the minimal relief provided by the twice-daily sips would be history. After tomorrow noon, the men up front who'd secretly sipped seawater would take greater draughts, no longer caring if they were seen. After tomorrow noon, the healthiest would sicken, the sick would fight delirium, and those battling unconsciousness would die.

After tomorrow noon, they'd begin the custom of the sea.

Samuel could not last another day. Henry gently raised his brother's head for his morning water and watched the drops dribble from the corners of his lips. The inside of his mouth was black; his tongue was a gnarled integument, a knob far back in his throat wriggling like a feeble worm. His forehead was burning hot; the scarlet rash that covered his skin made his body seem afire. "Samuel, drink," he urged, worried that his brother had strayed so far into unconsciousness that he'd never speak again. If Mitchell was right, they'd reach Hawaii by tomorrow; if wrong, all would die. Just one more day. What a heartless joke if Samuel, who'd taken this trip for his health, died one day short of rescue.

He couldn't let that happen, and vowed to keep his brother alive. But how? They had water enough for tonight's ration, then a few sips for morning—and then no more. He'd already divided his own morning ration, and constantly bathed his brother's forehead and face to cool his fever. He bent to his ear and talked as the hours passed . . . about their family and California, about how happy Miss Snow would be when he returned. "Think how her eyes will light up when you tell her about the waterspout," he whispered, but Samuel only groaned.

The more he talked, the less effect it seemed to have, and by afternoon Henry was in a panic of despair. The sun beat down without respite; he wet a handkerchief and tied it around Samuel's head. His aristocratic older brother resembled a grizzled pirate, and in any other circumstance he'd laugh. Not now. Samuel's breath was growing shallow; his spirit seemed to flutter in his chest with the delicacy of a bird. He was dying as Henry watched, burning to a cinder, and there seemed nothing Henry could do. He asked the captain if he could have his evening water ration early to give to Samuel. Mitchell nodded and Fred dipped the tin cup in the cask. "You won't have none yourself tonight," Clough advised him, almost tenderly.

"I can manage," Henry said.

Henry begged his brother to drink, but Samuel didn't hear; he rubbed his brother's cracked lips with a moistened finger, then poured a thin stream down his throat. Samuel's eyes fluttered momentarily; he choked and coughed, but seemed to revive. His hands reached for the cup; Henry held it steady as he drank the portion down.

Water was the only medicine available, but it seemed to do the trick. Henry made quick calculations in his mind. He'd used up his own evening rations on his brother, but Samuel's evening sip still remained. That and the evening cool would get him through the night. If he only had one more ration, it might carry Samuel through the afternoon.

He looked around him. He could ask the captain, who might hand over his ration in kindness, but they needed Mitchell alert and healthy to get them through. He asked the men up front for help, but they stared back without a word. *Please*, he begged, *he's my brother*. He can't die like this, not one day from rescue. He looked at Jimmy Cox and Mr. Thomas, at the Danish duke and Charlie Kaartman. But the survival instinct was too strong. "We're sorry," said several with whom he pleaded. "You're asking us to kill ourselves."

That left Fred. Henry turned to the guardian of the water cask, exhausted by his pleas. "I know you have a brother," he said. "You were going to Frisco to pan for gold with him." He dug into his pocket and grabbed his pocket watch. On impulse, he thrust it at the sailor. "I'll give you this in exchange."

Fred looked at his feet, embarrassed for Henry Ferguson. "Put your watch away."

"It'll bring a good price at a pawn shop. I'll give you more when we get to port."

"Put your damn watch away." And suddenly, with this second utterance, they all realized that Fred's answer would be different. Despite his disgust, he had not refused.

Perhaps he didn't know it yet, for Fred was angered beyond words. This is what it comes to, he thought: a high-hat's offer of money for something more precious than gold. He hated Henry in that instant as he stared back at the gaunt face, wide eyes, mouth frozen open in hope and surprise. Why didn't the little bastard just ask for water instead of going on about how much his watch would bring? As if there was a pawn shop here in the Pacific; as if he could eat the watch case and mainspring. That's what the rich always assumed of the poor—that they were slaves to the price of a trinket, lackeys to be bought and sold. It didn't work like that, not here. Sure it was easy to take money, but what people like Henry never understood was that you did so to survive. Survival was what ultimately mattered: the fuel that drove the anger, that primed the panic of starvation, that lurked in every shadow like a thug. Survival was the chasm dividing the rich and poor, a divide the rich would never bridge because they hadn't experienced what such a life did to a man. It twisted him to something brutal, turned him inside out with vengeance till he was ready to kill just to be heard. Eventually he assumed that killing was the *only* way to be heard. The gap would grow wider, the hatred deeper, until the entire world was like their little boat, swept by a wrath that raged like a furnace till nothing was left but ashes in a drifting hull.

Fred looked at his friends from the forecastle. They stared back, and he could read their minds. They wanted him to deny Henry. Let the brother die. Prove to the rich that gold couldn't buy off the Reaper. Let them know death as the true democracy.

He turned away, hating them for insisting that he make this choice. He hated Henry for reminding him that he too had a brother and forcing him into this spotlight before his friends. He hated Samuel Ferguson for coming so close to death, hated Sam Hardy for feeling sorry for sailors and cutting corners to start this whole mess, hated the captain for trusting so much in his charts and maps, hated the mapmakers for sitting at home with their quadrants and compasses instead of suffering for their mistakes, hated the birds and fish for not delivering themselves to his hunger, hated the rain for not falling down. All of life was just a cardhouse built of errors and all it took was the smallest jolt to knock it down.

"I don't want your watch," he snapped, then pulled back the lid of the cask, dipped out his evening ration, and handed it to Henry. He waved his hand in dismissal when Henry tried to thank him. He glanced up front and read the accusation in the eyes of his former friends.

The two extra water rations did help Samuel, at least for the remainder of that day. He returned to life and breathed easier. Henry told him what had happened. We do not know if he thanked Fred Clough: to do so would be to lower himself, but being granted another chance at life can change many things. For the first time in three days, Samuel scribbled a journal entry: "Very weak but very hopeful. Good wind and everything very promising."

Samuel slept better that night, but Henry barely slept at all. Like Fred, he'd looked in the eyes of his shipmates and had seen something frightening. They'd been cheated of life by one of their own. With that extra sip of water, Henry used up the last of his options. The next time his brother slipped into a coma, there'd be no way to save him. He'd delayed the inevitable by a day.

That night when he dreamed, it was of the inevitable. Its details were contained in "The Steward's Handbook," a slim volume left around the cabin by Henry Chisling. He'd read the passages on butchering fresh meat during the run down the Atlantic coast of South America. "Bleed the beast," the manual advised. "This is done by cutting up the gullet and severing the arteries and veins on each side of the neck. . . . The blood will now flow out quite freely."

He watched in his dream as the steward took a handful of Samuel's hair and plunged his knife into his neck; he jerked the blade sideways to sever the artery, then held a bowl against the neck to catch the blood. Sucking sounds arose from Samuel's throat; his white eyes stared up, unseeing. "Now make a slit in the stomach and run the knife right up. . . . Remove the fat from round the intestines and then pull out the intestines, paunch, and liver. Cut the gall bladder off the liver right away. Turn the kidney fat over and remove the kidneys. Now cut through the diaphragm, commonly called the skirt, which separates the organs within the chest from the intestines, and remove the lungs, heart, and thorax."

When it was over, the steward cut off Samuel's head and threw it overboard, followed by the large bones, genitals, and intestines. Henry could hear sharks fight beneath him.

The drawing of the lots would begin tomorrow. All Henry could do this last night was pray.

AT 9:00 A.M. ON FRIDAY, JUNE 15, a man up front lifted his head and said that he saw land.

Henry opened his eyes. What hoax was this? This was the day that their water ran out, when lots were cast and one would die. Must they be toyed with, too? Henry stared forward: he saw a low blue line in the west, but too often this had turned into a morning bank of cloud low on the horizon. He waved it off in disgust, weary of being deceived.

Mitchell kept his peace, knowing through experience how dangerous it was to speak. As all sank beneath the thwarts, Mitchell kept staring. His sight was dim: he wished he could see.

But by 10:30 A.M., the sailor's hopes were confirmed. "Land ho!" he shouted, this time with undisguised joy. This was no mirage. Hawaii, the easternmost island in the 1,400-mile volcanic chain, was rising from the water dead ahead. The snow-capped peak of Mauna Loa rose high into the ether; to the north, the even loftier Mauna Kea touched the clouds. There had been eruptions lately in Kilauea Crater, and steam rose in the south where lava poured into the sea.

One man fainted. Another said the sight was better than a day's rations. "Wake up," Henry rasped, running a cloth over Samuel's face. His brother's eyelids flickered. "Are we saved?"

"We are." Henry giggled like a maniac.

But they were far from saved. Mitchell knew from his charts that the port of Hilo opened somewhere in this blurry blueness, but the trades pushed them northwest and he feared skirting the island completely. He beat to the south as best his square sail let him, but by afternoon they were north of the settled areas and sailing along a desolate stretch of coast Hawaiians called "the windward side." Though he searched for a landing, only stark lava cliffs rose from the water. At the top he could see a green tableland filled with grass, trees, and fields, but down here, breakers smashed against the black cliffs with nothing at the base to provide even a handhold.

No one in the boat seemed to care. They couldn't believe the panorama spread before them, richer and more sumptuous than the false feasts of their dreams. After 43 days and eight hours of blue sky and ocean, they were overwhelmed by verdancy. The place was as lush as Eden, trembling with color, yet out of reach overhead. Down here, the sea smashed against the cliffs, but it didn't matter to them. "It's good to see green fields again," said a man in the bow.

Mitchell wasn't so easily satisfied. Running too close risked being crushed against the rocks; a reef ran parallel to the cliffs, without break, for miles. Attempting to land in daylight was treacherous enough. But evening approached, and making a night landing was suicide.

By 4:00 P.M., he thought he'd found his answer. He spotted an opening in the reef and beyond that the tiny village of Laupahoehoe, the only inhabited spot for 35 miles. The name itself meant "leaf of lava," an accurate description for the thin lava trail that had pushed into the sea along a narrow valley, the path of Mauna Kea's last volcanic convulsion eons ago. A white fringe of sand divided the black rock from the water: three rows of combers marked where the sea floor angled up and the reef formed a barricade. At the edge of the beach sprouted a grove of coconut trees; small cabins nestled among their trunks. They shouted for help, but no one seemed to hear.

"Maybe we can lower the sails and row in," Mitchell said. Mr. Thomas cut the halyard and the sail clattered down. Yet no sooner were they through the first break in the reef than they saw the impossibility of continuing. The reef was a hidden maze of deadly traps; jagged rocks rose from the surf like a mouthful of fangs. The place would chew them up, then spit out their carcasses to float to shore. "We have to go back," cried Mitchell, but they were too weak to raise the sail. They tried to ship the oars but discovered that not one of them—not even Peter Smith—had the strength any longer to row. Smith tried to turn the boat against the current, but a sweep was wrenched from his grasp and floated out of reach. They were turning broadside to the waves and reefs—they'd soon be cut to pieces.

On the beach, some people stepped from a cabin and stared. Such tiny figures, Henry thought: no more than toys. Harry Morris stripped off his shirt and waved it in the air. Another man did the same but tied it to the gaff like a flag. More people appeared from the cabins and waved back. "They think we're a fishing party," Morris said.

A huge roller lifted the boat until they were able to see the breaking waves and white sheets of water frothing up the incline of the beach, almost to the coconut trees. About 40 yards out from shore the waves began to break in earnest, a caldron of water where the waves seemed 20 feet high. Peter Smith did what he could with the remaining sweep and Mitchell hung tight to the tiller, but neither regained full control. "Stay close to the boat until she swamps," advised Mitchell, "then jump clear. Those who feel able, help the weakest ashore."

Henry pondered dying after all he'd been through, here at the very doorstep of safety. He looked from the beach to his shipmates; they did not seem afraid. If anything, they accepted the fact that for better or worse, their ordeal was nearly done. There was relief in that, but also something else—a singular expression of sadness in their faces, as if it wasn't fair to be allowed so close, only to hit this final barrier. The fact of their drowning seemed a waste and a shame.

A roller lifted them up and roared beneath them, sweeping them closer to shore. More people gathered and two men ran toward the water, magically shedding their clothes.

"They're coming to help," cried Jimmy.

"They'll never reach us," Mr. Thomas answered calmly.

Another huge wave lifted them up and the breakers pounded like thunder. The water boiled around them. Henry held on for dear life, scared to be pitched into the foam.

Mitchell stared at the men swimming toward them; he knew they'd never make it before the boat struck the first line of coral. He gazed at his men and realized that no one, not even Antonio Possene or Thomas Tate, showed a hint of fear. A wave of pride and gratitude swept him in that moment, a feeling he'd never known before. No matter what had been said or plotted on this boat, they'd survived together on the open ocean longer than seemed humanly possible. They'd never given up, even until the end. This was a kind of pinnacle and Death could take him if it wanted. He stood by the tiller, trying to make himself heard above the surf.

"This is it, boys," he cried. "Don't jump till I say." The Pacific reached for them greedily and he hung to the tiller with every ounce of his strength. "Steady, now."

13

THE ISLAND

SAM CLEMENS lay on his back, disgusted with life, luck, and the gods of journalism. A once-in-a-lifetime scoop had landed on his doorstep, but he was helpless to do a thing. It was the kind of story for which every writer prays: the Odyssey to Homer, the Ancient Mariner to Coleridge, and like both, emerging full-blown from the sea. But Clemens was laid up with an excruciating and humiliating case of saddle sores, and could not move from bed.

So far, Clemens only knew as much as the rest of Honolulu. According to the *Pacific Commercial Advertiser*, an Englishman named Gaston arrived on June 16 from the tiny fishing village of Laupahoehoe on the big island of Hawaii with an amazing tale. The survivors of the clipper ship *Hornet*, from New York to Frisco, had drifted to shore after 43 days and 8 hours at sea. "The entire party were in a state of starvation," said the one-paragraph story, and no wonder, since they'd floated more than 4,300 miles on ten days' rations. Sam knew Laupahoehoe: he'd ridden on horseback through there two weeks earlier and gazed east across the ocean, his thoughts passing over the poor wretches as they fought for their lives.

The situation was galling for an ambitious man like Clemens. He wanted to be the most famous writer in America, but by age 31 that path was beset by detours. He felt adrift himself, floating through life with no plotted course; there'd been promising starts, but all had come to nothing. He'd chronicled gold fever for papers in Nevada and California; in 1863, he had begun signing his work "Mark Twain"; he published his first short story, "Jim Smiley and His Jumping Frog," in the November 11, 1865, issue of the New York *Saturday Press.* Praise of the story whetted his appetite for fame. Ever since landing in Honolulu three months earlier, he'd written travel letters at $20 apiece on the ways of the islands for the *Sacramento Daily Union.* Yet by June 21, 1866, when he read the news from Laupahoe-hoe, he was still a footnote in the world of letters and would soon return to the mainland with no real jump on fame.

If there was a pattern to Clemens's life, it was the wave: unceasing crests and valleys like the ones that made him seasick on his steamship ride to "Kanaka land." His whole life seemed like that—one moment downing oysters in San Francisco's best hotels; the next, out of work, broke, and in jail for writing too accurately about local police brutality. One night in early 1866, as the *Hornet* was cruising south off the coast of Brazil, Clemens had grown despondent and placed a pistol to his head. A San Francisco newspaper editor had penned an attack calling him a deadbeat, drunk, and jailbird; he christened him a "Bohemian from the sage-brush" who'd been rolled in a whorehouse and possibly contracted venereal disease. "Even for an era of scurrilous journalism, this was a frightful attack," Twain's biographer, Justin Kaplan, observed.

Clemens did not pull the trigger, but quietly departed for Hawaii. On March 18, as the *Hornet* had begun to round Cape Horn, Sam rode the 1,993-mile track to the Sandwich Islands aboard the steamship *Ajax.* "The sea was very rough," he wrote. "I found twenty-two passengers leaning over the bulwarks vomiting and remarking, 'Oh, my God!'" But the islands were for him a place of romance: he found "no careworn, or eager, anxious faces" in this "unimaginably happy land." His dispatches to the *Sacramento Daily Union* included a profile of the ruling monarch, a description of the funeral ceremonies for Princess Victoria Kamamalu, a tour of the lava pits of Kilauea, and observations of the sugar and citrus industries, of interest to American investors.

Residents were uncertain whether the wildly gesticulating Missourian was crazy or drunk, but his visibility made him several important friends, including General Van Valkenberg, U.S. envoy to Japan, and Anson Burlingame, U.S. minister to China, both on a layover before continuing to their posts. Burlingame was especially friendly: suave, rich and opinionated, he was a fan through his son, who'd read "The Jumping Frog," and helped open doors. He told Clemens to "seek refinement of association" with "men of superior intellect and character"; he advised him never to "affiliate with inferiors" but to "always climb." Burlingame's praise was an anodyne to the self-loathing that drove Clemens to stare down the barrel of a pistol; he would forever after call him "a man who would be esteemed, respected and popular anywhere, no matter whether he were among Christians or cannibals." But in the process, Clemens absorbed something else: Burlingame's belief that the world was best served by a stewardship of "superior" men.

Clemens got the *Hornet* story, thanks to his benefactor. A few days after the first reports, some crewmen were moved to a hospital in Honolulu while Mitchell, the Fergusons, and Possene remained on the "Big Island." On June 25, Burlingame had Clemens's cot carried to the hospital: he interviewed the crew while Clemens took notes. Clemens stayed up all night writing what would be the most famous of his Hawaiian dispatches, and the bulky envelope with his manuscript was thrown on a steamer to California the next morning as it pulled from the dock for sea.

The main source was Mr. Thomas, though Jimmy Cox and another sailor contributed. The men were little more than skeletons; ten days after rescue, their clothes hung limp and "fitted them no better than a flag fits the flag-staff in the calm," the young reporter would later write when his transformation to Mark Twain was nearly complete. Despite his sympathy, he did not like the common sailors and called them a helpless bunch of "mixed aliens" who could not have survived by "any merit of their own, but by merit of the character and intelligence of the captain." In so saying, he parrotted Burlingame. At least one later critic would note that although Twain was "a fervent critic of hypocrisy and perverseness in individuals, he rarely recognized the conditions underlying such cancers in the social body." His blindness may have started that day.

Twain *was* taken with Thomas: he liked the third mate's intelligence and called him a "very cool and self-possessed young man." He took to heart Thomas's hatred of the "Portyghee" without once meeting the man. As Thomas talked for three hours straight, the marks of the ordeal still showed on his face: although he was only 24, Twain said he looked nearly ten years older, aging a decade in 43 days. Thomas described the fire aboard the *Hornet*, the decision to cut loose the quarter-boats, the stalking waterspout and swordfish, the storms, heat, thirst, and starvation. He mentioned the decision to hold a lottery, but left out the mutiny. He praised the Fergusons, the banished duke, and fisherman Joe Williams, but reserved his greatest praise for Mitchell. It was to the Captain's "good sense, cool judgment, perfect discipline, [and] close attention to the smallest particulars . . . that [the] boat's crew owe their lives," Twain concluded. "He has shown brain and ability that make him worthy to command the finest frigate in the United States, and a genuine unassuming heroism that [should] entitle him to a Congressional medal."

It was a classic example of journalism in service of prevailing needs and myths, and how this version becomes history. The sailors sugar-coated Mitchell's choices and their own revolt in hopes that they would not be punished for mutiny; the best way to do this was to praise the person who might report them. To the *Pacific Commercial Advertiser*, they expressed "the most unbounded confidence" in Mitchell, "and felt, like soldiers with their General, that so long as he led them, they were safe, and should reach land." Such statements were blatantly transparent, but the press ate it up. Before Twain ever met Mitchell, the myth had assumed a life of its own.

Twain's agenda was more subtle. Gone in his report was Mitchell's dependence on his crew's seamanship, no less equal than their dependence on his navigational skills. Gone was their survival as a team. Mitchell's choice to abandon the quarter-boats sprang from the same source as the crew's choice of cannibalism—both deemed necessary for the majority's survival. Twain's praise of Mitchell depended entirely on Thomas and descriptions by Burlingame; his dislike of the lower classes echoed his patron's. His account became a morality tale for the rule of law over the masses, and for the power of "superior" men over the mob.

Such themes percolated in his mind. "There is nothing of its sort in history that surpasses it in impossibilities made possible," he said in a piece for *Harper's New Monthly Magazine* later that year. "The interest of this story is unquenchable; it is of the sort that time cannot decay, for by some subtle law all tragic human experiences gain in pathos by the perspective of time."

The steamship voyage to Frisco took two and a half to three weeks, and Twain's manuscript arrived safely. But it was not the first word to the mainland about the castaways. A telegram was sent on July 15 from the U.S. consul in Honolulu to the San Francisco firm of George Howes & Co., co signee of the *Hornet*. Samuel Ferguson sent a second to his father: "We are saved, in good hands, and doing well." A day later, a detailed letter from

Mitchell arrived to George Howes. Relatives of crewmen had haunted his office, and now one father was rewarded for his diligence:

> An old man, whose son was one of the crew of the lost ship, had repeatedly called at the office of the cosignees to ask for tidings of her and gone away disappointed. On the day of the arrival of the news of the loss, he came in as the letter of the Captain was being read, and stood by the side of the reader too deeply anxious to trust his voice to ask a question, the while with suppressed breath, glancing eagerly down the page. At last his eye fell on the name of his son among the saved, and with the exclamation, "Thank God, my son is spared to me!" fainted from excess of emotion.

Twain's account appeared on the front page of the *Sacramento Daily Union* on July 19, a month and three days after the rescue. It was reprinted in newspapers across the United States, and in a letter to his family, Twain predicted "it will be published first all over the U.S., France, England, Russia and Germany—all over the world."

THE FACT THAT FAME would be their newest lot did not register at first, especially with Mitchell. His thoughts floated like the world around him, all unreal. Until the last second, their fate seemed certain: the longboat was within five yards of a reef sticking like fangs from the surf when their rescuers climbed aboard. They took over the boat as if the act of saving castaways were a daily occurrence, shaking hands, inquiring, "How do you do?" One took the last oar from Peter Smith; the other unwrapped the tiller from Mitchell's fingers. They easily threaded the reef and within 15 minutes the longboat ground to a halt on the white sandy shore.

The sudden appearance of a crowd seemed fantastic, too. A hundred Hawaiians pressed so close that their saviors shouted for breathing room. Henry stared, unbelieving—his ordeal was over, a fact that hit him like a bucket of water. "We made it, Samuel," he whispered, but his older brother could not drag his gaze away from the crowd. Eyes stared back that were wide, weeping, curious; people pressed up who were anxious, worried, and amazed. They communicated more with a look than all the eloquence he'd heard from pulpits; these people did not know him, might not share a common language, yet the same winds pushed them and his eyes filled with tears.

Henry tried to stand, but the island rocked beneath him and he was caught by the hands of strangers. The crowd carried them up the shore to the house of John Jones, local agent for the merchant firm of J. C. King & Co. Jones watched with his native wife and Charles Bartlett, his steward: the crowd placed them in the shade of the house and veranda, then rushed off for food.

Henry and the others were overwhelmed with food, so much that it threatened harm if they immediately ate, given the shrinkage of their bellies. The villagers brought potatoes, taro, bananas, poi, green coconuts, and flagons of clear water; the sailors reached for the bounty as fast as it piled up, but Jones and Bartlett kept grabbing it away from the starving men. It would be safer if each man took a little water, then eased into nourishment that night with some broth and tea, but the sailors weren't interested in Jones' caution. Possene downed six green bananas before the bunch was ripped from his fingers; Harry Morris and Joe Campbell smuggled a slab of pork around the side of the house; Jimmy Cox ate a coconut, which Mitchell tossed into the yard. Jimmy started to cry, the first tears anyone could recall from him, but watching that food fly out of reach was heartbreaking. "That's hard treatment, Captain," Jimmy sobbed.

There was more hard treatment to come. Recovery from starvation is a torturous denouement to rescue: their guts cramped to knots as their digestive tracts cranked back in gear. Not one of them had had a bowel movement in 18 days, several for 25 to 30, and one man for as long as 44. Now, visits to the head were announced with screams—trying to pass the undigested remnants of rags, butter casks and boot leather was not easy. "I had a good deal of pain and nearly fainted tonight," Henry wrote, "but the purgative medicines [Jones] had given me have done the work." All had lost 30 to 55 pounds apiece: now they regained weight, but in odd ways. Fat returned to their guts and fluid to their cells, but this initial water gain occurred as swelling in their feet and legs. It would take weeks before their feet thinned out to their old shoe size, even longer before their weight returned. They learned to resume activity slowly: their legs swelled like sausages and their pulses raced if they walked too far. Some discovered their hair falling out in clumps, while all learned that the scars from salt-water boils would not disappear for a year.

The most common complaint was their constant hunger. This plagues all starvation victims, even those in controlled conditions. Subjects in the Minnesota study found that, after the test, they always seemed to eat, and some had not returned to normal weight after three months of daily diets approaching 5,000 calories. Filling the stomach was the reason for life: even when full, it was hard to stop, a condition called "supernormal eating." One man stuffed himself "until he [was] bursting at the seams"; another had so little control over cravings that he never felt satiated, even when "stuffed to the gills." Viktor Frankl, a Holocaust survivor, recounted that cravings for food had to be satisfied instantly. "One starts to eat—for hours, for days, through half the night," he wrote.

Although Henry and the others recuperated quickly, Samuel, Mitchell, and Possene were prostrated physically and mentally. Henry's main complaint was an advanced set of nerves. He didn't like loud noises, too many questions, or unannounced visitors. Samuel and he roomed together in Jones' house, next to Mitchell, while the crew slept in Jones's sitting room. On the first night, Henry washed, donned clean clothes, and briefly told his story to a Belgian priest from a nearby village and to the English traveler named Gaston. Charles Bartlett had medical training and operated on Neil Turner's abscess, probably saving his life. "Charles . . . knows something of surgery and has doctored and cut him some and he is rather better," Henry said.

Henry dreamed throughout his first few nights on land. He once more felt the rocking of the boat, heard the waves lick against its side, smelled the salt air. He bolted upright, certain their rescue had been the dream. His destiny was to be trapped in the boat forever, but when he awoke he was in Laupahoehoe, swaddled in cool sheets, stretched on a soft bed.

In the quiet, he heard the talk of the men. He could not abide their version of the ordeal. "I wish we could get these men off soon, as some . . . already are terribly ungrateful," he wrote on June 16–17. "It will be a relief. . . . They are with some exceptions an ungrateful set of dogs."

More than anything else, he worried about Samuel. His brother was not getting better: he feared he might never heal. "Suffered considerably," Samuel wrote on June 16, then crossed out the line. His hacking cough had returned, accompanied by a copious green discharge. He checked his handkerchiefs for streaks of blood, but none yet appeared. "Improved, but very weak and emaciated," he wrote on June 18, three days after landing. "Weigh 81 pounds."

Ghosts cried out to Mitchell. Each night he heard Samuel cough and thought the poor man called, "Captain, Captain." No matter, he could not sleep anyway. Sleeplessness is a common aftermath of starvation, but he was haunted by more than recovery. Jones and the Belgian priest had grabbed a chart and discovered that although Laupahoehoe was 3,360 miles in a straight line from where the *Hornet* sank, their meandering route north and west had taken them 4,300 miles. It was a record, they said excitedly: Captain Bligh had traveled only 3,618 miles in his open boat, and although he'd been at sea for 53 days, there'd been several island stops along the way. Mitchell took no pride in the accomplishment. The cost had been too high. Each night he listened to the fear in the voices of his crewmen, terrified of a charge of conspiracy. Each morning he asked for word of Parr or Sam Hardy, but the answer was always, "None."

"I feel about as yesterday, resigned, cannot sleep," he wrote on June 16. "The island seems to rock like a boat. My head confused."

Rest was all he wanted. Rest from hardship, guilt, and responsibility. With the lifting of his vigilance, he became the feeblest of men. He felt cut off from others, his heart so chilled that he almost felt blood congeal beneath his nails. Unlike the crew, a captain was expected to be an island to himself. Mitchell felt cut off from *all* humanity, judged for what he'd done.

He stood in the veranda and listened as voices swirled in his head. He heard his men whisper in the sitting room, fearing jail and realizing they might not get paid. Poor devils, they'd lost everything, even the few relics of their past, when the ship took their sea chests to the bottom. If he testified against them, they'd lose their futures, too. All choices on the boat had been based on survival. The crew was ready to sacrifice him and the Fergusons, but he'd sacrificed two boats, and the 16 men in them, so that his boat would survive.

So he stood and listened, a deeper shadow in the tropical gloom. He listened to Samuel's coughs, to Henry's shouts from his dreams. He watched for signs of John Parr or Sam Hardy from the vastness of the ocean, but there would never be a sign of their fate, nothing but the testimony of that spar. He recalled the shriek of the whirlwind. The white waves paced back and forth in the moonlight, but he was tired and sad, and no longer wished to interpret their message.

One night he told Mr. Thomas that whatever was said or done in those final days was the result of delirium and, like their thirst and starvation, remained at sea. There'd be no charges from him: pass that along to the men. He told Henry and Samuel that whatever happened on the boat stayed on the boat. They'd been given a second chance at the expense of Sam Hardy, Henry Chisling, William Laing, and the others. Vengeance had no place in Laupahoehoe.

On the evening of Sunday, June 17, the clipper brig *Nahienaena* took his crew for a short stop in Hilo, then on to the hospital in Honolulu. Mitchell placed Mr. Thomas in charge: it was in Honolulu that Thomas was questioned by Anson Burlingame and Mark Twain. The departure brought Mitchell some peace—at least some voices were stilled. The next morning he wrote to A. Caldwell, the U.S. consul in Honolulu, and sent the letter to his San Francisco agents by steamer. Henry wrote a long letter to his father; Samuel, a shorter one. All were sent to Honolulu on June 18 aboard a fast whaler provided by the consul in Hilo. "Sam's cough improved a good deal during the voyage but was not entirely gone when the accident happened," Henry wrote, putting the best face he could on matters. "Thank God, I think it is no worse than when the ship burned but he is well and will . . . need much rest and recruiting. I am afraid to write more."

On Wednesday, June 20, Mitchell walked to the beach, the first time he'd done so since the day of rescue. It wasn't far: "perhaps 30 rods," a stroll of about 165 yards, or one and a half football fields, but to him it seemed miles. "Bad night, no sleep, nervous, trouble with brain," he wrote. "Body gains faster than head." He set out alone after dinner and came to the boat, keel upended, left where they'd landed. "Much affected," he wrote. Nothing more.

Above all else, he felt a loneliness he'd never experienced before. Mitchell missed the "either-or" of survival: nothing in his life would ever again be as clear-cut as those 43 days at sea. He wondered if he any longer had the ability or right to enter the "civilized channels of thought" again. The ordeal left him "with a sense of loss and lingering fear," and perhaps, like a later castaway, Mitchell took comfort "in the silent company of those who have suffered greater ordeals, and survived."

The next day, Mitchell sold the boat "as she lies" to an unidentified

Frenchman for $200. The money was split into twelve equal shares of $16.66 apiece for Mr. Thomas and the crew. Although this equals about $187 in current dollars, each man's expenses in Hilo and Honolulu were apparently deducted from the amount. Fred Clough, for example, the only crewman for whom there remains a record of payment, received $4.37 of the $16.66, or about $49 today. It may have been the only pay the survivors received. It was unusual for a crew to return without their ship, and the understanding was that the ship must come home if the sailor were to be paid.

Mitchell and the Fergusons stayed in the village until Friday evening, June 22, when a "new whale boat with a good crew" took them to Hilo. Parting with those who'd saved them was painful. How does one say "thank you" for such things? A touch of unconscious racism can be seen by the fact that their Hawaiian saviors were never identified (unlike John Jones and Charles Bartlett, the village's sole white residents), but the two men were never forgotten. A slow change began in Henry: a split from the elitism of his family and friends. Money and position did not matter to these people, nor race nor belief in an Episcopal god. All they'd seen were human wrecks floating on the water. The hatreds and prejudices that had come within a heartbeat of killing everyone on the longboat seemed obscene beside such kindness. He looked at the people who'd nursed him back to health and humbly said: "May they never want for friends."

Shortly after midnight, they docked at Hilo and re-entered the world.

THE WORLD WELCOMED THEM as heroes. Mitchell and the Fergusons stopped at the house of "Captain Spencer," who, with the American consul, arranged for their needs. "Balmy air, tropical trees and plants with most luxuriant foliage," Henry marveled. "Flowers in great variety." Spencer's house was perched on a bluff overlooking the beach; Mitchell could rise and stare at the lovely turquoise ocean that tried so hard to kill him. It was "the Eden of the world," he mused. "If Susan was only here, she would never desire to leave."

They stayed eleven days. Henry attended church, was visited by well-wishers, told their story until a sore throat set in. But there was a *quid pro quo*: he grilled the curious about the world he'd left behind. Half a year had passed since they'd left New York City, and he felt like Rip Van Winkle. He read in the Honolulu and Frisco papers of violence in the Reconstruction South, of a society of hooded Southern "patriots," of a rumored conspiracy to free Jefferson Davis from his Virginia prison cell. There was war and rumor of war. The "Five Civilized Tribes" of Indians were forced to give up half of present-day Oklahoma; Swedish scientist Alfred Nobel invented dynamite; Otto von Bismarck engineered a seven-week war with Austria to gain all of northern Germany. The first transoceanic cable was laid across the Atlantic, while backers announced the Suez Canal would be completed in three years. The world was smaller, more scientific, and more ruthless than when he'd left. Editorialists called it the dawn of a modern age.

By June 30, two weeks after rescue, Henry felt strong enough for a horseback ride to a local sugar cane plantation. "I think my ride jogged me up a little," he said, feeling queasy afterward. He also regained his interest in girls—and they in him, if his visitor list was an indication. There was an 18-year-old "Miss Cohen," plus "two young ladies of about the same age, schoolmates of hers." In the back of his journal he drew a portrait of a pretty "Miss Cotton" with almond-shaped eyes, dark brows, thick hair in a bun, and an aquiline nose. If not for his worries about Samuel, it would have been the best of all possible worlds.

But Samuel refused to heal. The deterioration that had begun on the boat could not be halted. He coughed all night, great hacking bouts that left him without sleep and inspecting his handkerchief for blood. A "Dr. Wetmore" gave him pills to induce sleep, but the coughs defeated medication. He refused to gain weight, grew increasingly impatient, fell prey to what Henry called "queer fancies." Mitchell was more blunt: "Poor fellow, I fear he will never reach home."

Mitchell did little better. He couldn't sleep until Dr. Wetmore prescribed an unidentified soporific; one of his arms briefly became paralyzed and his head grew "very giddy" after reading. His fatigue remained, and he was plagued by sudden bouts of emotion. He was a clipper captain, by God, accustomed to hiding his feelings for the good of his ship and its owners, but now he broke into tears at the least provocation and thought of himself as a mewling girl.

With such preparation, or lack of it, they boarded a schooner on July 3 and left Hilo for Honolulu. They arrived at 4:00 P.M., July 4. There were fireworks over the ocean that night. Among the American community, it was Independence Day.

NOW THEIR RECEPTION turned white-hot, most of the spotlight focused on the captain. Samuel and Henry were given a room at the American Hotel, while Mitchell was spirited away by the editor of the Honolulu *Advertiser* and "Burlingame, Van Valkenberg and Co." Mitchell learned of Twain's lengthy article in a mainland paper; he did not approve of the young writer, so doted on by Burlingame, yet under Burlingame's urging acceded to letting him copy his journal for a longer article in a national magazine. The myth-making was underway, with or without his approval. His captaincy of the longboat was recast by Burlingame and Van Valkenberg as proof of the need for a ruling class, a thin line separating man from chaos, and was called a living lesson "on the moral power of the government of the men." It was "a very high compliment," Mitchell protested, but one he felt "undeserved, for all was God's mercy."

But humility has no place in myth, especially to its makers. Mitchell's protests fell on deaf ears. On Saturday, July 7, the two ministers to the distant East left belatedly for their posts, but not before upgrading the praise. "They were very kind to me," Mitchell recounted. "Said I was one of the great men of the age and flattered me a good deal." The accolades did not end with their departure. Mitchell explored the town, paid $30 for a suit of clothes, sat for pictures in the newspapers, and was invited to the homes of the important, bored, and kind. On Tuesday, July 10, he was overwhelmed "with a purse containing $310 in gold collected for me. I felt like a criminal upon receiving it [and] was completely overcome. The first time in my life I was ever in such a situation. Could not refuse it. There is some true charity in the world yet."

He needed such charity more than he realized. The $310, worth $3,500 today, was a timely gift, for there would be problems in payment upon his return. The ever-frugal Mitchell, who recorded every credit and debit down to $5 for "under clothes," made no record of payment from George Howes & Co. on returning to Frisco. He twice made enigmatic notes that he "extended protest," possibly to Lawrence & Giles in New York over nonpayment of salary, but nothing more is mentioned. More intriguing are indications that a sizable investment sank with the *Hornet*. Clipper captains grew rich by owning shares in their ship, or by shipping their own cargo, sometimes netting three or four times their pay and bonuses.

Mitchell had been with the *Hornet* long enough that a small fortune in invested savings may have been lost forever when she went down. Before the disaster, Mitchell and his family were well off, but within a year of his return, he would write: "You ask, my dear girls, if we are poor. . . . [W]e are rich in the great love we *bear to each other*, better than all else in life." But he conceded, "times have so changed within the last few years and expenses so large . . . that comparatively we are poor."

More than anything else, he wanted to go home. "All I desire is to get my letters from home and know how my dear family are getting along," he said in a letter to his wife on July 8. He thought of Honolulu in terms of Susan and the future. "Wish I could go there and live," he wrote. "How happy my wife would be there. It may be yet."

The Fergusons wanted out of Honolulu also, but for a different reason. The air was too hot and Samuel's condition worsened. "I am too weak to do anything but take a short walk," he said. Gone was the philosopher taking pleasure in a sunset; now Samuel took pleasure in a doctor's prescription of whiskey beaten with an egg and milk, for it soothed his throat and acted "as a strengthener and stimulant." His system was failing, warned the doctor, his consumption made worse by his 43 days on the boat and possibly beyond healing. "He has been fearfully reduced by our exposure and famine," Henry mourned. It was imperative that he leave the tropics for cooler and drier climes, like parts of California. "God grant that the change may be for the best," Henry wrote, "and that he may find some place in California where he will regain his strength and make headway against his dreadful disease."

Samuel seemed to realize that it may have been too late by then. He rarely wrote in his diary, and was suddenly adamant that Henry leave him in Hawaii to return to school. Bitter arguments rose between them, and Henry backed down. "I hope and trust he will improve and get strong and that I may not have to leave him sick on the island in the hands of strangers," he wrote. "He is much set to have me go immediately and I don't know but that it may be the best, though it will break my heart to do it." Given Samuel's affection for his younger brother, it is likely that he didn't want Henry to watch him die.

On July 13, the three sat for a photograph. The image is solemn, almost funereal. Mitchell sits on the left and Samuel on the right, with Henry standing between them. Mitchell wears his new frock coat, starched collar, and white duck trousers, eyes drawn off-camera, eager to leave. Henry stands straight and dapper, his face long and gaze steady, arm placed lightly on the back of Mitchell's chair. They are a unit, linked by touch and sight lines. Samuel sits to the side. He is shrunken and diminished, forehead bulging, eyes sunken. He stares blankly at the camera, face a bony mask, hands emerging from his black coat like claws. He stares past the lens, into infinity.

On the previous day, July 12, Mitchell watched his crew depart for San Francisco; he undoubtedly told the Fergusons of this by the photo sitting. Except for Jimmy Cox, Fred Clough, and one mention of John Ferris, it is the last we hear of them—as if they drop off the face of the earth, subsumed by the hive that is Sailortown or swallowed by the sea. Did Peter Smith regain his dukedom? Did Mr. Thomas move up the ladder to a captaincy? We do not know, but a curse seems to follow. The *Hornet* would remain famous into the 1930s, when Depression, war, and tales of shipwrecked Allied sailors gained prominence, yet even so nothing more is heard of the crew, the common fate of Burlingame's "lesser men."

We do know this—in seven years, Mitchell would write that only three still lived. Most seemed healthy and happy when they left Hawaii, yet their days were already numbered. Mr. Thomas, Peter Smith, Antonio Possene, young Thomas Tate—all disappeared as completely as those companions who had vanished on the quarter-boats in the doldrums. Even Jimmy Cox was dead—the most loyal among them, who risked death for his loyalty. Strange rumors arose with his return: that he fell heir to a fortune during the ordeal, that an insane impostor would take his identity. But what could engulf and destroy men that even an ocean could not kill?

There was at that time no diagnosis for what today is called post-traumatic stress disorder, but its indicators were evident among those surviving disaster. They included "emotional tension (anxiety, insecurity, nightmares, excessive startle responses, phobias), cognitive impairment (apathy, poor memory, preoccupation, retardation, confusion), somatic complaints (chiefly headache, gastrointestinal distress, backache), and rarely, conversion phenomena (ataxia, stuttering, weakness, anesthesia)." This description, compiled after World War II by two English psychiatrists, has a shopping-list quality, as if one can stroll down the aisle and choose any response to stress, but all were reactions so debilitating that sufferers no longer led normal lives. They were first systematically studied when doctors noticed similarities between the "combat exhaustion" of soldiers and airmen and the torments of Holocaust survivors and former prisoners of war. For many, disaster persisted mentally and never let them free, as if the true site of suffering were the mind. Doctors studying men involved in the Guadalcanal evacuation found that every survivor developed some neurosis: fifteen years after combat, 70 percent had developed symptoms, with one-third unemployed and another third leading unstable or unhappy lives. A study of 40 torpedoed seamen found that 75 percent experienced "severe persisting reactions"; a smaller study of seven peacetime castaways lost for 13 days found that "of the seven men, five have developed formal psychiatric disorders for the first time in their lives," including depression, insomnia, severe alcoholism, impotence, drug addiction, "survivor's guilt," and violent spouse abuse. "The experience of a disaster . . . may carry a price," the authors said.

The most intimate portrait of the mind of disaster victims was Robert Jay Lifton's study of the *hibakusha*, the survivors of Hiroshima, for whom the idea of being a "survivor" was a mystical experience in which one touched death yet remained alive. Even so, death stayed with them daily. Theirs was a life of grief, forever mourning the known and anonymous dead, yet this was not survivor's guilt or fear of future annihilation. It was a need to placate the dead. Lifton imagined their train of thought: "I was almost dead . . . I should have died . . . I did die or at least am not alive." A bargain was struck with the dead to justify life: "By living as if dead, I take the place of the dead and give them life."

Such a continued relationship with death is not dissimilar to the Jonah, disgorged by the sea. Those who escape once are never truly free. They are marked, and the sea waits patiently for their return.

ON JULY 19, Mitchell and the Fergusons finally left for San Francisco aboard the bark *Smyrniote*, Mark Twain in tow. Samuel ultimately decided to return to the mainland, probably at his doctor's urging. They left on the same day Twain's scoop appeared on the front page of the *Sacramento Daily Union*, and by the time they arrived on August 13, the story was printed in newspapers across the nation and working its way through English-language papers around the globe. Samuel and Henry apparently liked Twain better than had Mitchell; at least they found him diverting. Samuel

remarked that while many of the bark's 16 passengers fell sick after weighing anchor, "Mark Twain [was] suffering other than seasickness," a polite
reference to his lingering saddle sores. Twain asked to copy their journals
for his magazine article, and Henry agreed provided any "sensational matter such as the potential for cannibalism" be omitted. Twain either misun-
derstood Henry or simply broke his promise, unable to resist the siren
song of good material, and the December article in *Harper's* trumpeted
Henry's fears. Forever after, he felt that Twain had "done him dirt," and
reportedly never forgave him.

The voyage to San Francisco seemed interminable, filled with seasickness and tedium. Henry practiced his Greek, while Mitchell wrote letters
to his family to be posted on arrival. He vowed to make a new beginning
with Susan, possibly in Hilo. "How much I have thought of you every day
since I got into that [long]boat," he wrote. "I shall know everything when
I get to San Francisco and see Harry. . . . That I shall enjoy my home more
than ever—God grant it."

It is sad to view men's lives in retrospect, knowing what will come.
Hardship leads to hope, hope to despair, and this to a tragic nobility. They
ran ahead of their fate as if the blind god Whirl sought them out—Samuel
was the first to sense that something implacable still stalked him over the
sea. He wanted to go home before it caught up. Perhaps he thought Stamford was a safer place. Most likely, he wished to say goodbye.

His final journals are filled with impatience and urgency, displaying the
irritable, dismissive Samuel Ferguson, not the observant philosopher.
"Ship a very nice one, though very small after the *Hornet*," he said of the
Smyrniote. "Cabin, of course, uncomfortable for gents." His entry on July
20 would be his last: "Staterooms very small and hot though each has a
'Bull's Eye,'" a piece of thick glass set flush in the deck to let light below.
"Lady passengers still continue sick. . . . Babies sick and crying, making
being in the cabin anything but delightful."

They landed at 4:00 P.M. on Monday, August 13. The brothers, captain,
and writer made their goodbyes. In his restless fashion, Twain was first to
leave Frisco: he'd returned to the site of his ignominious departure five
months earlier, "without means and without employment," and wracked
his brain for ways to stave off creditors. His first act was to present his editors at the *Sacramento Daily Union* with a bill of $300 for the *Hornet* scoop,
an unheard-of amount at $100 per column. The owners "laughed, in their

jolly fashion, and said it was robbery, but . . . it was a grand 'scoop.'" To his surprise, they paid in full. For two or three weeks he roamed California and Nevada on a lecture tour, relating to packed houses his impressions of Hawaii and the tale of the *Hornet*. He returned to New York via the Isthmus of Panama, a trip he was lucky to survive "for the cholera broke out among us . . . and we buried two or three bodies at sea every day." But home was a dreary place, and once again he felt adrift. Within a year he began a world tour that provided material for his first significant book, *The Innocents Abroad*.

Before that, "Forty-Three Days in an Open Boat" was published in the December *Harper's*, yet fame did not come as planned. The article was published without a byline, as was the style; however, the year's list of contributors was published in the following issue, and as he opened the page he anticipated a flood of accolades. Unfortunately, he had not written "Mark Twain" distinctly and a printer's devil listed the author as "Mark Swain." He later lamented, "I was not celebrated . . . I was a Literary Person, but . . . a buried one; buried alive."

Mitchell hung around San Francisco another two weeks, conducting business, visiting his son Harry. He wrote and wired to Susan, but there was only silence. "I think Mother is sick," said Harry, but had no other details. Mitchell looked up the crew to pay them their share of the longboat, and on August 22 found and paid Fred Clough. Fred was living with his mother in the Mission District, and contemplated work as a carriage maker. "I don't think I'm going to sea again, Captain," he said. "At least not for awhile." He could not help but feel that if he did, he would never return—a fear that nagged at Mitchell, too. Clough's mother was outraged by Twain's article in the Sacramento paper that mentioned how the sailors—her son included—had planned to draw lots to devour each other if they hadn't made landfall that day. It was a scandal: How was a mother to show her face outside? She made Freddy promise never to tell the story for publication as long as she lived. Mitchell assured her that by guarding the water cask, Fred had been essential to their survival. "Your boy has fists like sledgehammers, Mrs. Clough," he said. "No one stole a sip of water. You should be proud, not ashamed." He left Fred, feeling sorry for the boy: he had a haunted look and was scared of the sea, the only world he really knew.

Three days later, Mitchell took a train 40 miles south to the Warm Springs sulfur baths in Santa Clara, where Samuel and Henry had repaired. "Found Mr. Ferguson . . . about the same," he said. He took a warm sulfur bath and "felt first-rate," then returned to San Francisco. On August 30, he cast off on the Isthmus route aboard the Pacific Mail Steamship Company's sidewheel steamer *Golden City*, which would go down in flames four years later. He arrived in New York on September 19, and stepped off the train in Freeport on September 25.

Samuel died in Santa Clara on October 1. The voyage of recovery had killed him; the last best hope hastened his end. Of those in the boat, he'd been the most spiritually inclined, transforming the sea's beauty into a pastel frame on the page. Yet he'd been rigid in his thinking, dismissing those in lower circumstances unless they adhered to the rules of "better" society. His rules, that is. By doing so, he helped inflame the raw emotions and innate tensions of the boat. Mitchell always had the highest praise for Henry, but for Samuel there was silence and pity.

It seems hard to sympathize with Samuel, even in death, unless one remembers that he was a deeply disappointed man. He'd played by the rules of society, yet still felt cheated by God. For all of his intelligence, he refused to look beyond the class lines that tore America apart in the coming decades. He never understood the drama of the boat, never acknowledged Fred's gift of water or his exile from his friends by that act of mercy. One wonders if mercy like Fred's would even occur to him.

It had occurred to Henry: all of it—Fred's mercy, the irony of Samuel's death, his own family's ossified values, the anger and savagery of men. He was heartbroken by Samuel's fate, and his turmoil was recorded by his silence. He placed his brother in a "cooler coffin" and accompanied the body home. Later that year, Samuel was buried in the St. Andrews' churchyard in Stamford, the youngest, and first, of the five Ferguson brothers to die.

Henry never wrote about Samuel's death, but it changed everything. In *Essays in American History,* one of his two books, echoes of his older brother creep onto the page. About the Quakers, he wrote: "For the constancy of the Quakers themselves, their endurance and their fortitude, one can feel nothing but admiration," a passage that describes Samuel's stoicism as he wasted away. Of Cotton Mather's relation to nature, he said, "Every storm, every meteor . . . was a portent," as Samuel had felt when reading the skies.

Of the despised Loyalists during the Revolutionary War, he ended with a discourse on hope, a quality Samuel rarely went without:

> "Why did you come here, when you and your associates were almost certain to endure the sufferings and absolute want of shelter and food which you have now narrated?" asked an American gentleman of one of the last settlers of St. John, near Brunswick, a man whose life . . . was without a stain. "Why did we come here?" replied he, with emotion that brought tears; — "for our loyalty; think you that our principles were not as dear to us as were yours to you?"

Despite his pride and faults, Samuel had risen above himself. No one had taken as many torments with him into the longboat, and no one had endured them as well. Henry had watched his brother's torment, and the act of witnessing changed him. Samuel's last, best mark on the world was Henry.

MITCHELL RETURNED HOME to his own tragedy.

Susan was dying. The wait since her husband's ship disappeared had been too much to endure. Rigid with fear and hoping against hope, she waited for days, weeks, and months; anxiety, fear, and sorrow conspired against her already fragile health. "My poor wife is sick," he wrote on his return to Freeport, "which accounts for my not getting letters."

The long wait affected all who hoped for news. At Chatham on Cape Cod, Sam Hardy's wife and child prayed for his safe return. When the news did arrive, she was devastated and ruined. Funeral services were held in the village church, not just for her husband, but for all lost on the *Hornet*. A brief inscription placed on the tombstone told what little she ever learned.

Susan Mitchell's suffering dragged on for nearly a month after Josiah's return. She was nauseous by day, screaming in pain at night. His daughters arrived, replaced after a week by a girl with experience in nursing the terminally ill. It is hard to know from what she suffered. By October 16, two doctors had diagnosed her condition as dropsy in the abdomen, a condition marked by an excess of fluid in the body cavities, but the pain and swelling also suggest cancer. It was horrible for Mitchell to watch—doubly horrible after escaping himself from such torment just to find his wife succumbing to her own ordeal. On October 17, he wrote: "Poor wife growing weaker hourly. Cannot swallow anything. Impossible, she can live many days this way. God grant if she cannot be raised, that she may not suffer."

By October 21, Susan made it clear she was "anxious to die." She could take no fluid or nourishment, "not even a drop of water." What he would have given for a drop, and now Susan treated it like poison. She suffered "beyond description, and at times exceedingly happy and joyful. Much in the spiritual, and O so anxious to go and yet so drawn to earth." By October 23, the doctors finally gave her morphine to kill the pain.

She died at 2:30 A.M. on October 31. She lay quiet under the effects of the morphine and slipped away easily. Outside her window, a storm had raged for nearly three days. "Very heavy gale from S.E., and rain," Mitchell wrote as if still at sea. He recognized such weather, the sudden storms that drove ships upon the rocks, that tore mainmasts from their roots and set strong men adrift and confused. "O my own dear wife, why am I so stricken and left when as you said, we all ought to rejoice," he wrote. "God strengthen and comfort us all. Cannot write, mind not in a fit state."

Weeks later, as he went through her effects, he came upon her diary. He flipped through the yellowing pages filled with the spidery hand and dried flowers pressed between the leaves. The book fell open to the last entry: August 8, 1866, nearly three months before she died. There is no mention of Josiah's rescue, but she would have known by then. Her daughter Mary knew what his disappearance had done to her mother: she watched her slip deeper into hopelessness, and had taken her to the Great Lakes to dispel the gloom. The region's beauty had affected Susan deeply, yet she had seemed resigned in a way Mary had never seen. Maybe Susan had known she was dying, and the only question was whether she'd outlast the tides of poison until Josiah's return.

Mitchell ran his finger down the lines of cursive until nearly reaching the end, when he read something that made him feel "shook up aloft," as he tended to say. She'd been reflecting on the gulfs that tear men apart when suddenly it seemed as if she'd been transported to the longboat and had seen the divisions that nearly killed them all:

How great a wrong we do each other by not studying the natures and dispositions of those around, so that we may know how to [effect] their greatest good. Little do we know the eternal *injury* we do by neglecting the study of *human nature.* The penalty of the crime will not end here; it will go on in cycles to generations yet unborn.

Then Susan mocked herself, as was her way—an ability Josiah never possessed, and which he'd loved her for. He could see her laugh to herself as she finished the lines and gaze out of the window. "But I digress," she ended—

"I could write volumes."

THE FLOATING WORLD

TIME DESERTS THE CASTAWAY, as it did the *Hornet* survivors. They re-entered a nation that seemed to them faster and somehow alien; it was easy to imagine they'd missed Hawaii and kept drifting, and what they took for waking was only dying dreams. In the months and years to come, the United States would enter a watershed period that transformed government, business, and religion—and how the individual related to each. The Indian Wars and a new sense of destiny dominated public thought; mass production cheapened goods; health advances lengthened life. It seemed a safety net was being woven beneath Americans. Like nets strung beneath ships to snag drunken sailors, it would catch them should they fall.

Yet promises demand a price, and the landscape of the longboat became that of America and the world. The age of steel and steam split haves and have-nots as never before, concentrating untold wealth and power in the hands of a few, seeing the rudimentary labor movement founded by sailors and longshoremen mushroom into labor groups of every shade. Ironically, sailors, whose rage presaged the unions, were the last to organize. The income gap became a battleground: attempts by owners to suppress the unions led to further violence, while workers seemed eager to go to war. Dynamite bombs, dubbed the "proletariat's artillery," became the weapon of choice. As the Gilded Age lost its glitter, terror became part of the rhetoric and compromise gave way to an annihilation dubbed "propaganda by the deed."

By then, clipper ships had virtually disappeared from the shipping lanes, victims of their greatest asset—speed. The racehorses of the sea were outstripped by the world they created. The 1869 opening of the transcontinental railroad and final dominance of steamships in the 1880s ended the Age of Sail. As steamships took their business, clippers became tramp freighters, hauling lumber, grain, coal, and other bulk goods. Their numbers dwindled through attrition: the *Lightning* burned in 1869 while loading wood in China, the *Great Republic* sank in 1872 off Bermuda, the *Flying Cloud* wrecked off Newfoundland in 1874. Others were dismasted and used as coaling barges for steamships, or suffered the ultimate indignity and were relegated to the guano trade. The only surviving clipper today is the *Cutty Sark*, permanently docked in 1949 as a museum ship in Greenwich, England, site of the prime meridian, center of the sailing world.

The mythical islands bedeviling the longboat went the way of the clippers, too. In November 1875, Sir Frederick Evans, newly appointed hydrographer of the British Navy, ordered 123 doubtful islands banished from Admiralty Chart 2683 of the Pacific Ocean. All disappeared, including three real islands that had to be restored. Among the victims were the American Group, but American mapmakers would not emulate their counterparts for 24 years. In 1899, the steamer *Albatross* sounded the area, finding nothing shallower than 2,776 fathoms; the U.S. Hydrographic Office struck all traces from the charts and replaced them with the *Albatross's* figures. There was excitement in 1902 when the *Australia* reported shoal waters, but the cruiser *Tacoma* investigated two years later and found nothing, sinking the islands forever. By then, John DeGreaves, the man who claimed to have dined there with a dancer, worked in a Honolulu morgue. He'd contracted leprosy and anticipated ending his days at the leper colony on Molokai.

By then, the island paradise Mitchell loved had been forever changed. On April 30, 1900, Congress annexed Hawaii and appointed Sanford Dole, a planter who led the 1893 overthrow of the monarchy, as first colonial governor. By then, the die for the longboat's saviors was already cast: unable to cope with alien concepts of taxes, land ownership, and discrimination, the native *Kanaka* dwindled. In 1778, there were an estimated 300,000 Hawaiians on the islands. By 1930, that number had dropped to 60,000. Survivors had a saying for what happened. *Na Kanaka 'oko 'o wale aku no I kau 'uhane*: "The people freely dismissed their souls and died."

ON DECEMBER 3, 1873, Mitchell wrote a short letter to Fred Clough:

> My Dear Friend and Shipmate—
> I believe there are but three of us left; at least I know of no
> more. I saw Henry Ferguson last summer. He had about finished
> his study for the ministry. He inquired after you. Cox is dead. We
> certainly had a wonderful and providential escape, and nothing
> but God's grace sustained us—not a particle of credit is due to me.
> I only did what any other man must have done under the circum-
> stances. It was the long, constant watchfulness that broke me
> down more than all the rest.

Mitchell was slightly misinformed. John Ferris was still alive and settled in Modesto, California, according to a 1901 letter to Henry. And there
was someone who passed himself off as "Captain James Cox, friend of
Mark Twain." A brief story in the December 25, 1925, *New York Tribune*
would say that Captain James Cox, 79, an "eccentric character" known as a
friend of Twain's, died in bed of heart trouble at a sanatorium in Westport,
Connecticut. The pseudo-Cox, Twain's alleged "source of inspiration in
several short stories and anecdotes," said he was the *Hornet*'s sole survivor:
"He passed forty-three days in an open boat in the Pacific, his only companion the ship's dog, until he was cast away on one of the Sandwich
Islands."

By the time of his letter, Mitchell had returned to sea. Shortly after
Susan's death, he sought work in Washington, D.C., and moved his family
there. His son, who owned a coal and lumber yard, would take his horse on
Pennsylvania Avenue to race other horse fanciers. Harry lived for speed,
like his father—just not at sea. Mitchell's daughter Mary installed herself
as housekeeper. But Mitchell was not happy on land. In January 1867, he
accepted captaincy of the 1,600-ton ship *General McClelland*, owned by old
friends at Lawrence & Giles. "Were it not for my girls, I would rather be on
board a good ship at sea than anywhere," he wrote. "I feel more at home on
board than anywhere else." Harry pressured him to sell the family home in
Freeport, and in February 1867, he relented. "I have disposed of the old
place . . . and I hope that you will not shed so many tears . . . as I do myself."

Although he mourned the decision, he admitted that "I could never feel happy there, everything constantly reminding us of the Lost One." Years later, Freeport natives swore that the upper story was haunted, close to the bedroom where Susan died.

So he drifted. "I am lost, Mary, with no home I can call my own," he wrote. "I have arrived at that pass where I enjoy being alone a great part of the time, communing with myself and thinking of those that are so dear to me." In late summer of 1869, Mitchell left New York on a clipper ship to Frisco, the first time he'd taken this route since the *Hornet* burned three years earlier. The idea of making that trip called up every superstitious fear of the sea awaiting its Jonah, but this was no "picnic" trip and he was allowed little time for imagination. One day into rounding the Horn, his ship got stuck in a two-week maelstrom of shrieking winds and "mountainous seas." By November 1, they were trapped in the doldrums, and on November 8, he passed over the spot where the *Hornet* had burned:

> We have passed over that part of the ocean where I had that terrible accident in the *Hornet* and that awful experience in the boats, and have lived it all over again in memory. . . . Daily do I ask myself—Why has God been so good to me when so many others—*all*, who chose the sea for a profession at the time I did, of my friends and acquaintances are gone before me? I pray and hope and trust that I may not be a Castaway at last.

By then, he was lost, financially and emotionally. In 1873, the year of the letter to Clough, his son Harry finally decided not to be a captain, a decision heightening Mitchell's isolation. He'd passed his skills and knowledge on to Harry, but his son turned away. That same year, Sarah Abbie—his second daughter, whose birth nearly killed Susan—herself died in childbirth at 27. Suddenly the sea itself could not hold his despair. "I am so sick and tired of being at sea," he wrote. "I am longing for a change of scenery."

Sarah's death and the great financial panic of 1873 called forth the fatalism he'd shown in the longboat, but now tinged with finality. "I am already beginning to have a great longing for the quiet of the ocean," he wrote to a friend. "It would not trouble me to be buried there, after 44 years passed upon its bosom. It is the largest of all cemeteries, and the same waves roll over all—the same requiem of the ocean is sung to the honor of all." The next year he remarried, but even this did not halt his wandering. The bride was Katie M. Thyng, a former neighbor in Freeport. She was 41; he was 61. Katie had helped doctor Susan during her last weeks, and was said to be religious. But their bond was given little time to develop, for by now his travels assumed a desperate stamp, as if he were searching for something that did not exist. Within two years, he was dead.

The end did not come quickly. He lingered as long and painfully as Susan. By 1875, his health was failing: the fact that he was one of the few veteran captains left from the clipper's glory days gave him pause. Even so, he didn't contemplate the thought for long. On August 1, 1875, he assumed command of the 1,812-ton ship *Ellen Austin*, bound from San Francisco to the Peruvian guano ports, then round the Horn to London. He sensed it might be his last command. "A long, perplexing and hard voyage for me with my poor health to undertake," he wrote: "Were it not for fear the Owners might be displeased and think me ungrateful and attribute my leaving to other causes, I should most assuredly leave—for I am weak and most miserable, and feeble, than is known to any but myself." He knew he should relinquish command but considered it a point of honor to stay at his post. He missed his children, and envisioned being reunited with his wife and daughter "never more to be separated, being in a house of our own." But he could also hope that such thoughts were just a fit of the doldrums. "I hope to feel better after getting to sea."

The guano islands were the worst place for an ailing man: they did to him what the longboat did to Samuel Ferguson. The *Ellen Austin* beat to the south, then waited for months for a turn beneath the guano chutes. As the cloud of yellow dust spread over his ship, his bodily weakness spread; there were days when he could not leave his cabin. Finally, Mitchell turned the ship over to his mate and booked a steamship to New York, desperate to make it home.

He never got that far. The steamship docked and he was carried to the house of a brother-in-law in Washington Heights; his wife and daughters made it to his bedside with barely a day to spare. Mitchell died in New York on July 23, 1876, a little over ten years after the ordeal that made him famous and ruined his life forever.

Despite the earlier fame, Mitchell's death was unheralded. A brief notice was included in the *New York Herald*'s "Marriages and Deaths" listing. That day, stories covered the deaths in the city of five people from sun-stroke; an inquest into several deaths aboard the wrecked yacht *Mohawk*; and the murder conviction of three Molly Maguire assassins in Pennsylvania, an early glimpse of labor wars to follow. The big news was still the mourning for those slain in the Custer Massacre nineteen days earlier: funds for a monument were solicited. "It is true that we have dealt wrongly with the red men," lamented the *Herald,* "but now we are forced to deal with the results of our own blunders. . . . We must subdue the hostile warriors or have our military and civil government disgraced in the eyes of the world." The extermination of the Indian began in earnest—like the Hawaiians, they would dismiss their souls and die.

Few knew of the captain's death years after the fact. The man who made him famous did not know. In November 1899, Mark Twain was asked by *Century Magazine* to write "My Debut as a Literary Person," a retelling of the *Hornet* wreck and its part in Twain's career. The article was then incorporated into *The Man That Corrupted Hadleyburg and Other Stories and Essays,* which appeared next year. Twain's tribute to Mitchell came at the outset: the ordeal was "a very remarkable trip, but it was conducted by a captain who was a remarkable man, otherwise there would have been no survivors. . . . I remember him with reverent honor. If he is alive he is eighty-six years old now."

Mitchell was forever associated in Twain's mind with Hawaii, which had become for him a spiritual home. "For me, its balmy airs are always blowing, its summer seas flashing in the sun," he wrote to a friend. "In my nostrils still lives the breath of flowers that perished twenty years ago." Twain was 64 and world famous; his Hawaiian letters were said to mark the transition between Sam Clemens, the disappointed journalist, and Mark Twain, the writer and public man. The islands floated in his memory like dreams. By then, he'd lost his daughter Susie, and his beloved wife Olivia, who died in 1904, had begun her downhill slide. The past was a happier place, cast in a simple light of heroes and scoundrels. Like Josiah Mitchell, he was a castaway.

By the time of the *Century* article, Twain was privately writing stories with protagonists whose dreams turned into frightening reality. A rich and happy man falls asleep and in that brief moment his house burns around him, he becomes bankrupt, his happy life becomes one of disgrace and horror. In another, a man wakes to find himself on a chartless voyage, lost for years. When he is rescued, all of his fellow passengers are dead or insane. A man goes on a voyage in a drop of water and becomes a parasite floating in God's intestines; he becomes a micro-organism adrift in the bloodstream of a hobo named Blitzowski. The dream tales dealt with responsibility and hidden guilt, with extremes that destroy identity. What if man were just a dream himself, a dream within a dream? Perhaps man never existed at all.

During this time, Twain also wrote "The Mysterious Stranger," published posthumously. The ultimate nightmare of floating, the novella was his most bitter dream. "It is true," said Satan to the narrator, "there is no God, no universe, no human race, no heaven, no hell: "It is all a dream—a grotesque and foolish dream. Nothing exists but you. And you are but a *thought*—a vagrant thought, a useless thought, a homeless thought, wandering forlorn among the empty eternities!"

The publication of Twain's *Century* article returned Henry to the limelight, too. The twin ordeal of the *Hornet* and watching Samuel's death had driven him to God. He traveled through California and possibly as far as Nevada after Samuel died, drifting and distraught, wondering what to do with his life. He apparently visited Fred Clough and his mother, informing Fred what had happened to his brother and solidifying a friendship that would last. By fall he'd decided to return to Trinity and graduate with his class in 1868. He entered the Episcopal ministry, was pastor at two New Hampshire churches, studied at Bonn, Oxford, and the Sorbonne, and in 1883 returned to Trinity as a professor of history and political economy. He married in 1873 and had four children. He named his first son Samuel.

Henry's seemed a settled, accomplished life, and he acquired the reputation of peacemaker, a level-headed fellow who could mediate the most bitter conflicts between academic peers. His approach was that no grievance should be allowed to fester; after too much time, the knives were drawn. He did not tell his colleagues that such convictions sprang from flashbacks that seemed too real. He was reading by a fire at home when suddenly he'd be praying desperately in the boat, for with the morning lots would be drawn. No one could ever convince him that prayer was not effective: he had proof, though others called it coincidence. His feelings toward Harry Morris and Joe Campbell had even mellowed, especially after asking Mitchell why he didn't charge them with mutiny. "These poor devils live hard lives," said Mitchell, and no one—not shipowners, captains, legislators, or the society that depended on their labor—lifted a finger to make their lot easier. What they'd seen on the longboat was a warning, Mitchell said. In time the whole world might go the way of the longboat: drawing lots, sharpening knives.

So Henry tried to forgive and forget, but Twain's article did not allow him that luxury. He'd always resented Twain's breach of confidence in playing up cannibalism in the *Harper's* piece; he'd seen Twain in the 1880s when both lived in Hartford, but never mentioned his feelings, figuring it would only cause resentment at that late date. The *Century* article caught him by surprise: when he heard it would be included in a book, he decided that something needed to be said. On November 8, 1899, he sent his complaint to Twain, then living in London:

> My dear Mr. Clemens,
>   I was surprised to see so much of my own and my brother's diaries republished in your article in the November number of the *Century*. Perhaps you never knew how unexpected it was to us that they should appear in *Harper's* magazine 33 years ago without allowing us to edit them previously. We had no thought of improving the English or "polishing them up" but did not wish names to appear in any way that could do harm nor did we wish anything purely personal to be made public. What was published did do harm, I am informed, to one man of the party, and caused grief to another.

One to suffer from Twain's account was Fred Clough. The intended cannibalism and mention of his name as one of the conspirators trailed him like a doppelganger. Forgotten was his charity to Henry and Samuel, and even hardened San Francisco shivered at the thought of a cannibal walking among them. Clough and another crewman, never identified, lost employment, job prospects, and possibly even love due to their portrayal as monsters. "I have never before mentioned the matter to you," Henry continued, "thinking that the harm was done and could not be mended, but now that there seems to be a probability of the extracts being put in permanent form, and given the wide circulation that naturally will come from your literary reputation, I have felt that I should make an attempt to prevent the perpetuation of what has always been a source of . . . annoyance

and grief to me, and has caused injury to others." He told Twain of
Mitchell's death, and asked that the names of crewmen be omitted from
future versions.

Twain was livid, his initial response petty. "My dear Professor Ferguson," he wrote on November 20, 1899. He told Henry that he had copied
the journals "in the sweltering heat of the Pacific" with the understanding
that proceeds from the article's sale go to "an Episcopal church in Stamford," most probably St. Andrews. Henry was not aware of this condition,
which must have been made by Samuel. Twain said he fulfilled this condition, and continued:

> The home-voyage lasted 28 days; there was abundance of time for the
> editing of the diaries: that you did not offer to edit them, and did not put
> upon me any restrictions or limitations of any kind, was your fault, not
> mine. If you were surprised, afterward, that you neglected to edit them,
> that was your affair—and remains so.
>
> The whole first page of your letter is made up of pure imaginings,
> with not a supporting fact behind them. They make against me, by
> innuendo, a charge of discreditable conduct, and I will ask you to with-
> draw it.
>
> Your second page begins with the remark that the publication did
> harm to one man of the party and caused great distress to another—a
> suggestion that I am to blame for that, too. I am in no way responsible
> for it—you should have edited those things out if you didn't want them
> left in. I had no interest in imposing [upon] anyone, and nothing to
> gain by it.

Twain continued in this vein throughout the letter, but in the end offered to
do exactly what Henry asked: to "suppress" the crewmen's names. Henry
could have taken offense at Twain's response, but he'd gotten what he
wanted and apologized for any unintended slur. A number of more cordial
letters followed through 1900, all concerned with details. Henry also
wrote his old friend at St. Andrews, Pastor Braithwaite, and asked whether
Twain ever made the payment to which he alluded. "I have gone through
every book and paper likely to throw any light on the subject," Braithwaite
responded on December 11, 1899, "and can find *nothing—absolutely nothing*.
If such an amount was ever paid, there is no record or note of any kind."

Henry never mentioned this to Twain. It was not his style. For the 18 years left after their correspondence, he quietly fixed problems before they became too great, and tried to plug leaks as institutions foundered. His instincts were not destructive, as could have been said if he'd sullied Twain's reputation with his discovery. In 1906, he left Trinity to become rector of the financially troubled St. Paul's School in Concord, the institution he'd attended as a boy. He shored up its finances and guided it to safer shores. In 1911, he retired and went home to Hartford.

By then he was feeling old and tired. He remembered the sailors' tales of Fiddler's Green, the Heaven of Jack Tar, and figured he'd visit it soon. He died at home on March 30, 1917, seven years after Twain's death and 51 years after the *Hornet* beat north in a strong wind off the Chilean coast, headed for her doom. There'd been a full eclipse of the moon on that night in 1866, and he had looked up in wonder at the first such eclipse he'd ever seen. The solar bodies had lined up and the sky had blacked out; they had floated in darkness, the sea like space as he drifted through the stars. It was the strangest experience, as if he weren't real at all, just a figment in a dream.

Henry was buried on Palm Sunday, on a hill overlooking St. Paul's School. His funeral was attended by many. Reverend F. S. Luther, Trinity's president, called Henry "the friend of all that is good in all the world." Henry rarely said as much, but everything important in his life was learned aboard the longboat. "Perhaps his greatest work . . . resulted from his gift of friendship," Luther eulogized. "He was always smoothing out rough places, explaining misunderstandings, correcting the mistakes of others or minimizing the consequences of those mistakes."

Henry thought about this often: how quickly evil spread, like a fire that enveloped the world. "Though we talk of the progress that the race has made in learning and enlightenment," he wrote, "it is alarming to notice . . . how germs which men deem dead really lurk dormant for ages, and then develop themselves with startling rapidity when they find the proper menstruum":

Man, like others animals, seems to exhibit from time to time a tendency to revert to the original type . . . with their fears and their hatreds, their low spiritual conceptions and their dominant animal passions. It is the work of education, of civilization, and of religion to strive against this tendency. We can only hope that as men have . . . made steady progress in many directions, and have conquered and are conquering the animal that is in them, they may in time get the better of all the evil legacies which their primeval ancestors have bequeathed them.

Even Henry's family didn't realize the extent of his fears. Although his children asked, he rarely talked about his famous ordeal. "My own first-hand knowledge of the *Hornet* story is vague because my father seldom talked about it," his first-born son, Samuel, later said. "Whenever he spoke of it, he was unable to sleep at night. But it did not frighten him of the sea. He often traveled after that, and he even took his family on a three-months' voyage on a sailing ship." Henry's son paused, and perhaps had a revelation. "But he was always afraid of fire."

That left Fred Clough. He surfaced briefly in 1900, after the release of Twain's article. He was a carriage maker in San Francisco, and his mother had recently died, releasing him from his promise never to tell his story for publication while she still lived. A local journalist looked him up: Fred had put on weight, lost hair, and exhibited the venous tracery and florid complexion of the heavy drinker. He'd never gotten over the disaster: "The telling of his experiences is still so painful to the old sailor that he often sheds a tear in the recital," the 1900 article about him said.

In the weeks before his death, Henry heard that Clough had fallen on hard times. He directed the Phoenix Mutual Life Insurance Company of Hartford to find Samuel's savior and pay him, for the rest of his life, an annuity of $100 per year. Henry's purchase of the annuity was one of his last acts.

But finding Clough was a challenge. By now he was a different kind of castaway, one of the homeless and alcoholic old salts drifting among the waterfront's shabby rooming houses, earning pennies for liquor as courtesy "captains" steering sightseers through Frisco's sailors' dens. When the Phoenix agents found him, they could not locate a birth certificate, considered necessary. But Fred was notorious among old citizens. Oh yes, the *Hornet* survivor who was almost a cannibal, they said. The front office *could* make exceptions in extraordinary cases, and few were more extraordinary than this. He was paid quarterly for the rest of his days.

Fred drifted like that for another nine years. On July 14, 1926, he was found dying in a rooming house on Kearny Street, near San Francisco's notorious Barbary Coast. By then he was 80, the longest-lived and only remaining *Hornet* survivor, pushed from island to island on waves of grain alcohol. "Old cronies of the mariner, smoking their pipes in the sun in front of Billy Lyons' bail bond shop in Merchant Street, learned he was dead at Central Emergency Hospital," said the *San Francisco Call & Post.* The official cause of death was pneumonia, another way to drown. He struggled awhile, as had his friends in the quarter-boats, until exhaustion overcame him, too.

Near the end, the *Hornet* no longer scared him. The furnace in the night no longer haunted his dreams. He was the "sturdy sailor lad" who survived one of the longest castaway dramas on record, the boy "with the sledge-hammer fists" who guarded the water cask and saved them all. People liked to hear that story. The telling gave him identity. He was someone again.

It gave him an income as well. Each quarter the bank draft came, and with its arrival he remembered Henry's last act of kindness. His eyes teared up, whether from alcohol or emotion was hard to tell, and he was transplanted elsewhere. The floating world swayed beneath his feet, but such rocking soothed him now. "He gave me $100 a year for life," Fred rasped, and his voice trembled. "Just for a moment of kindness. Just for a drink of water."

There was a hush in the waterfront dive as old sailors remembered friends lost to the sea. But silence is threatening. Newcomers clamored for Fred to tell his famous story. A tourist bought a beer and set it before him on the bar.

"C'mon, old timer," he said, one hopes with some kindness. "Maybe this will loosen your tongue."

APPENDIX I

---•◦•---

DAILY POSITION OF THE HORNET'S LONGBOAT, FROM MITCHELL'S NOON READINGS AND LATER ESTIMATES MADE FROM CREW INTERVIEWS WITH MARK TWAIN

Day 1   Thu., May 3, 1866: Lat. 2°04' N, Long. 112°00' W
(site of the *Hornet*'s sinking)

Day 2   Fri., May 4: Lat. 2°50' N, Long. 112°45' W

Day 3   Sat., May 5: Lat. 4°00' N, Long. 111°30' W

Day 4   Sun., May 6: Lat. 5°11' N, Long. 111°05' W

Day 5   Mon., May 7: Lat. 6°12' N, Long. 110°00' W

Day 6   Tue., May 8: Lat. 6°21' N, Long. 109°99' W

Day 7   Wed., May 9: Lat. 6°50' N, Long. 108°00' W

Day 8   Thu., May 10: Lat. 7°03' N, Long. 110°32' W

Day 9   Fri., May 11: Lat. 7°00' N, Long. 109°03' W

Day 10   Sat., May 12: Lat. 7°00' N, Long. 109°00' W

Day 11   Sun., May 13: Lat. 8°08' N, Long. 109°00' W

Day 12   Mon., May 14: Lat. 9°06' N, Long. 109°00' W

Day 13   Tue., May 15: Lat. 9°40' N, Long. 109°40' W

Day 14   Wed., May 16: Lat. 10°16' N, Long. 110°18' W

Day 15   Thu., May 17: Lat. 10°40' N, Long. 109°30' W

Day 16   Fri., May 18: Lat. 11°12' N, Long. 109°10' W

Day 17   Sat., May 19: Lat. 11°20' N, Long. 110°00' W

Day 18   Sun., May 20: Lat. 12°10' N, Long. 110°50' W

Day 19   Mon., May 21: Lat. 13°00' N, Long. 111°40' W

Day 20   Tue., May 22: Lat. 13°20' N, Long. 112°35' W

Day 21   Wed., May 23: Lat. 13°45' N, Long. 113°25' W

Day 22   Thu., May 24: Lat. 14°18' N, Long. 114°20' W

Day 23   Fri., May 25: Lat. 14°45' N, Long. 115°00' W

Day 24   Sat., May 26: Lat. 15°50' N, Long. 115°00' W

Day 25   Sun., May 27: Lat. 16°06' N, Long. 117°24' W

Day 26   Mon., May 28: Lat. 16°24' N, Long. 118°15' W

Day 27   Tue., May 29: Lat. 16°44' N, Long. 119°20' W

Day 28   Wed., May 30: Lat. 17°17' N, Long. 121°00' W

Day 29   Thu., May 31: Lat. 17°45' N, Long. 123°00' W

Day 30   Fri., June 1: Lat. 18°00' N, Long. 124°30' W

Day 31   Sat., June 2: Lat. 18°09' N, Long. 126°20' W

Day 32   Sun., June 3: Lat. 17°54' N, Long. 128°30' W

Day 33   Mon., June 4: Lat. 17°06' N, Long. 130°30' W

Day 34   Tue., June 5: Lat. 16°46' N, Long. 132°10' W

Day 35   Wed., June 6: Lat. 16°30' N, Long. 134°00' W

Day 36   Thu., June 7: Lat. 16°36' N, Long. 136°00' W

Day 37   Fri., June 8: Lat. 17°15' N, Long. 138°00' W

Day 38   Sat., June 9: Lat. 17°52' N, Long. 140°20' W

Day 39   Sun., June 10: Lat. 18°36' N, Long. 142°30' W

Day 40   Mon., June 11: Lat. 19°23' N, Long. 145°00' W

Day 41   Tue., June 12: Lat. 19°52' N, Long. 147°20' W

Day 42   Wed., June 13: Lat. 20°10' N, Long. 149°50' W

Day 43   Thu., June 14: Lat. 20°00' N, Long. 152°00' W

Day 44   Fri., June 15 (a partial day at sea): Lat. 19°55' N, Long. 154°30' W (landing at Laupahoehoe in Hawaii)

SOURCES: Diary of Josiah Mitchell; Diary of Samuel Ferguson; Diary of Henry Ferguson; Alexander Crosby Brown, *Longboat to Hawaii: An Account of the Voyage of the Clipper Ship HORNET of New York Bound for San Francisco in 1866* (Cambridge, Md: Cornell Maritime Press, 1974). Brown's valuable book contains the journal entries of Mitchell and the two Fergusons, as well as Twain's occasional notes, divided as best as possible day by day.

APPENDIX II

THE <u>HORNET</u>'S CREW LIST, BY BOAT, RATING,* AND POINT OF ORIGIN

JOSIAH MITCHELL'S BOAT

Josiah A. Mitchell, shipmaster, Freeport, Maine.

Samuel Ferguson, passenger, Stamford, Connecticut.

Henry Ferguson, passenger, Stamford, Connecticut.

John Sidney Thomas, third mate, Richmond, Maine.

Harry Morris, able-bodied seaman, Havre, France.

John Campbell (misspelled as "Cambell" in Mitchell's notes),
able-bodied seaman, Fultonville, Massachusetts.

Joseph Williams ("a native of Madeira"), seaman, New Bedford,
Massachusetts.

Frederick Clough, ordinary seaman, Thomaston, Maine.

John Ferris, seaman, Port Madeira.

Antonio Possene (alternately spelled "Antone" Possene, also known
as the "Portyghee"), seaman, Cape Verde Islands.

Peter Smith (the "banished duke"), seaman, Denmark.

Charles H. Kaartman (misspelled as "Kartman" in Mitchell's notes,
also known as "Charley Irons"), seaman, Denmark.

Neil Turner, seaman, New York City.

Thomas Tate, apprentice seaman, Portsmouth, New Hampshire.

---

*The crewmen's ratings as able-bodied or ordinary seamen are not listed in Mitchell's notes and letters, and where given are simply informed speculation, based upon facts about each man's duties and experience included in the Fergusons' journals. A seaman's rating would be included in the ship's manifest, but such records are spotty at best, and the *Hornet*'s manifest for this voyage apparently no longer exists.

SAMUEL HARDY'S BOAT

Samuel F. Hardy, first mate, Chatham, Cape Cod, Massachusetts.

Henry Chisling, steward, New York City.

Joseph A. Washington (misidentified as "George Washington" in Mitchell's notes), cook, New York City.

George Whitworth, seaman, London, England.

William Lintern (misidentified as "William Linten" in Mitchell's notes), seaman, New York City.

Joseph Frank, seaman, Spain.

Joseph Collagan (misspelled as "Joseph Callagan" in Mitchell's notes), seaman, Spain.

Charles Beale, seaman, New York City.

William Laing, apprentice seaman, New York City. In some later accounts, Laing was identified as a passenger, like the Fergusons, but this was an assumption based not on the ship's manifest or Mitchell's notes, but on Laing's upper-class upbringing as the son of a New York stockbroker. The confusion was compounded by Mark Twain's notes, in which he accidentally mixed the identities of Laing and Thomas Tate. Laing was like his predecessor (and possibly his inspiration), Richard Henry Dana, a child of privilege drawn by the romance and excitement of the sea.

JOHN PARR'S BOAT

John H. Parr, second mate, North Shields, England.

Ben Laarson (also identified as "Ben Lawson"), ship's carpenter, Sweden.

Joachim Behnke (also identified as "Betinke"), seaman, Hamburg, Germany.

John Noldt (also identified as "Notat"), seaman, Hamburg, Germany.

A. J. Andersen (also identified as "Anderson"), seaman, Sweden.

James A. Mathson, seaman, Denmark.

Peter Paulson, seaman, Denmark.

James Cox, apprentice seaman, New York City. On May 22, Cox moved to Captain Mitchell's boat.

APPENDIX III

GLOSSARY

bark (also "barque"): a three-masted sailing vessel with the aftermost mast (mizzenmast) rigged fore-and-aft like a schooner, and the fore and main masts square-rigged. Smaller than a "ship."

beam-end: the "beams" of a sailing ship are the strong pieces of timber stretching across the vessel to support the deck. Thus, to be "on beam-ends" is the situation of a ship, almost always in a violent storm, when she is turned so that her beams are inclined toward the vertical and her masts are horizontal to the sea.

block: a wooden pulley with wheels, or **sheaves**, through which the rigging passes to add purchase.

chip log: a knotted piece of line attached to a triangular chip, which is thrown overboard and timed. When the time is up, the number of "knots" fed out are counted to determine speed, thus the term for nautical miles per hour.

clew: the lower corner of a square sail.

clew-iron: the shackle or iron ring attached to the **clew** of a sail.

clipper ship: a fast, three- or four-masted oceangoing sailing ship, with raking bows and masts, specifically built for speed. "Extreme" clippers, like the *Hornet*, were the longest of this type of ship, and even more narrow in profile.

dead reckoning: the method of estimating a ship's position by compass and distance in the log when more direct observation is not possible.

donkey's breakfast: a sailor's mattress, made from straw, considered part of his gear.

fall: the hanging, hauling part of a rope.

fathom: a nautical measure of six feet, primarily used for depth, or soundings. The British Parliament once defined a fathom as "the length of a man's arms around the object of his affections."

forecastle: the part of the upper deck forward of the fore mast. Also, the forward part of the vessel where the sailors live, as opposed to the officers, who live in the "afterdeck" or "aftercabin."

gunwale (or "gunnel"): the upper rail on the side of a boat or ship.

halyard: the rope running up the mast that pulls up the sail.

hawse-hole: the hole in the bows through which the anchor cable runs. To "come up through the hawse-hole" is a term used to describe a ship's captain who started at the very bottom, as a common sailor or even a green hand.

jibboom: the spar set forward on a ship, beyond the bowsprit, to which is rigged a triangular sail, or "jib."

leeward: the lee side of a boat, or the side opposite that from which the wind blows.

longboat: the largest boat in a merchant vessel, usually carried between the fore and main masts. A longboat usually measures 20 feet in length or more, and is the principal lifeboat in a sailing ship, able to carry the greatest number of men and largest quantity of stores.

mizzentop: a "top" is a platform, placed over the head of a lower mast and supported by strong timbers, or "trestle-trees," for the convenience of the men aloft. Thus, the **mizzentop** is that platform on the aftermost mast, or "mizzenmast."

pooped: a vessel is "pooped" when a sea breaks over her stern. The "poop" itself is the deck raised over the after part of a ship.

port: the left side of a vessel, looking forward. Originally "larboard," but later changed in common usage to avoid confusion with **starboard,** the right side of a vessel.

prime meridian: the meridian from which longitude is reckoned and, since 1794, fixed at Greenwich, England. Longitude 0°.

quarter-boat: the smaller boats in a merchant vessel, approximately half the size of a longboat.

ratline: any of the small lines strung across the shrouds of a sailing ship like ladder-rungs and used to climb the rigging.

reeve (or "rove"): to pass a line through a block.

saloon: the messroom in a sailing ship, usually in the aftercabin, where the officers are served their meals.

sea anchor: an open-ended canvas cone, or "drag," used to stabilize a boat in a storm.

seaway: the open sea, implying unhindered passage. Sometimes, a rough sea, as in "in a seaway."

sheaves: the wheels of a wooden pulley, or **block**.

slush: the grease, skimmed from the top of boiling salt meat, used to lubricate masts and yards.

soger: to goof off or goldbrick in order to escape work, usually by pretending an illness or injury.

spanker: the fore-and-aft after sail of a ship or bark, set with a gaff and boom.

spar: a general term for masts, yards, gaffs, booms, and so forth.

speak: to hail another ship on the open sea. To "speak" another ship usually entailed lying to and relaying such information as destination, general conditions aboard ship, and gossip, as well as messages to owners and families.

starboard: the right side of a vessel, looking forward.

studding sail: light sails set outside the square sails, on booms rigged especially for that purpose. Studding sails were set in a fair wind and in moderate weather, and were often used on clipper ships for extra speed.

sweeps: the large oars carried on longboats, used for extra leverage in forcing them ahead.

thwart: the seats going across a longboat.

tiller: the bar of wood or iron used to move the rudder.

windward: the side of a vessel or boat from which the wind blows. Opposite of **leeward**.

yard: a long piece of timber hung by its center to the mast, upon which is spread a square sail.

yard arms: the extremities of a yard.

NOTES

PREFACE

xiii **era of dynamite.** Richard Maxwell Brown, "Historical Patterns of Violence in America." In *The History of Violence in America: A Report to the National Commission on the Causes and Prevention of Violence,* Hugh Davis Graham and Ted Robert Gurr, ed, (New York: Bantam Books, 1969), p. 74.

xiii **the United States had the bloodiest** Philip Taft and Philip Ross, "American Labor Violence: Its Causes, Character and Outcome." In *The History of Violence in America: A Report to the National Commission on the Causes and Prevention of Violence,* Hugh Davis Graham and Ted Robert Gurr, ed, (New York: Bantam Books, 1969), p. 281.

xiv **"When it came night the white waves."** Stephen Crane, "The Open Boat." In *The Norton Anthology of Short Fiction,* ed. R.V. Cassill (New York: W.W. Norton & Company, 1978), p. 371.

PROLOGUE   A FIRE AT SEA

2 **Of all classes of men, the mariner.** Ship's steward Washington Fosdick's memoirs were quoted in Margaret Scott Creighton, *The Private Life of Jack Tar: Sailors at Sea in the Nineteenth Century* (a dissertation published for the Boston University Graduate School, 1985), p. 12.

2 **The constant threat of an unpredictable environment.** Creighton, *The Private Life of Jack Tar,* p. 12.

2 **the voyage was made under such strange circumstances.** Leigh H. Irvine, "The Lone Cruise of the HORNET Men: The Personal Narrative of Frederick Clough." *The Wide World Magazine,* London (vol. 5, no. 30), September 1900, p. 573.

3 **In the 1870s, when marine insurers.** Charles P. Kindleberger, *Mariners and Markets* (New York: New York University Press, 1992), p. 37. His analysis was drawn from the British Parliament's "Loss of Life Commission" findings of 1887.

4 **walked the waters like a thing of life.** Quoted in A.B.C. Whipple and the editors of Time-Life Books, *The Clipper Ships* (Alexandria, Va.: Time-Life Books, 1980), p. 6.

4 **give him a passage to the other world.** The hatred of sharks by sailors was best described in Richard Henry Dana Jr., *Two Years Before the Mast: A Personal Narrative of Life at Sea* (New York: Penguin Books, 1983, first printed 1840), p. 168.

10 **a man of rare caution.** Quoted in Irvine, "The Lone Cruise of the HORNET Men," *The Wide World Magazine,* p. 572.

CHAPTER 1   THE PICNIC CRUISE

16 **Mitchell had commanded the *Hornet*.** The information on the *Hornet*'s previous voyages under Prince Harding and Josiah Mitchell were found in William Armstrong Fairburn's *Merchant Sail*, vol. 6 (Fairburn Marine Educational Foundation, 1945–1955), in the section "Chamberlain & Phelps," pp. 3808–3811.

16 **or nearly $4.4 million in today's dollars.** This and all later conversion to present-day, or inflation-adjusted, dollars are calculated by using an "Inflation Adjustor" developed by Professor Robert Sahr of the Oregon State University Political Science Department and included in the Resources section of the *Columbia Journalism Review's* site on the World Wide Web, URL: http://www.cjr.org.

16 **notices of wreck and ruin.** The shipwrecks of January 9–11 were all recorded in the shipping columns of *New York Herald*, January 11–13, 1866.

17 **an average sustained speed of six knots.** As all good mariners know, but many landlubbers do not, nautical miles and land miles are different. A nautical mile equals 1.15 statute miles, or miles on land, and speeds and wind velocities are stated in knots, or nautical miles an hour. Thus, 20 knots equals 23 mph, and 22 knots equals 25.3 mph.

17 **high-duty freight composed of smaller, more valuable items.** James P. Delgado, *To California by Sea: A Maritime History of the California Gold Rush* (Columbia, S.C.: University of South Carolina Press, 1990), p. 44. During the Gold Rush, "measurement goods" commanded a freight rate of $1 per cubic foot, while an average of $60 to $70 a ton was charged for bulkier cargo. Also, Robert Evans, Jr., "'Without Regard for Cost,' The Returns on Clipper Ships," *Journal of Political Economy* (February 1964), p. 33ff.

18 **Robert Evans, Jr., has argued that even after costs.** Robert Evans, Jr., "'Without Regard for Cost,' The Returns on Clipper Ships," *Journal of Political Economy* (February 1964), p. 42. Also, the rate of returns on clipper ships was quoted in Evans, "'Without Regard for Cost'," Pp. 41–42.

19 **Edmund, the third brother, left an estate.** Interview, June 2001, with Henry Ferguson.

20 **sweet, insipid, or saltish.** Quoted from a popular medical textbook in the mid-1800s, in Katherine Ott, *Fevered Lives: Tuberculosis in American Culture since 1870* (Cambridge, Mass.: Harvard University Press, 1996), p. 25.

20 **his body assumed the classic proportions of the dying.** The description and quotation were drawn from medical textbooks of the 1800s, quoted in Ott, *Fevered Lives*, p. 10.

21 **Decay and disease are often beautiful.** Quoted in Ott, *Fevered Lives*, p. 13.

21 **When the doors of the slaughter-houses.** John Cadman, *The Round Trip by Way of Panama* (New York: G.P. Putnam's Sons, 1879), p. 113.

21 **scarcely ever heard of, and never expected** Michael E. Bell, *Food for the Dead: On the Trail of New England's Vampires* (New York: Carroll & Graf Publishers, 2001), p. 32. Bell quotes from Logan Clendening, comp., *Source Book of Medical History* (New York: Dover Publications, Inc., 1960), p. 434.

21 **when Roman orator Cicero spat blood.** Quoted in Thomas Dormandy, *The White Death: A History of Tuberculosis* (New York: New York University Press, 2000), p. 105.

21 **the seeking of life under more gentle skies.** Stevenson is quoted more extensively in Dormandy, *The White Death*, p. 105. Like Samuel, he also took a sea voyage to the tropics, though his trip was far less of an ordeal.

21 **Go West and Breathe Again!** Dormandy, *The White Death*, p. 120.

22 **the shipping press described her.** Quoted in William Armstrong Fairburn, *Merchant Sail*, vol. 6 (Fairburn Marine Educational Foundation, 1945–1955), p. 3808.

23 **a high grade reflecting her 15 years of service.** Evans, "Without Regard for Cost," p. 37. Evans was able to determine the average life-span of clippers by looking at the records of 223 out of approximately 425 such ships. The life of a ship was considered ended when it was listed as wrecked, went ashore, was condemned and sold for salvage, or was rebuilt in another form. The life expectancy for a clipper at launching ranged from 13.1 years for medium clippers to 17 years for regular ones; after ten years, that diminished from 9.5 years for extreme clippers to 14.1 years for regular ones. In 1866, the *Hornet* was 15 years old, which by Evans' figures put her past her prime.

23 **A ship is born when she is launched** *Tucker* v. *Alexandroff*, 183 U.S. 424 (1902): "A ship is born when she is launched, and lives so long as her identity is preserved. Prior to her launching she is a mere congeries of wood and iron—an ordinary piece of personal property—as distinctly a land structure as a house, and subject only to mechanics' liens created by a state law and enforceable in the state courts. In the baptism of launching she receives her name, and from the moment her keel touches the water she is transformed, and becomes a subject of admiralty jurisdiction. She acquires a personality of her own; becomes competent to contract, and is individually liable for her obligations, upon which she may sue in the name of her owner, and be sued in her own name. Her owners' agents may not be her agents, and her agents may not be her owners' agents. She is capable, too, of committing a tort, and is responsible for damages therefor. She may also become a quasi-bankrupt; may be sold for the payment of her debts, and thereby receive a complete discharge from all prior liens, with liberty to begin a new life, contract further obligations, and perhaps be subjected to a second sale."

23 **swift little pilot boats clustered at the harbor mouth.** Regulations drafted in 1694 required the presence of pilots aboard all in- and outbound ships to the New York Harbor, but left open the means by which the pilots were paid. Thus, the swift little pilot boats clustered outside the harbor like towtrucks around auto wrecks today. Their pay was based on the length and draft of each vessel they guided into port, and so when a larger ship—such as a clipper or transatlantic steamer—appeared above the horizon they raced to be first, leaving the smaller ships for losers.

24 **Clipper cabins could be luxurious.** Joan Druett, *Hen Frigates: Wives of Merchant Captains Under Sail* (New York: Simon & Schuster, 1998), p. 52–53.

26 **half open, as though just ready to grasp a rope.** Dana, *Two Years Before the Mast*, p. 41.

26 **and probably scarred.** Ira Dye, "Early American Merchant Seafarers." In *Proceedings of the American Philosophical Society* 120 (October 1976), p. 357.

26 **The history of Thomaston, Maine** From "Thomaston—The Town That Went to Sea." World Wide Web, URL: www.mint.net/thomastonhistoricalsociety /wentto.ktm.

27 **One exterminator hired to clean out a nest of rats.** A.B.C. Whipple, *The Challenge* (New York: William Morrow and Company, 1987), p. 122.

27 **they could digest anything small enough to swallow.** Frederick Pease Harlow, *The Making of a Sailor, or Sea Life Aboard a Yankee Square-Rigger* (Mineola, New York: Dover Publications, 1988, reprint from 1928 edition). The joys of salt beef and other foremast delicacies are delineated on pp. 147–149.

27 **Prejudice among groups was rampant.** Margaret Baker, *The Folklore of the Sea* (London: David & Charles, 1979), p. 178.

28 **The close of the war with our resources.** Quoted in Shelby Foote, *The Civil War, A Narrative: Red River to Appomattox* (New York: Vintage Books, 1974), p. 1042.

29 **deputized each and every American.** Jimmy M. Skaggs, *The Great Guano Rush: Entrepeneurs and American Overseas Expansion* (New York: St. Martin's Griffin, 1994), p. 224

30 **the toughest class of men in all respects.** Quoted in Whipple, *The Clipper Ships*, p. 84.

30 **They were a class of humans incapable of self-regulation.** Creighton, *The Private Life of Jack Tar*, p. 97.

31 **to raise themselves above their betters.** Whipple, *The Clipper Ships*, p. 127.

32 **They say I hung my mother.** "Hanging Johnny," Harlow, *The Making of a Sailor, or Sea Life Aboard a Yankee Square-Rigger*, pp. 253–254.

32 **to be numbered neither with the living nor the dead.** Quoted in Greg Dening, *Mr. Bligh's Bad Language: Passion, Power and Theatre on the Bounty* (New York: Cambridge University Press, 1992), p. 56.

32 **a distant and peculiar species.** Creighton, *The Private Life of Jack Tar*, p. 170.

CHAPTER 2   DEAD RECKONING

39 **as if we hadn't any home anymore.** Mark Twain, "Burning of the Clipper Ship *Hornet*," *Sacramento Daily Union*, July 19, 1866.

41 **changes were occurring that were nowhere more apparent.** Most immigrants in midcentury were from Ireland, still fleeing the effects of the Great Famine of 1848. By 1860, 1,611,304 Irish lived in America, and one in eight of them, or 203,740, were crammed into Manhattan.

41 **The nation is . . . in a state of Revolution.** *Washington Times*, quoted in "The New York Draft Riots" on the World Wide Web, URL: www.civilwarhome.com /draftriots.htm

41 **When the riot ended, at least 2,000** Although the statistics on injury and damage resulting from the Draft Riots are general, many of the details were taken from Herbert Asbury, *The Gangs of New York: An Informal History of the Underworld* (New York: Alfred A. Knopf, 1927, reprint 1998 by Thunder's Mouth Press), pp. 154–155.

42 **They have manifested a degree of tenderness.** Journal of Avery Parker, quoted in Creighton, *The Private Life of Jack Tar*, p. 97.

42 **A framework of statutes.** A whole host of laws that circumscribed the rights and lives of American and British sailors from colonial times until the Civil War is included in Jesse Lemisch, "Jack Tar in the Streets: Merchant Seamen in the Politics of Revolutionary America," *William and Mary Quarterly* 25 (July 1968), pp. 377–380, text and footnotes.

44 **The elasticity of feeling which he breathed.** Matthew Fontaine Maury, *Explanations and Sailing Directions to accompany the Wind and Current Charts*, vol. I and II, 8th edition (Washington: William A. Harris, Printer, 1858), p. 40.

44 **The rays of the torrid sun.** Maury, *Explanations and Sailing Directions*, p. 56.

47 **Samuel copied a list of islands.** The list of seven islands and their real, or erroneous, positions can be found in Nathaniel Bowditch, *The New American Practical Navigator*, 29th ed. (New York: E. & G.W. Blunt, 1860), p. 375.

54 **That Sunday morning, Mitchell also dreamed.** Josiah Mitchell never reported his dream in his journal, and apparently never mentioned it to his family. But immediately after his rescue, he seemed desperate to be fully understood and so described the dream to Twain, who outlined it in his notes. However, when writing up the *Hornet* disaster for the *Sacramento Daily Union* and *Harper's Monthly Magazine*, Twain omitted all mention of it, possibly because the dream did not make sense to him or did not fit his image of Mitchell's character. Twain always emphasized Mitchell's courage and steadfastness, but rarely his doubts and certainly never his abiding sense of guilt. Mark Twain, *Mark Twain's Notebooks and Journals, vol. 1 (1855–1873)*, ed. Frederick Anderson, Michael B. Frank, and Kenneth M. Sanderson (Berkeley, Calif.: University of California Press, 1975), p. 156.

CHAPTER 3   THE DOLDRUMS

55 **There is in a gael.** James Boswell, *The Life of Samuel Johnson, LL.D.* (Modern Library Edition; first published 1791), p. 589.

58 **speck of terrain.** *The North Pacific Pilot*, quoted in Alexander Crosby Brown, "Isles of Vain Hope," *The Log of Mystic Seaport* (October 1976), p. 75.

58 **from what was listed in the charts.** *Bowditch* listed Clipperton Island at 10°28' N and 109°19' W, while the true fix determined by satellite positioning is 10°17' N and 109°10' W.

58 **immense castle.** James M. Imray, *The North Pacific Pilot, Part II* (London, 1870), p. 279.

58 **They were very large.** Sir Edmund Belcher's notes on Clipperton Island are quoted in Alexander George Findlay, *A Directory for the Navigation of the North Pacific Ocean*, 3rd ed. (London, 1886), p. 1029.

59 **By 1866, a three-way tug-of-war existed.** The first permanent settlement occurred with Oceanic Phosphate's arrival in 1893, and even then, the island was hostile. The largest number of deaths ever associated with an American guano operation

occurred there when 100 Japanese workers died from drinking contaminated water, a disaster never officially corroborated.

60 **He was paid not to have doubt.** The subject of Mitchell's pay raises questions. There are no records of the bonus given to Mitchell, but Captain PrinceHarding's sudden sickness and the cargo, already insured at $400,000, virtually insures that some private arrangement beside wages was arranged. The planned cruise, from New York to San Francisco, and then back home via China and England, would have taken almost a year: such absences placed stress on captains' families, and to have a man leave suddenly before his affairs were in order made the leavetaking doubly stressful. At least one scholar, A.C. Brown, thought that the "Fergusons' father probably made some private arrangement with the owners," since the *Hornet* was not a passenger carrier. *Letter: A.C. Brown to Deborah A. Berger, U.S. Naval Institute, Annapolis, MD, Oct. 23, 1978, A.C. Brown Collection, folder 27, The Mariners Museum.*

60 **profound depression and indifference that.** Stephen Crane, "The Open Boat." In *The Norton Anthology of Short Fiction*, ed. R.V. Cassill (New York: W.W. Norton & Company, 1978), p. 353.

60 **individuals swing between feelings.** Warren Kinston and Rachel Rosser, "Disaster: Effects of Mental and Physical State," *Journal of Psychosomatic Research*, 18 (1974), p. 442.

60 **absence of emotion, inhibition..** Kinston and Rosser, "Disaster: Effects of Mental and Physical State," p. 442.

61 **decided, calculating mischief.** Owen Chase's account of the sinking of the *Essex*, quoted in Nathaniel Philbrick, *In the Heart of the Sea, The Tragedy of the Whaleship Essex* (New York: Viking, 2000), p. 108.

61 **The psychologist William James.** James's actual quotation regarding the inevitability of myth was as follows: "I realize now how inevitable were men's earlier mythological versions [of disaster] and how artificial and against the grain of our spontaneous perceiving are the later habits which science educates us." Quoted in Philbrick, *In the Heart of the Sea*, p. 108.

63 **Lang was sunk in a depression.** Twain's notes on William Laing, the "young gentleman sailor." Included in Mark Twain, *Notebooks and Journals, vol. 1 (1855–1873)*, ed. Frederick Anderson, Michael B. Frank, and Kenneth M. Sanderson (Berkeley, Calif.: University of California Press, 1975), p. 148.

63 **prayed out fervently to God to protect and save us.** Quoted in William Jeffrey Bolster, *Black Jacks: African American Seamen in the Age of Sail* (Cambridge, Mass.: Harvard University Press, 1997), p. 125.

63 **'Oh, God, get me out of this.'** Scott Henderson and Tudor Bostock, "Coping Behavior after Shipwreck," *British Journal of Psychiatry*, 131 (1977), p. 17.

63 **the two-masted schooner Nimrod on August 26, 1858.** There is a second wreck that Chisling could have been referring to, the sinking on November 3, 1863, of the two-masted schooner *Gulielma*, which struck a breakwater at Buffalo Harbor during a storm and was pounded to pieces by the waves. However, Chisling's statement that he was also aboard the *Dreadnaught* with famous clipper captain Samuel Samuels makes the timing of his presence aboard the *Nimrod* more likely. Information on both

the *Nimrod* and the *Gulielma* wrecks contained in "The Great Lakes Shipwreck Research Foundation: David Swayze Great Lakes Shipwreck File," on the World Wide Web. URL: www.ghost-ships.org.

64 **'wasting beef,' 'burning a pudding,' and 'boiling rotten eggs.** Quoted in Margaret Creighton, *The Private Life of Jack Tar*, p. 99.

64 **stamped him and hammered him.** Quoted in Creighton, *The Private Life of Jack Tar*, pp. 100–101.

64 **'presume upon his equality"** Quoted from several contemporary texts and journals in Bolster, *Black Jacks*, p. 165.

65 **British cooks were said to skim £50 in slush.** Charles P. Kindleberger, *Mariners and Markets*, p. 43.

65 **Last night I dreamed of home.** Benson's journals are quoted extensively in Michael Sokolow, *"What a Miserable Life a Sea Fareing Life Is": The Life and Experiences of a Nineteenth-Century Mariner of Color* (a dissertation for the Boston University Graduate School of Arts and Sciences, 1997) p. 129.

66 **You and the children must have things.** Sokolow, *"What a Miserable Life a Sea Fareing Life Is,"* p. 130.

66 **three times, but it was dark.** Quoted in Margaret Creighton, *The Private Life of Jack Tar*, p. 55.

CHAPTER 4   CHIMERAS

70 **The first indication of a deficiency.** Quoted in Ancel Keys et al., *The Biology of Human Starvation* 2 vols. (Minneapolis: University of Minnesota Press, 1950), p. 786.

70 **molasses-like feeling of being stuck in endless time.** Maggie Scarf, *Unfinished Business: Pressure Points in the Lives of Women* (New York: Doubleday and Co., 1980), p. 347, quoted in Edward T. Hall, *The Dance of Life: The Other Dimension of Time* (Garden City, N.Y.: Anchor Press, 1984), p. 132.

70 **Studies of fishing crews subject to isolation.** Jan Horbulewicz, "The Parameters of the Psychological Autonomy of Industrial Trawler Crews." In *Seafarer and Community: Toward a Social Understanding of Seafaring*, ed. Peter H. Fricke (London: Croom Helm Ltd., 1973), p. 74.

71 **his famous predecessor William Bligh.** Bligh's rages are described in Dening, *Mr. Bligh's Bad Language*, p. 58.

72 **every man, against every man?** Thomas Hobbes, *Leviathan*, ed. Michael Oakeshott (Oxford, 1955), p. 82.

72 **life, health, liberty, or possessions.** John Locke, *Two Treatises of Government*, ed. Thomas I. Cook (New York, 1947), p. 44.

CHAPTER 5   THE STALKING SEA

77 **his lip quivered.** Although this passage did not appear in the three journals, it was told to Twain by Mitchell and later appeared in his notes: "Capt. said the boys

[Fergusons] were good grit. Henry's lip never quivered but once, and that was when he was told that there was barely a shadow of a chance for their rescue—and then the feeling he showed was chiefly at the thought that he was never to see his college mates any more." Mark Twain, *Mark Twain's Notebooks and Journals*, p. 142.

81 **A great black dragon is seen.** John of Brompton is quoted in Fletcher S. Bassett, *Legends and Superstitions of the Sea and Sailors: In All Lands and at All times* (Chicago & New York: Belford, Clarke & Co., 1885), p. 30.

82 **"shot the dragon"** Quoted in Margaret Baker, *The Folklore of the Sea* (London: David & Charles, 1979), p. 164.

86 **the copper sheathing, the felt.** Quoted in Gudger, "The Alleged Pugnacity of the Swordfish and the Spearfishes as Shown by Their Attacks on Vessels," *Memoirs of the Royal Asiatic Society of Bengal*, vol 12, no. 2, 1940, p. 232.

86 **penetrated to a depth of 30 inches.** *New York Herald*, May 11, 1871.

86 **neither to be trusted.** E.W. Gudger, "The Perils and Romance of Swordfishing: The Pursuit of Xiphias Gladius with the Trident in the Strait of Messina," *The Scientific Monthly*, July 1940, vol 51, p. 38.

87 **It not unfrequently happens.** Gudger, "The Alleged Pugnacity of the Swordfish," p. 235.

87 **It quickly turned and rushed at and under the boat.** Quoted in Gudger, "The Alleged Pugnacity of the Swordfish," p. 271.

CHAPTER 6   THE FIRST PARTING

89 **It is like losing a limb.** Richard Henry Dana, Jr.,*Two Years Before the Mast*, p. 77.

90 **Sailors are almost all believers.** Dana, *Two Years Before the Mast*, p. 78.

90 **To work hard, live hard.** Dana, *Two Years Before the Mast*, p. 78.

92 **According to the Talmud.** Jewish Battlefield Ethics," URL: www.aleph-institute.org/html/MARCHMEN.HTM. Specific verses are: "His life is no less valuable than your own" (Pesachim 25b); and, "What makes you think his blood is more red than yours?" (Sanhedrin 75a). The authors also drew examples from Alfred J. Kolatch, *The Second Jewish Book of Why*.

92 **the need to refuse to accept death.** Scott Henderson and Tudor Bostock, "Coping Behavior after Shipwreck," *British Journal of Psychiatry*, p. 17.

93 **At first my thoughts dwell.** Quoted in Ancel Keys, *The Biology of Human Starvation*, p. 817.

93 **You can't humble the soul if you don't ration the bread.** Peter France, *Hermits: The Insights of Solitude* (New York: St. Martin's Press, 1997), p. 35.

93 **Father Tertullian of the early church.** Walter Vandereycker and Ron Van Deth, *From Fasting Saints to Anorexic Girls: The History of Self-Starvation* (New York: New York University Press, 1994), p. 15.

94 **In general,wrote Lewis Petrinovich.** Lewis Petrinovich, *The Cannibal Within* (New York: Aldine de Gruyter, 2000), p. 49.

94 **After thirty-two years I find.** Mark Twain, "My Debut as a Literary Person," *Century Magazine*, November 1899 (vol. 59, no. 1).

95 **his smiling visage and adventurous spirit.** Dougal Robertson, *Survive the Savage Sea* (Dobbs Ferry, N.Y.: Sheridan House, Inc., 1994), p 15.

95 **Left to your own devices.** Robertson, *Survive the Savage Sea*, p. 86.

95 **If you disobey an order again, I'll hit you with this!** Robertson, *Survive the Savage Sea*, p. 157.

97 **Death is at all times solemn.** Richard Henry Dana, Jr., *Two Years Before the Mast*, p. 77.

98 **public, independent, dependent on rituals.** Dening, *Mr. Bligh's Bad Language*, pp. 80–81.

101 **The world lives on death.** Joseph Campbell, *The Masks of God: Primitive Mythology* (New York: Penguin Books, 1976), p. 177.

CHAPTER 7   THE SECOND PARTING

110 **More than anything else, they felt as if they were 'growing old.'** Keys, *The Biology of Human Starvation*, p. 828.

110 **unusual vindictiveness.** Cited in Keys, *The Biology of Human Starvation*, p. 909.

110 **the *combat* personality.** Cited in Keys, *The Biology of Human Starvation*, p. 909.

110 **intoxicating blindness.** The words of castaway Owen Chase, first mate aboard the doomed whaler *Essex*, quoted in Nathaniel Philbrick, *In the Heart of the Sea*, p. 159.

112 **pleasant dream.** James Lowson is quoted in Sebastian Junger, *The Perfect Storm: A True Story of Men Against the Sea*, pp. 143–145.

112 **An immense energy pulls at my mind** Steven Callahan, *Adrift: Seventy-Six Days Lost at Sea* (Boston: Houghton Mifflin, 1986), p. 149.

112 **as a terrier dog does a rat.** David Livingstone recounted the attack by the lion in his 1857 *Missionary Travels and Researches in South Africa*, quoted in Sherwin B. Nuland *How We Die: Reflections on Life's Final Chapter* (New York: Vintage Books, 1995), p. 134.

113 **Nothing would please me more.** Nuland, *How We Die*, p. 138. My own grandfather, Charles Arthur Jackson, experienced one such "near-death" moment during his first massive heart attack in 1978. The sequence was the same as that described by Kenneth Long and Sherwin Nuland—darkness, bright light, entering the light—and then a lush field, a kind of "Fiddlers' green," split by a clear stream. On the other side of the water stood his sister Mary and brother Joe, both of whom had predeceased him; when he started across the stream they held up their hands and Mary said, "Go back, Charlie, now is not your time." Reluctantly, he returned. My grandfather had quietly been a skeptic before this incident; he was no more. I, too, am a skeptic, but it makes me wonder. With all the violent death I've seen in my life, perhaps there's more in the end than that final, terror-filled, terminal gasp. If nothing else, my grandfather no longer seemed frightened of death after his encounter by the water. He was more at peace with the death that would not come for another ten years. Perhaps the end as we know it, he said, is not really an end.

CHAPTER 8   ALONE

115 **The dark side of a man's mind.** Richard E. Byrd, *Alone* (New York: Ace Books, 1938), p. 127.

117 **The jar of meal will not be emptied, and the jug of oil will not fail.** I Kings 17:13–14.

117 **This widow was observed.** The widow at the Temple is described in Mark 12:42–44.

117 **battleground for the soul of man.** Daniel E. Sutherland, *The Expansion of Everyday Life: 1860–1876* (New York: Harper & Row, Publishers, 1989), p. 127.

117 **home beyond the skies.** Sutherland, *The Expansion of Everyday Life*, pp. 127–128.

118 **Physical pain does not simply resist language.** Elaine Scarry, *The Body in Pain* (New York: Oxford University Press, 1985), p. 4.

119 **a bitter memory of how Possene.** Thomas's thoughts and calculations were given to Mark Twain in the "Burning of the Clipper Ship 'Hornet' at Sea: Detailed Account of the Sufferings of Officers and Crew, as given by the Third Officer and Members of the Crew," *Sacramento Daily Union*, July 19, 1866.

120 **Isn't the situation romantic enough.** Twain's remarks are quoted in Alexander Crosby Brown, *Longboat to Hawaii: An Account of the Voyage of the Clipper Ship HORNET of New York Bound for San Francisco in 1866* (Cambridge, Md: Cornell Maritime Press, 1974), p. 151. Brown's book is neither a narrative nor an interpretation of events, but it is a helpful daily compendium of three journals by Mitchell and the Ferguson brothers, as well as commentary from Twain's writings.

121 **nature's flophouses for the outcast.** William Sill, "The Anvil of Evolution," *Earthwatch*, August 2001, p. 27.

122 **stirred up by impressment gangs.** Richard Maxwell Brown, "Historical Patterns of Violence in America." In *The History of Violence in America: A Report to the National Commission on the Causes and Prevention of Violence*, ed, Hugh Davis Graham and Ted Robert Gurr, (New York: Bantam Books, 1969), p. 73.

122 **the lower class were beyond measure enraged.** Lemisch, "Jack Tar in the Streets," p. 391.

122 **the nature of protest had changed largely to work stoppage.** Briton C. Busch, "Brace and Be Dam'd: Work Stoppages on American Whaleships, 1820–1920," *International Journal of Maritime History* 3, no. 2 (December 1991), p. 102.

126 **while its graceful folds float.** Florence G. Thurston and Harmon S. Cross, *Three Centuries of Freeport, Maine* (Freeport, Maine: 1940), p. 78.

127 **great white racehorses of the sea.** Harold Waldo, "Yankee Captain and Southern Pilot," *Overland Monthly and Out West Magazine*, May 1924, p. 200.

127 **the capacity to be alone.** Jan Horbulewicz, "The Parameters of the Psychological Autonomy of Industrial Trawler Crews." In *Seafarer and Community: Toward a Social Understanding of Seafaring*, ed. Peter H. Fricke (London: Croom Helm Ltd., 1973), p. 72.

127 **doomed to sad thoughts.** Mary Putnam's diary, quoted in Joan Druett,

Hen Frigates: Wives of Merchant Captains Under Sail (New York: Simon & Schuster, 1998), p. 190.

128 **To have a seaman's chest.** Quoted in Lisa Norling, *Captain Ahab Had a Wife: New England Women and the Whalefishery, 1720–1870* (Chapel Hill, N.C.: University of North Carolina Press, 2000), p. 192.

128 **uniquely pious.** Norling, *Captain Ahab Had a Wife*, p. 170.

129 **crucible of female strength.** Quoted in Lisa Norling, *Captain Ahab Had a Wife*, p. 193.

130 **We can scarcely conceive.** Quoted in Lisa Norling, *Captain Ahab Had a Wife*, p. 193.

130 **poisonous to her existence, and sink too deeply into the breast to be eradicated.** Quoted in Lisa Norling, *Captain Ahab Had a Wife*, p. 194.

CHAPTER 9   THE THEFT

135 **The most conspicuous psychological abnormality.** The British psychological report of the survivors of Bergen-Belsen is quoted in Ancel Keys, *The Biology of Human Starvation*, p. 798.

135 **Nothing else counted.** Quoted in Herbert A. Bloch, "The Personality of Inmates of Concentration Camps," *American Journal of Sociology* (1947), p. 338.

CHAPTER 10   THE AMERICAN GROUP

141 **Passivity is itself.** John Leach, *Survival Psychology* (New York: New York University Press, 1994), p. 167.

141 **Think if you like of the distance.** Bligh's statement, recorded in survivors's journals, was quoted in Charles Nordhoff and James Norman Hall, *Men Against the Sea* (1934), compiled in Nordhoff and Hall, *The Bounty Trilogy: Comprising the Three Volumes "Mutiny on the Bounty," "Men Against the Sea," & "Pitcairn's Island"* (Boston: Little, Brown & Company, 1964), p. 356. Although a work of fiction, the *Bounty Trilogy* was an ambitious work of psychological investigation based on copious use of historical sources to answer the enigmas of both Mr. Bligh and Mr. Christian.

141 **Since no estimate I have heard of.** Robertson, *Survive the Savage Sea*, p. 205.

141 **The enormous difference.** Robertson, *Survive the Savage Sea*, p. 205.

141 **The barrier of bitterness.** Robertson, *Survive the Savage Sea*, p. 143.

142 **the ideal distance between people.** Michael Stadler, *The Psychology of Sailing: The Sea's Effects on Mind and Body* (Camden, Maine: International Marine Publishing Co., 1987), p. 97.

142 **Rats, the most social of mammals.** Quoted in *Virginian-Pilot*, January 26, 2002, p. A12.

142 **behavioral sink.** John R. Calhoun, "Population Density and Social Pathology," *Scientific American* 206 (February 1962), p. 144.

143 **moved through the community like somnambulists.** Calhoun, "Population Density and Social Pathology," p. 146.

148 **the relieving gift of self-expression.** Hilde O. Bluhm, "How Did They Survive?" *American Journal of Psychotherapy,* 2, no. 1 (1948), p. 10.

148 **a strange mood took possession.** Leon Szalet, *Experiment "E," a report from an extermination laboratory* (New York: Didier Press, 1945), p. 137.

150 **Historians have noticed an intimate, familial.** Edmund Fuller, "The Nature of Mutiny," *Mutiny!: Being Accounts of Insurrections, Famous and Infamous, on Land and Sea, from the Days of the Caesars to Modern Times,* (New York: Crown Publishers, 1953), p. ix.

151 **The contract of a sailor.** *Robertson* v. *Baldwin,* 165 U.S. 275 (1897), popularly known as the *Arago* case. The High Court's decision did not occur in a vacuum, however, but evolved out of a lineage of ancient and medieval sea laws almost as old as records of the sea. They included the Law of Rhodes of the third century B.C., then were codified over the next 1,800 years in the Ordinances of Triani, the Judgment of Oleron, the Maritime Laws of Wisby, the Maritime Laws of Damme, and the Consolato del Mare. British sea laws evolved from these continental codes, and American sea laws evolved in turn from the British. Jay M. Pawa, "The Jefferson Borden Pirates and Samuel Gompers: Aftermath of a Mutiny," *The American Neptune: A Quarterly Journal of Maritime History* 27 (January 1967), p. 49ff, and "Robertson v. Baldwin," URL: www.guncite.com/court.fed/sc.

152 **the disturbance of minds.** Leonard F. Guttridge, *Mutiny: A History of Naval Insurrection* (Annapolis, Md: Naval Institute Press, 1992), p. 5.

152 **Mutiny in my ship.** Quoted in Guttridge, *Mutiny: A History of Naval Insurrection,* p. 2.

153 **the unwholesomeness of the victual.** Guttridge, *Mutiny: A History of Naval Insurrection,* p. 7.

153 **The adage that idleness is the root of evil.** Guttridge, *Mutiny: A History of Naval Insurrection,* p. 7.

153 **incoherent protest.** Fletcher Pratt, "Mutiny—A Study," *United States Naval Institute Proceedings,* April 1932, vol. 58, no. 4, p. 532.

CHAPTER 11   DELIRIUM

159 **do not taste good.** Konrad Lorenz, *On Aggression,* trans. Marjorie Kerr Wilson (New York: Bantam Books, 1963, 1966), p. 115.

159 **Darius, after he got the kingdoms of [Persia].** Herodotus, *Histories,* 3:38. Quoted in Peter France, *Hermits: The Insights of Solitude* (New York: St. Martin's Press, 1997), pp. 10–11.

160 **this mania for eating people.** Abd al-Latif is quoted in Neil Hanson, *The Custom of the Sea* (New York: John Wiley & Sons, 1999), p. 121, and Reay Tannahill, *Flesh and Blood: A History of the Cannibal Complex* (New York: Stein and Day, 1975), pp. 49–51.

161 **the carcasses of four human beings.** Quoted in Hanson, *The Custom of the Sea,* p. 123.

162 **away from the tranquility of Paradise.** Frank Lestringant, *Cannibals: The*

Discovery and Representation of the Cannibal from Columbus to Jules Verne (Berkeley, Calif.: University of California Press, 1997), pp. 28–29.

162 **poor wretches forced to abandon.** Quoted in Julia F. Burch, *Sink or Swim: Shipwreck narratives, survival tales, and postcultural subjectivity* (a dissertation for doctoral requirements, University of Michigan, 1994), p. 30.

162 **driven to the horrid alternative.** Quoted in Burch, *Sink or Swim*, p. 38.

163 **That affectionate, peaceable temper.** Quoted in Philbrick, *In the Heart of the Sea*, p. 171.

163 **dreamed maniacal dreams of hunger.** George B. Stewart, *Ordeal by Hunger: The Story of the Donner Party* (Boston, New York: Houghton Mifflin, 1988), p. 104.

163 **Slaves were eaten first.** Hanson, *The Custom of the Sea*, pp. 131–132.

164 **they were going to fetch succor.** "Shipwreck of the Medusa," facsimile of the penny-press edition, 1816. Research library of the Mariners' Museum, Newport News, Va., p. 21.

164 **those whom death had spared.** Quoted in Hanson, *The Custom of the Sea*, pp. 125–126.

164 **cruel mathematics.** Philbrick, *In the Heart of the Sea*, p. 173.

CHAPTER 12   THE LOTTERY

169 **An Italian researcher in 1890.** Max Kleiber, *The Fire of Life: An Introduction to Animal Energetics* (New York: John Wiley and Sons, 1961), p. 11.

171 **cleaving to the roof of my mouth.** Quoted in A.V. Wolf, *Thirst: Physiology of the Urge to Drink and Problems of Water Lack* (Springfield, Ill.: Charles C. Thomas, Publisher, 1958), p. 219 ff.

172 **the focus of a burning-glass.** Quoted in A.V. Wolf, *Thirst*, p. 228.

173 **his ribs edged out.** W.J. McGee, "Desert Thirst as Disease," *Interstate Medical Journal* (March 1906), pp. 279–300. This is hard to find and is also quoted in Wolf, *Thirst*, pp. 386–389.

174 **A 1943 British survey of shipwreck deaths.** MacDonald Critchley, *Shipwreck Survivors: A Medical Study* (London: Churchill, 1943), quoted extensively in Wolf, *Thirst*, p. 274–275.

185 **Bleed the beast . . . and remove the lungs.** The "Steward's Handbook" is quoted in Hanson, *The Custom of the Sea*, pp. 118–119.

CHAPTER 13   THE ISLAND

191 **Even for an era of scurrilous journalism.** Justin Kaplan, *Mr. Clemens and Mark Twain: A Biography* (London: Jonathon Cape, 1967), p. 15.

191 **The sea was very rough.** Mark Twain, *Mark Twain's Letters from Hawaii*, ed. A. Grove Day (Honolulu: University of Hawaii Press, 1966), p. 6.

191 **no careworn, or eager, anxious faces.** Edgar Marquess Branch, *The Literary Apprenticeship of Mark Twain* (Urbana, Ill.: University of Illinois Press, 1950), p. 158.

192 **a man who would be esteemed.** Twain, *Sacramento Daily Union*, July 16, 1866.

192 **fitted them no better than a flag.** Mark Twain, "My Debut as a Literary Person," *Century Magazine*, November 1899 (vol. 59, no. 1), pp. 76–88.

192 **mixed aliens.** Mark Twain, "Forty-Three Days in an Open Boat," *Harper's New Monthly Magazine*, December 1866 (vol. 34), pp. 104–113.

192 **a fervent critic of hypocrisy.** Branch, *The Literary Apprenticeship of Mark Twain*, p. 181.

193 **good sense, cool judgment.** Mark Twain, "Burning of the Clipper Ship *Hornet* at Sea," *Sacramento Daily Union*, July 19, 1866.

193 **the most unbounded confidence.** *Pacific Commercial Advertiser*, June 30, 1866.

193 **There is nothing of its sort in history.** Twain, "Forty-Three Days in an Open Boat," *Harper's New Monthly Magazine*.

194 **An old man, whose son.** Report from unidentified San Francisco newspaper, quoted in Alexander Crosby Brown, *Longboat to Hawaii: An Account of the Voyage of the Clipper Ship HORNET of New York Bound for San Francisco in 1866* (Cambridge, Md: Cornell Maritime Press, 1974), p. 172.

194 **it will be published first all over.** Letter to Mrs. Jane Clemens and Mrs. Moffett in St. Louis, June 27, 1866.

196 **until he [was] bursting.** Ancel Keys, *The Biology of Human Starvation*, pp. 846–847.

196 **One starts to eat—for hours, for days.** Viktor Frankl is quoted in Hilde O. Bluhm, "How Did They Survive?" p. 29.

198 **civilized channels of thought.** Robertson, *Survive the Savage Sea*, p. 176.

198 **with a sense of loss.** Steven Callahan, *Adrift*, p. 234.

202 **You ask, my dear girls.** Letter from Josiah Mitchell to his daughters, Liverpool, April 1867.

203 **Even Jimmy Cox was dead.** Letter of Marion Mitchell to A.C. Brown, December 14, 1939. The rumor of Cox's fortune circulated without verification in Mitchell's family for decades, long after the captain died.

203 **emotional tension.** Warren Kinston and Rachel Rosser, "Disaster: Effects of Mental and Physical State," p. 446.

204 **Doctors studying men.** H.C.D. Archibald, et al , "Gross stress reactions in combat, 15 year followup," *American Journal of Psychiatry*, 119, 317 (1963).

204 **severe persisting reactions.** Sydney Margolin, Lawrence Kubie, et al, "The Nature and Incidence of Acute Emotional Disturbances in Torpedoed Seamen of the Merchant Marine Who are Continuing at Sea," *Journal of Nervous and Mental Disease* 97, January-June 1943, p. 581.

204 **of the seven men** Scott Henderson and Tudor Bostock, "Coping Behavior after Shipwreck," *British Journal of Psychiatry* 131 (1977), pp. 18–19.

204 **I was almost dead.** R.J. Lifton, *Death in Life: Survivors of Hiroshima* (New

York: Random House, 1967), quoted in Kinston and Rosser, "Disaster: Effects of Mental and Physical State," p. 447.

205 **sensational matter such as the potential for cannibalism.** Letter from A.C. Brown to Thomas McCance, quoting members of the Ferguson family, December 12, 1972.

205 **without means and without employment.** Mark Twain, *Roughing It* (NewYork: New American Library, reprint edition 1962), p. 415.

205 **laughed, in their jolly fashion.** Mark Twain, "My Debut as a Literary Person," from *The Man That Corrupted Hadleyburg and Other Stories and Essays* (New York: 1900), quoted on the World Wide Web, "Mark Twain," URL: www.marktwain.miningco.com.

206 **for the cholera broke out among us.** Twain, *Roughing It*, p. 422.

206 **I was not celebrated.** Twain, "My Debut as a Literary Person." In "Mark Twain," URL: www.marktwain.miningco.com.

207 **For the constancy of the Quakers.** Henry Ferguson, *Essays in American History* (New York: James Pott and Co., 1894), p. 49.

207 **Every storm, every meteor.** Henry Ferguson, *Essays in American History*, p. 67.

208 **Why did you come here?** Henry Ferguson, *Essays in American History*, p. 198.

208 **At Chatham on Cape Cod.** William Roos, *The Hornet's Longboat* (Boston: Houghton Mifflin, 1940), p. 238.

EPILOGUE   THE FLOATING WORLD

212 **In 1778, there were an estimated 300,000 Hawaiians.** Statistics and translation in Benjamin B.C. Young, "The Hawaiians." In *People and Cultures of Hawaii: A Psychocultural Profile*, ed. John F. McDermott, Jr., Wen-Shing Tseng, and Thomas W. Maretzki (Honolulu: University of Hawaii Press, 1980), p. 10.

213 **My Dear Friend and Shipmate.** Mitchell's letter is originally quoted in Leigh H. Irvine, "The Lone Cruise of the HORNET Men: The Personal Narrative of Frederick Clough," *The Wide World Magazine*, London (vol. 5, no. 30), September 1900, p. 572.

313 **eccentric character . . . his only companion.** "Capt. James Cox, Friend of Mark Twain, Is Dead," *New York Tribune*, December 25, 1925.

214 **I am already beginning to have a great longing.** Mitchell's letter is quoted in Harold Waldo, "Yankee Captain and Southern Pilot," p. 201.

216 **a very remarkable trip.** From Twain, "My Debut as a Literary Person," in *The Man That Corrupted Hadleyburg and Other Stories and Essays* (New York: 1900). Mitchell would actually have been 88 or 89 at the time of writing.

216 **For me, its balmy airs.** Quoted in Edgar Marquess Branch, *The Literary Apprenticeship of Mark Twain*, p. 160.

217 **'It is true' said Satan.** Mark Twain, "The Mysterious Stranger." In *Selected Shorter Writings of Mark Twain*, ed. Walter Blair (Boston: Houghton Mifflin, 1962), p. 388.

218 **My dear Mr. Clemens.** Letter from Henry Ferguson to Samuel Clemens, November 8, 1899. "Henry and Samuel Ferguson" files, Yale Collection of American Literature, Beinecke Rare Book and Manuscript Library, Yale University Library.

219 **in the sweltering heat of the Pacific.** Letter from Samuel Clemens to Henry Ferguson, November 20, 1899, "Henry and Samuel Ferguson" files, Yale Collection of American Literature, Beinecke Rare Book and Manuscript Library, Yale University Library.

219 **I have gone through every book.** Letter from Fr. Braithwaite to Henry Ferguson, December 11, 1899. "Henry and Samuel Ferguson" files, Yale Collection of American Literature, Beinecke Rare Book and Manuscript Library, Yale University Library.

220 **Though we talk of the progress that the race has made.** Henry Ferguson, *Essays in American History*, pp. 101–102.

221 **My own first-hand knowledge.** Quoted in George W. Bragdon, "Epic of 'Hornet's' Men 43 Days in Open Boat," *Hartford Times*, Monday, November 27, 1939.

221 **The telling of his experiences is still so painful.** Leigh H. Irvine, "The Lone Cruise of the HORNET Men," p. 571.

222 **Old cronies of the mariner.** *San Francisco Call & Post*, July 14, 1926.

BIBLIOGRAPHY

I. CONCERNING THE *HORNET* AND HER CASTAWAYS

American Lloyds' Registry of American and Foreign Shipping (New York: GW Blunt, 1862).

Barnitz, William S., ed. "The Hornet's 21-foot longboat . . . sailed 4000 miles in 43 days. Her captain was Josiah Angier Mitchell, an Alumnus of Hebron Academy." HEBRON SEMESTER, Hebron, Maine (vol. 2, no. 2), Spring 1956, pp 20–24.

Brown, Alexander Crosby. Historical research collection of Alexander Crosby Brown, 1940–1984. The Mariners' Museum, Newport News, Va.: Box 1A, Folders 26, 27, 30, 31, 32.

——"The HORNET Journals." *The American Neptune* (vol. 1, no. 2), April 1941, pp. 164–165.

——"Isles of Vain Hope." *The Log of Mystic Seaport* (October 1976), pp. 74–85.

——*Longboat to Hawaii: An Account of the Voyage of the Clipper Ship HORNET of New York Bound for San Francisco in 1866* (Cambridge, Md: Cornell Maritime Press, 1974).

——"Shipwreck and Survival: Fasting and Prayer—A True Story of the Loss of the Clipper Ship Hornet." Alexander Crosby Brown Collection, Folder 31, Mariners' Museum, Newport News, Va.: An unpublished manuscript given as an address at St. Andrews Episcopal Church, Newport News, April 1976.

"The Clipper Ship HORNET." *The Lookout* (vol. 30, no.9), September 1939, pp. 4–6.

Crane, J.R. "They Rowed Four Thousand Miles." *The Lookout* (vol. 61, no. 6), July–August 1970, pp. 11–13.

Davis, J.D. *A Most Remarkable Mix: Sketches of Notable Freeporters* (Freeport, Maine: Freeport Historical Society, 2000).

Fairburn, William Armstrong. *Merchant Sail*, vol. 6 (Fairburn Marine Educational Foundation, 1945–1955).

Ferguson, Henry. *Essays in American History* (New York: James Pott and Co., 1894).

——*The Journal of Henry Ferguson, January to August 1866* (Hartford, Conn.: privately printed by the Case, Lockwood & Brainard Co. for Samuel Ferguson II, 1924).

Foot, George. "Six Weeks in a Lifeboat." *AHI Magazine*, issue unknown, copy kept at the historical research collection of Alexander Crosby Brown, 1940–1984. The Mariners' Museum, Newport News, Va.

Hall, James Norman. *The Tale of a Shipwreck* (Boston and New York: Houghton Mifflin Company, 1934). A letter to Hall from Marian Mitchell, capts' granddaughter, is printed on pp. 128–133.

"Henry Ferguson." *Horae Scholasticae*, May 5, 1917, pp. 154–155. A publication of St.

Paul's School, Concord, N.H., in an editorial published after Henry Ferguson's death.

Irvine, Leigh H. "The Lone Cruise of the HORNET Men: The Personal Narrative of Frederick Clough." *The Wide World Magazine*, London (vol. 5, no. 30), September 1900, pp. 571–577.

Mitchell, Josiah A. *The Diary of Captain Josiah A. Mitchell* (Hartford, CT: Privately printed, 1927).

Mitchell. Mary Angier. *Diary kept on board ship Hornet by Miss Mary A. Mitchell on a voyage to Bristol, England, March 1861.* This handwritten diary, kept during 1861 and 1862, was never published. It is kept in the possession of Judith Elfring, Josiah Mitchell's great-great granddaughter.

Mitchell, Sarah Abbie. *The Diary of Sarah Abbie Mitchell, aged 16.* This handwritten diary, kept during 1862 and 1863, was never published. It is kept in the possession of Judith Elfring.

Mitchell, Susan R. *The Diary of Susan R. Mitchell.* This handwritten diary, kept from 1861 to 1865, was never published. It is kept in the possession of Judith Elfring.

New York Marine Register: A Standard Classification of American Vessels, and Other Such Vessels as Visit American Ports (New York: R.C. Russet, Anthony and Co., 1857).

Parmenter, Charles. "Clipper Ship Hornet." *The Lookout* (vol. 31, no. 9), September 1940, p 3.

"The Rector's Letter." *Alumni Horae*, vol. 65, no. 2, St. Paul's School, Summer 1985.

Roos, William. *The Hornet's Longboat* (Boston: Houghton Mifflin, 1940). This is a work of fiction drawn from Mitchell's diary and written by his nephew. But not all is fiction: family tales passed down from Josiah Mitchell are incorporated in the text.

Thurston, Florence G., and Cross, Harmon S. *Three Centuries of Freeport, Maine* (Freeport, Maine: 1940), pp. 93–123. Chapter XX is about Josiah Mitchell.

Twain, Mark. "Burning of the Clipper Ship 'Hornet' at Sea: Detailed Account of the Sufferings of Officers and Crew, as given by the Third Officer and Members of the Crew." *Sacramento Daily Union*, July 19, 1866.

——"Forty-Three Days in an Open Boat," Mislabeled authorship, "Mark Swain." *Harper's New Monthly Magazine*, December 1866 (vol. 34), pp. 104–113.

——*Mark Twain's Letters from Hawaii*, ed. A. Grove Day (Honolulu: University of Hawaii Press, 1966).

——*Mark Twain's Notebooks and Journals*, Vol. 1 (1855–1873), ed. Frederick Anderson, Michael B. Frank and Kenneth M. Sanderson (Berkeley, Calif.: University of California Press, 1975).

——"My Debut as a Literary Person." *Century Magazine*, November 1899 (vol. 59, no. 1), pp. 76–88.

——*Roughing It* (New York: New American Library, reprint edition 1962). Although *Roughing It* does not contain mention of the *Hornet* and her crew, the Hawaiian chapters give a general sketch of Twain's journey around the islands and his state of mind.

——"Short and Singular Rations." From *The Celebrated Jumping Frog of Calaveras*

County and Other Sketches (New York: C.H. Webb, 1867), reprinted on the World Wide Web, URL: http://marktwain.miningco.com.

Waldo, Harold. "Yankee Captain and Southern Pilot." *Overland Monthly and Out West Magazine,* May 1924, pp. 199, 200, 201, 233.

II. SOURCES

Ackerman, Diane. *The Natural History of the Senses* (New York: Random House, 1990).

Albion, Robert G.; Baker, William A.; and Labaree, Benjamin W. *New England and the Sea* (Middletown, Conn.: Wesleyan University Press, 1972).

Alexander, David."Literacy Among Canadian and Foreign Seamen, 1863–1899." In *Working Men Who Got Wet,* ed. Rosemary Ommer and Gerald Panting (Memorial University of Newfoundland: Maritime History Group, 1980), pp 1–34.

Altman, I., and Haythorn, W. "The Ecology of Isolated Groups." *Behavioral Science,* 12 (1967), p. 169–82.

Archibald, H.C.D.; Long, D.M.; Miller, C.; and Tuddenham, R.D. "Gross stress reactions in combat, 15 year followup." *American Journal of Psychiatry,* 119, 317 (1963).

Asbury, Herbert. *The Gangs of New York: An Informal History of the Underworld* (New York: Alfred A. Knopf, 1927, reprint 1998 by Thunder's Mouth Press).

Baker, Margaret, *The Folklore of the Sea* (London: David & Charles, 1979).

Barnaby, K.C. *Some Ship Disasters and Their Causes* (London: Hutchinson & Co., 1968).

Bassett, Fletcher S. *Legends and Superstitions of the Sea and Sailors: In All Lands and at All times* (Chicago and New York: Belford, Clarke & Co., 1885).

Battick, John F. "A Study of the Demographic History of the Seafaring Population of Belfast and Searsport, Maine, 1850–1900." In *Working Men Who Got Wet,* ed. Rosemary Ommer and Gerald Panting (Memorial University of Newfoundland: Maritime History Group, 1980), pp. 229–261.

Baudelaire, Charles. *Les Fleurs du Mal,* trans. George Dillon and Edna St. Vincent Millay (New York: Washington Square Press, 1962).

Beal, Timothy K. "Our Monsters, Ourselves." *The Chronicle of Higher Education,* November 9, 2001, pp. B18–19.

Beck, Horace. *Folklore and the Sea* (Edison, N.J.: Castle Books, 1973).

Behrman, Cynthia Fansler. *Victorian Myths of the Sea* (Athens, Ohio: Ohio University Press, 1977).

Bell, Michael E. *Food for the Dead: On the Trail of New England's Vampires* (New York: Carroll & Graf Publishers, 2001).

Bennett, F.D. *Narrative of a Whaling Voyage Round the Globe . . . 1833 to 1836,* vol. 1 (London, 1840).

Bloch, Herbert A. "The Personality of Inmates of Concentration Camps." *American Journal of Sociology* (1947), pp. 335–341.

Bluestone, H., and McGahee, C.L. "Reaction to Extreme Stress: Impending Death by Execution." *American Journal of Psychiatry* 119 (1962), pp. 393–96.

Bluhm, Hilde O. "How Did They Survive?" *American Journal of Psychotherapy* 2, no. 1 (1948), pp. 3–32.

Bolster, William Jeffrey. *Black Jacks: African American Seamen in the Age of Sail* (Cambridge, Mass.: Harvard University Press, 1997).

———"The Changing Nature of Maritime Insurrection." *Log of Mystic Seaport* 32:1 (Spring 1979), p. 14–21.

———"Every Inch a Man: Gender in the Lives of African American Seamen, 1800–1860." In *Iron Men, Wooden Women: Gender and Seafaring in the Atlantic World, 1700–1920*, ed, Margaret S. Creighton and Lisa Norling (Baltimore, Md: The Johns Hopkins University Press, 1996), pp. 138–168.

Boswell, James. *The Life of Samuel Johnson, LL.D.* (Modern Library Edition, first published 1791).

Bowditch, Nathaniel. *The New American Practical Navigator*, 29th ed. (New York: E. & G.W. Blunt, 1860).

Branch, Edgar Marquess. *The Literary Apprenticeship of Mark Twain* (Urbana, Ill.: University of Illinois Press, 1950).

Brown, Richard Maxwell. "Historical Patterns of Violence in America." In *The History of Violence in America: A Report to the National Commission on the Causes and Prevention of Violence*, ed. Hugh Davis Graham and Ted Robert Gurr (New York: Bantam Books, 1969), pp. 45–84.

Burch, Julia F. *Sink or Swim: Shipwreck Narratives, Survival Tales, and Postcultural Subjectivity* (a dissertation for doctoral requirements, University of Michigan, 1994).

Busch, Briton C. "Brace and be Dam'd: Work Stoppages on American Whaleships, 1820–1920." *International Journal of Maritime History* III, no. 2 (December 1991), pp. 95–107.

Byrd, Richard E. *Alone* (New York: Ace Books, Inc., 1938).

Cadman, John. *The Round Trip by Way of Panama* (New York: G.P. Putnam's Sons, 1879).

Calhoun, John R. "Population Density and Social Pathology." *Scientific American* 206 (February 1962), pp. 139–148.

Callahan, Steven. *Adrift: Seventy-Six Days Lost at Sea* (Boston: Houghton Mifflin Company, 1986).

Campbell, Joseph. *The Masks of God: Primitive Mythology* (New York: Penguin Books, 1976).

Caughey, John W., and May, Ernest R. *A History of the United States* (Chicago: Rand McNally & Co., 1964).

Chapelle, Howard I. *The Search for Speed Under Sail, 1700–1885* (New York: W.W. Norton & Company, 1967).

Clark, Arthur H. *The Clipper Ship Era: An Epitome of Famous American and British Clipper Ships, Their Owners, Builders, Commanders, and Crews, 1843–1869* (New York: G.P. Putnam's Sons, 1911).

Crane, Stephen. "The Open Boat." In *The Norton Anthology of Short Fiction*, ed. R.V. Cassill (New York: W.W. Norton & Company, 1978), pp. 352–371.

Creighton, Margaret Scott. "Davy Jones' Locker Room." In *Iron Men, Wooden Women: Gender and Seafaring in the Atlantic World, 1700–1920*, ed, Margaret S. Creighton and Lisa Norling, (Baltimore, Md: The Johns Hopkins University Press, 1996), p. 118–137.

——*The Private Life of Jack Tar: Sailors at Sea in the Nineteenth Century.* A dissertation published for the Boston University Graduate School, 1985.

Critchley, MacDonald. *Shipwreck Survivors: A Medical Study* (London: Churchill, 1943).

Cutler, Carl C. *Five Hundred Sailing Records of American Built Ships* (Mystic, CT: The Marine Historical Association, Inc., 1952).

——*Greyhounds of the Sea: The Story of the American Clipper Ship.* (New York: G.P. Putnam's Sons, 1930).

Daly, R.J. "Samuel Pepys and Post-Traumatic Stress Disorder." *British Journal of Psychiatry* 143, 1983, p. 64–68.

Dana, Richard Henry, Jr. *The Seaman's Friend: A Treatise on Practical Seamanship* (Mineola, New York: Dover Publications, 1997, first printed 1879).

——*Two Years Before the Mast: A Personal Narrative of Life at Sea* (New York: Penguin Books, 1983, first printed 1840).

Davies, James C. "The J-Curve of Rising and Declining Satisfactions as a Cause of Some Great Revolutions and a Contained Rebellion." In *The History of Violence in America: A Report to the National Commission on the Causes and Prevention of Violence,* Hugh Davis Graham and Ted Robert Gurr (New York: Bantam Books, 1969), pp. 690–730.

Delgado, James P. *To California by Sea: A Maritime History of the California Gold Rush* (Columbia, S.C.: University of South Carolina Press, 1990).

Dening, Greg. *Mr. Bligh's Bad Language: Passion, Power and Theatre on the Bounty* (New York: Cambridge University Press, 1992).

De Tocqueville, Alexis. *Democracy in America,* ed. Richard D. Heffner, (New York: Mentor Books, 1956).

Dodge, Ernest S. *Beyond the Capes: Pacific Exploration from Captain Cook to the Challenger (1776–1877)* (Boston: Little, Brown, and Co., 1971).

——*Islands and Empires: Western Impact on the Pacific and East Asia* (Minneapolis, Minn.: University of Minnesota Press, 1976).

Dormandy, Thomas. *The White Death: A History of Tuberculosis* (New York: N.Y. University Press, 2000).

Drimmer, Frederick, ed. *Captured by the Indians: 15 Firsthand Accounts, 1750–1870* (Mineola, New York: Dover Publications, 1961).

Druett, Joan. *Hen Frigates: Wives of Merchant Captains Under Sail* (New York: Simon & Schuster, 1998).

Dye, Ira. "Early American Merchant Seafarers." *Proceedings of the American Philosophical Society* 120 (October 1976), pp. 331–60.

Evans, Robert, Jr.. "'Without Regard for Cost,' The Returns on Clipper Ships." *Journal of Political Economy* (February 1964), pp 32–43.

Feuer, A. B. "A Question of Mutiny." *Naval History* (March/April 1994), vol 8, no 2, pp. 22–27.

Findlay, Alexander George. *A Directory for the Navigation of the North Pacific Ocean,* 3d ed (London, 1886).

Fischer, Lewis B. "A Dereliction of Duty: The Problem of Desertion on Nineteenth Century Sailing Vessels." In *Working Men Who Got Wet*, ed, Rosemary Ommer and Gerald Panting (Memorial University of Newfoundland: Maritime History Group, 1980), pp. 51–70.

Foote, Shelby. *The Civil War, A Narrative: Red River to Appomatox* (New York: Vintage Books, 1974).

France, Peter. *Hermits: The Insights of Solitude* (New York: St. Martin's Press, 1997).

Fuller, Edmund. "The Nature of Mutiny." *Mutiny!: Being Accounts of Insurrections, Famous and Infamous on Land and Sea, from the Days of the Caesars to Modern Times*, ed. Edmund Fuller (New York: Crown, 1953), pp. ix–xiii.

Garn, S.M., and Block, W.D. "The Limited Nutritional Value of Cannibalism." *American Anthropologist* 72, no. 106 (1970), pp. 106–107.

Garrett, Laurie. *The Coming Plague: Newly Emerging Diseases in a World Out of Balance* (New York: Farrar, Straus and Giroux, 1994).

Genovese, Eugene D. *Roll, Jordan, Roll: The World the Slaves Made* (New York: Vintage Books, 1976). See esp. Part I, "On Paternalism," pp. 3–7.

Gerstenberger, Heide. "Men Apart." *International Journal of Maritime History*, vol. 8, no. 1 (June 1996), pp. 173–182).

Gudger, E.W. "The Alleged Pugnacity of the Swordfish and the Spearfishes as Shown by Their Attacks on Vessels." *Memoirs of the Royal Asiatic Society of Bengal*, vol.12, no. 2, 1940, pp. 215–315.

———"The Perils and Romance of Swordfishing: The Pursuit of Xiphias Gladius with the Trident in the Strait of Messina." *The Scientific Monthly*, July 1940, vol.51, pp. 36–48.

Guttridge, Leonard F. *Mutiny: A History of Naval Insurrection* (Annapolis, Md: Naval Institute Press, 1992).

Hadfield, Robert L. *Mutiny at Sea* (London: Geoffrey Bles, 1937).

Hall, Edward T. *The Dance of Life: The Other Dimension of Time* (Garden City, N.Y.: Anchor Press, 1984).

Halpine, C.G., and Taylor, H.H. *A Mariner's Meteorology* (Princeton, N.J.: D. Van Nostrand Company, Inc., 1956).

Hanson, Neil. *The Custom of the Sea* (New York: John Wiley & Sons, Inc., 1999).

Harlow, Frederick Pease. *The Making of a Sailor, or Sea Life Aboard a Yankee Square-Rigger* (Mineola, N.Y.: Dover Publications, Inc., 1988, reprint from 1928 edition).

Harris, M.A. *A Negro History Tour of Manhattan* (New York: Greenwood Publishing Corp., 1968).

Hassell, Martha. *The Challenge of Hannah Rebecca: An account of the experiences of the wife of a clipper ship captain, with quotations from her personal journal* (Sandwich, Mass.: Sandwich Historical Society, 1986).

Henderson, Scott, and Bostock, Tudor. "Coping Behavior after Shipwreck." *British Journal of Psychiatry* 131 (1977), pp. 15–20.

Hobbes, Thomas. *Leviathan* ed. Michael Oakeshott (Oxford, 1955).

Horbulewicz, Jan. "The Parameters of the Psychological Autonomy of Industrial Trawler Crews." In *Seafarer and Community: Toward a Social Understanding of Seafaring*, ed. Peter H. Fricke (London: Croom Helm Ltd., 1973), pp. 67–84.

Howe, Octavius T., and Matthews, Frederick C. *American Clipper Ships 1833–1858* (New York: Argosy Antiquarian Ltd., 1967/1927).

Hugill, Stan. *Shanties from the Seven Seas: Shipboard Work-Songs and Songs Used as Work-Songs From the Great Days of Sail* (Mystic, Conn.: Mystic Seaport Museum, 1994).

Huntington, Rev. E.B. *History of Stamford, 1641–1868*, (Harrison, N.Y.: Harbor Hill Books, 1979, reprint of 1868 edition).

Imray, James M. *The North Pacific Pilot, Part II* (London, 1870).

Johnson, James Weldon. *Black Manhattan* (New York: Alfred A. Knopf, 1930).

Junger, Sebastian. *The Perfect Storm: A True Story of Men Against the Sea* (New York: W.W. Norton & Co., 1997).

Kanas, Nick. "Psychosocial Support for Cosmonauts." *Aviation, Space, and Environmental Medicine*, April 1991, pp. 353–356.

Kaplan, Justin. *Mr. Clemens and Mark Twain: A Biography* (London: Jonathon Cape, 1967).

Keys, Ancel; Brozek, Josef; Henschel, Austin; Michelson, Olaf; and Taylor, Henry Longstreet. *The Biology of Human Starvation* 2 vols. (Minneapolis: University of Minnesota Press, 1950).

Kindleberger, Charles P. *Mariners and Markets* (New York: New York University Press, 1992).

Kinston, Warren, and Rosser, Rachel. "Disaster: Effects of Mental and Physical State." *Journal of Psychosomatic Research*, 18 (1974), p 437–56.

Kleiber. Max. *The Fire of Life: An Introduction to Animal Energetics* (New York: John Wiley and Sons, Inc., 1961).

Kotsch, William J., and Henderson, Richard. *Heavy Weather Guide*, 2d ed. (Annapolis, Md: Naval Institute Press, 1984).

Laing, Alexander. *Clipper Ship Men* (New York: Duell, Sloan and Pearce, 1944).

Lauring, Palle. *A History of the Kingdom of Denmark*, trans. David Hohnen (Copenhagen: Host and Sons Forlag, 1960).

Leach, John. "Psychological First-Aid: a Practical Aide-Memoire." *Aviation, Space, and Environmental Medicine*, July 1995, pp. 668–74.

——*Survival Psychology* (New York: New York University Press, 1994).

Lemisch, Jesse. "Jack Tar in the Streets: Merchant Seamen in the Politics of Revolutionary America." *William and Mary Quarterly* 25 (July 1968): pp. 371–407.

Lestringant, Frank. *Cannibals: The Discovery and Representation of the Cannibal from Columbus to Jules Verne* (Berkeley, Calif.: University of California Press, 1997).

Lewis, R.W.B. *The American Adam: Innocence, Tragedy, and Tradition in the Nineteenth Century* (Chicago: University of Chicago Press, 1955).

Litwack, Leon F. *North of Slavery: The Negro in the Free States, 1790–1860* (Chicago: University of Chicago Press, 1961).

Locke, John. *Two Treatises of Government*, ed. Thomas I. Cook (New York, 1947).

Lorenz, Konrad. *On Aggression*, trans. Marjorie Kerr Wilson (New York: Bantam Books, 1963, 1966).

Lundy, Derek. *Godforsaken Sea: The True Story of a Race Through the World's Most Dangerous Waters* (New York: Anchor Books, 1998).

Margolin, Sydney; Kubie, Lawrence S.; Kanzer, Mark; and Stone, Leo. "The Nature and Incidence of Acute Emotional Disturbances in Torpedoed Seamen of the Merchant Marine Who are Continuing at Sea." *Journal of Nervous and Mental Disease* 97, January–June 1943, pp. 581–86.

Maury, Matthew Fontaine. *Explanations and Sailing Directions to accompany the Wind and Current Charts*, vol. 1 and 2, 8th ed. (Washington, D.C.: William A. Harris, Printer, 1858).

——*The Physical Geography of the Sea, and Its Meteorology*, ed. John Leighly (Cambridge, Mass.: Belknap Press of the Harvard University Press, reprint 1963).

McGee, W.J. "Desert Thirst as Disease." *Interstate Medical Journal* (March 1906), p 279–300.

McNeill, William H. *Plagues and Peoples* (New York: Anchor Books, 1976).

Michaud, M. "Observations on Waterspouts." *Naval Chronicle*, vol 22, 1809, pp 328–333.

Miller, Robert. "Religious Significance of the Mast." *Mariners' Mirror* 83, no. 3, August 1997, p. 337.

Moseley, Caroline. "Images of Young Women in Nineteenth-Century Songs of the Sea." *Log of Mystic Seaport* 35 (1984), pp. 132–139.

Nalivkin, D.V. *Hurricanes, Storms and Tornadoes: Geographic Characteristics and Geological Activity* (Rotterdam: A.A. Balkema, 1986).

Neider, Charles. *Great Shipwrecks and Castaways: Authentic Accounts of Adventures at Sea* (New York: Harper and Brothers Publishers, 1952).

Nicholas, John M., and Penwell, Larry W. "A Proposed Profile of the Effective Leader in Human Spaceflight Based on Findings from Analog Environments." *Aviation, Space and Environmental Medicine*, January 1995, pp. 63–72.

Noble, Peter, and Hogbin, Ros. *The Mind of the Sailor: An Exploration of the Human Stories Behind Adventures and Misadventures at Sea* (Camden, Maine: International Marine, 2001).

Nordhoff, Charles, and Hall, James Norman. *The Bounty Trilogy: Comprising the Three Volumes "Mutiny on the Bounty," "Men Against the Sea," & "Pitcairn's Island."* (Boston: Little, Brown & Company, 1964).

Norling, Lisa. "Ahab's Wife: Women and the American Whaling Industry, 1820–1870." In *Iron Men, Wooden Women: Gender and Seafaring in the Atlantic World, 1700–1920*, ed, Margaret S. Creighton and Lisa Norling (Baltimore, Md: The Johns Hopkins University Press, 1996), pp. 70–91.

——*Captain Ahab Had a Wife: New England Women and the Whalefishery, 1720–1870* (Chapel Hill, N.C.: University of North Carolina Press, 2000).

Nuland, Sherwin B. *How We Die: Reflections on Life's Final Chapter* (New York: Vintage Books, 1995).

Oliver, Sandra L. *Saltwater Foodways: New Englanders and their food, at sea and ashore, in the nineteenth century* (Mystic, Conn.: Mystic Seaport Museum, Inc.,1995).

Ommer, Rosemary E. "Composed of All Nationalities: The Crews of Windsor Vessels, 1862–1899." In *Working Men Who Got Wet*, ed. Rosemary Ommer and Gerald Panting (Memorial University of Newfoundland: Maritime History Group, 1980), pp. 191–227.

Ott, Katherine. *Fevered Lives: Tuberculosis in American Culture since 1870* (Cambridge, Mass.: Harvard University Press, 1996).

Paine, Albert Bigelow. *Mark Twain: A Biography* (New York: Harper & Brothers, 1912).

Park, Steven H. "'The Ship Without Liberty': Mutiny and the Clipper *Contest*," *American Neptune: A Quarterly Journal of Maritime History*, vol. 55, no. 2, pp. 123–132.

Pawa, Jay M. "The Jefferson Borden Pirates and Samuel Gompers: Aftermath of a Mutiny." *The American Neptune: A Quarterly Journal of Maritime History* 27, (January 1967), pp. 46–60.

Petrinovich, Lewis. *The Cannibal Within* (New York: Aldine de Gruyter, 2000).

Philbrick, Nathaniel. *In the Heart of the Sea: The Tragedy of the Whaleship* Essex (New York: Viking, 2000).

Pratt, Fletcher. "Mutiny—A Study." *United States Naval Institute Proceedings*, April 1932, vol. 58, no. 4, pp. 520–532.

Radil-Weiss, Tomas. "Man in Extreme Conditions: Some Medical and Psychological Aspects of the Auschwitz Concentration Camp." *Psychiatry* 46 (1983), pp. 259–69.

Ramsay, Raymond H. *No Longer on the Map: Discovering Places that Never Were* (New York: Viking, 1972).

Robertson, Dougal. *Sea Survival, A Manual* (New York: Praeger Publishers, 1975).

——*Survive the Savage Sea* (Dobbs Ferry, New York: Sheridan House, 1994).

Rothman, Sheila M. *Living in the Shadow of Death: Tuberculosis and the Social Experience of Illness in American History* (New York: BasicBooks, 1994).

Rousseau, Jean-Jacques. *The Social Contract and Discourses*, trans. G.D.H. Cole (London: Everyman's Library, 1947).

Samuels, Captain Samuel. "A Crew of the 'Bloody Forties." In *Mutiny!: Being Accounts of Insurrections, Famous and Infamous, on Land and Sea, from the Days of the Caesars to Modern Times*, ed. Edmund Fuller (New York: Crown Publishers, Inc., 1953), pp. 221–233.

Scarry, Elaine. *The Body in Pain* (New York: Oxford University Press, 1985).

Seidman, David. *The Complete Sailor: Learning the Art of Sailing* (Camden, Maine: International Marine, 1994).

Shay, Frank. *A Sailor's Treasury: Being the Myths and Superstitions, Lore, Legends and Yarns, the Cries, Epithets, and Salty Speech of the American Sailorman in the Days of Oak and Canvas* (New York: W.W. Norton & Company, 1951).

Sherwood, Herbert F. *The Story of Stamford* (New York: The States History Company, 1930).

"Shipwreck of the Medusa." Facsimile of the penny-press edition, 1816. Research library of the Mariners' Museum, Newport News, Va.:

Sill, William. "The Anvil of Evolution." *Earthwatch*, August 2001, pp. 24–31.

Simons, Gerald, general editor, and the Editors of Time-Life Books. *The Blockade: Runners and Raiders*, part of the series *The Civil War: 1861–1865* (Alexandria, Va.: Time-Life Books, 1983).

Skaggs, Jimmy M. *The Great Guano Rush: Entrepreneurs and American Overseas Expansion* (New York: St. Martin's, 1994).

Sokolow, Michael. *"What a Miserable Life a Sea Fareing Life Is": The Life and Experiences of a Nineteenth-Century Mariner of Color* (a dissertation for the Boston University Graduate School of Arts and Sciences, 1997).

Sontag, Susan. *Illness as Metaphor* (New York: Farrar, Straus & Giroux, 1978).

Spallanzani."Observations on Waterspouts." *Naval Chronicle*, vol 2, 1799, pp. 601–606.

Spears, John R. "Mutinies on Merchant Ships." *Muncey's Magazine*, 1900, pp. 678–688.

Stadler, Michael. *The Psychology of Sailing: The Sea's Effects on Mind and Body* (Camden, Maine: International Marine Publishing Co., 1987).

Steefel, Lawrence D. *The Schleswig-Holstein Question* (Cambridge, Mass.: Harvard University Press, 1932).

Stewart, George B. *Ordeal by Hunger: The Story of the Donner Party* (Boston: Houghton Mifflin, 1988).

Stommel, Henry. *Lost Islands: The story of islands that have vanished from nautical charts* (Vancouver, B.C.: University of British Columbia Press, 1984).

Sutherland, Daniel E. *The Expansion of Everyday Life: 1860–1876*. The Everyday Life in America series, ed. Richard Balkin (New York: Harper & Row, 1989).

Szalet, Leon. *Experiment "E." a report from an extermination laboratory* (New York: Didier Press, 1945).

Taft, Philip and Ross, Philip. "American Labor Violence: Its Causes, Character and Outcome." In *The History of Violence in America: A Report to the National Commission on the Causes and Prevention of Violence*, ed. Hugh Davis Graham and Ted Robert Gurr (New York: Bantam Books, 1969), pp. 281–395.

Takla, Nader K.; Koffman, Robert; and Bailey, Dean A. "Combat Stress, Combat Fatigue and Psychiatric Disability in Aircrew." *Aviation, Space, and Environmental Medicine*, September 1994, pp 858–65.

Tannahill, Reay. *Flesh and Blood: A History of the Cannibal Complex* (New York: Stein and Day, 1975).

Twain, Mark. "The Mysterious Stranger." In *Selected Shorter Writings of Mark Twain*, ed. Walter Blair (Boston: Houghton Mifflin, 1962), pp. 306–388.

U.S. Congress, House. *Merchant Seamen*. Report no. 438, 44th Congress, 1st session, April 21, 1876.

U.S. Dept. of Commerce, Bureau of the Census. *Historical Statistics of the United States: Colonial Times to 1970*, parts 1 and 2 (Washington, D.C.: U.S. Bureau of the Census, 1975).

Van Dorn, William G. *Oceanography and Seamanship*, 2d ed. (Centreville, Md: Cornell Maritime Press, 1993).

Vandereycker, Walter, and Van Deth, Ron. *From Fasting Saints to Anorexic Girls: The History of Self-Starvation* (New York: New York University Press, 1994).

Ward, R. Gerard, ed. *American Activities in the Central Pacific, 1790–1870* (Ridgewood, N.J.: The Gregg Press, 1966).

Wendell, George Blunt. *George Blunt Wendell: Clipper Ship Master, letters and journals.* (Mystic, Conn.: Mystic Seaport Museum, 1949).

Whipple, A.B.C. *The Challenge* (New York: William Morrow and Company, 1987).

Whipple, A.B.C., and the editors of Time-Life Books. *The Clipper Ships* (Alexandria, Va.: Time-Life Books., 1980).

White, T.H., ed. *The Book of Beasts: Being a Translation from a Latin Bestiary of the Twelfth Century* (New York: G.P. Putnam's Sons, 1954; Dover Publications, 1984).

Williams, James H. *Blow the Man Down!: A Yankee Seaman's Adventures Under Sail*, ed. Warren F. Kuehl, (New York: E.P. Dutton & Co., Inc., 1959).

Wolf, A.V. *Thirst: Physiology of the Urge to Drink and Problems of Water Lack* (Springfield, Ill.: Charles C. Thomas, Publisher, 1958).

Young, Benjamin B.C. "The Hawaiians." In *People and Cultures of Hawaii: A Psychocultural Profile*, ed, John F. McDermott, Jr., Wen-Shing Tseng, and Thomas W. Maretzki (Honolulu: University of Hawaii Press, 1980), pp. 5–24.

III. ARCHIVES AND LIBRARIES

Freeport Historical Society, Freeport, Maine. Files: "Josiah A. Mitchell."

The Mariners' Museum, Newport News, Va.: Historical research collection of Alexander Crosby Brown, 1940–1984. Box 1A, Folders 26, 27, 30, 31, 32.

Stamford Room, Ferguson Library, Stamford, Conn. File: "John Day Ferguson."

Watkinson Library, Trinity College, Hartford, Conn. Files: "Henry Ferguson" and "Samuel Ferguson."

Yale Collection of American Literature, Beinecke Rare Book and Manuscript Library, Yale University Library. File: "Henry and Samuel Ferguson."

IV. NEWSPAPERS

Hartford Times, Monday, November 27, 1939."Epic of 'Hornet's' Men 43 Days in Open Boat," by George W. Bragdon.

New York Herald, January 11–16, 1866; July 23–24, 1876.

New York Times, October 15, 1917. "Drink of Water Brings Reward."

New York Tribune, December 5, 1925. "Capt. James Cox, Friend of Mark Twain, Is Dead."

Pacific Commercial Advertiser, Honolulu, Hawaii, June 23, 1866, "Ship Burned at Sea"; June 29, 1866, "Loss of the Hornet"; June 30, 1866, "Burning of the American ship Hornet."

Sacramento Daily Union, August 18, 1866.

Stamford Advocate, April 8, 1922.

Syracuse Sunday Herald, November 26, 1899.

Virginian-Pilot, January 26, 2002, "For 25,000 Living Aboard, Ship is Truly 'Tight.'"

V. WORLD WIDE WEB

Columbia Journalism Review, "Resources: Inflation Adjustor." http://www.cjr.org.

"The Great Lakes Shipwreck Research Foundation: David Swayze Great Lakes Shipwreck File." www.ghost-ships.org.

"Jewish Battlefield Ethics." www.alephinstitute.org/html/MARCHMEN.HTM.

"Mark Twain." www.marktwain.miningco.com.

"The New York Draft Riots." www.civilwarhome.com/draftriots.htm.

"Robertson v. Baldwin." www.guncite.com/court.fed/sc.

"Thomaston—The Town That Went to Sea." www.mint.net/thomastonhistorical society/wentto.ktm.

VI. INTERVIEWS

Judith Elfring, Yarmouth, Maine. Great-great-granddaughter of Captain Josiah Mitchell.

Henry Ferguson, Albany, New York.

ACKNOWLEDGMENTS
AND SOURCES

―――――◦◇◦―――――

S TORIES LIKE THIS are nothing without insight into those who spoke
from their distress, and the descendants of the Fergusons and Captain
Josiah Mitchell have often wondered what their illustrious ancestors
endured. Judith Elfring of Yarmouth, Maine, the great-great-granddaughter of Captain Josiah Mitchell, kept a treasure-trove of material on
the man. Especially helpful were unpublished diaries by Mitchell's wife,
Susan, and two of his daughters. In addition, I'd like to thank Henry Ferguson of Albany, New York, Ferguson family historian, who helped place
for me the brothers Ferguson in their day and age.

A project like this would also not have been possible without the generous aid of far-flung friends and acquaintances. Dr. Walter Dudley, director of the Pacific Tsunami Museum in Hilo, Hawaii, first got me interested
in the tale of the castaways. Jim Passon, of Kailua-Kona, Hawaii, played literary detective, digging up century-old newspaper stories; he and his wife,
Marilinda, gave me more insight into the Hawaiian islands than I could
have gotten alone. Connie Jones of Norfolk, Virginia, who will be an Episcopal priest by the time this is published, set me straight on church history
and loaned me her family copy of The Book of Common Prayer. I also
tapped the minds of several scholars at Virginia Wesleyan College in Norfolk: Dr. Steven and Henriette Emmanuel on Danish history; Dr. Craig
Wansink on religious fasting; Dr. Dan Margolies on the joys and politics
of guano. I'd like to thank them all.

The bulk of information in this book was found in archives, especially the Mariner's Museum in Newport News, Virginia. The archivists there were generous with their time and knowledge, especially during the confusion of renovations. Other archives and archivists include: Randall Wade Thomas, curator of the Freeport Historical Society, Freeport, Maine; Peter Knapp of the Watkinson Library at Trinity College, Hartford, Connecticut; Patty Kugan of the Mark Twain House, Hartford, Connecticut; Ernie DiMattia at the Stamford Room, Ferguson Library, Stamford, Connecticut; the Stamford Historical Society; the G.W. Blunt White Library at Mystic Seaport, Connecticut; the Ohrstrum Library at St. Paul's School, Concord, New Hampshire; and the Yale Collection of American Literature, Beinecke Rare Book and Manuscript Library, Yale University Library.

Special thanks go to the staff of the Thurber House in Columbus, Ohio, where I was visiting writer in spring 2001. I finished my second book while there and started this, my third. It's amazing how much work one can do alone in a garret apartment. As always, thanks go to my agent, Noah Lukeman, and to Elizabeth Stein and Rachel Klayman, editors at Free Press. And, of course, love and thanks go to Kathy and Nick, who lived with me while I wrote, and to my dog Noodle, who slept beneath the desk during several revisions and served as an efficient, if crowded, footwarmer.

INDEX

ABOUT THE AUTHOR

Five-time Pulitzer Prize nominee **Joe Jackson** is the author of *Leavenworth Train*, a finalist for the 2002 Edgar Award for Best Fact Crime, and coauthor with William F. Burke of *Dead Run*. From 1985 to 1997, he was an investigative reporter for the *Virginian-Pilot* and now lives in Virginia Beach with his wife and son.